Business and Peace-Building

In a world struggling to adapt to seismic social and environmental changes, the time is now for businesses to prioritise creating local conditions of peace. This book builds on original research foregrounding 'peace' as a core business outcome for natural resources industries. Especially in non-warlike situations where natural resources industries have exacerbated or caused conflict, foregrounding peace as a core business outcome can bring substantial benefits. Peace is a concept external and internal stakeholders understand. Consequently, research shows that when natural resources sector CSR professionals start reframing their day-to-day decisions in terms of peace outcomes, they are more likely to create efficient and cost-effective solutions to environmental, social and economic business challenges.

This book provides both theory and practical suggestions for how to reframe day-to-day CSR activities of natural resources companies as peace-focused, business decisions. Especially in the remote and rural regions of the world, where natural resources industries have the greatest impact, businesses can lead the way in contributing to conditions of peace while bringing much-needed resources to the market.

Carol Janson Bond is a Lecturer in Management at the University of Queensland Business School, Australia. Dr Bond's diverse research areas include: business ethics, peace-building responsibilities of business, leadership and Indigenous wisdom traditions. Carol's research focuses on large-footprint industries, including mining, coal seam gas, petroleum pipelines and large infrastructure projects.

Routledge Studies in Management, Organizations and Society

This series presents innovative work grounded in new realities, addressing issues crucial to an understanding of the contemporary world. This is the world of organized societies, where boundaries between formal and informal, public and private, local and global organizations have been displaced or have vanished, along with other nineteenth-century dichotomies and oppositions. Management, apart from becoming a specialized profession for a growing number of people, is an everyday activity for most members of modern societies.

Similarly, at the level of enquiry, culture and technology, and literature and economics, can no longer be conceived as isolated intellectual fields; conventional canons and established mainstreams are contested. **Management, Organizations and Society** addresses these contemporary dynamics of transformation in a manner that transcends disciplinary boundaries, with books that will appeal to researchers, students and practitioners alike.

Recent titles in this series include:

Relational Research and Organisation Studies
Charlotte Øland Madsen, Mette Vinther Larsen, Lone Hersted and Jørgen Gulddahl Rasmussen

Organizational Space and Beyond
The Significance of Henri Lefebvre for Organization Studies
Edited by Sytze F. Kingma, Karen Dale, and Varda Wasserman

The Organization of Craft Work
Identities, Meanings and Materiality
Edited by Emma Bell, Gianluigi Mangia, Scott Taylor, and Maria Laura Toraldo

Business and Peace-Building
The Role of Natural Resources Companies
Carol Janson Bond

For a full list of titles in this series, please visit www.routledge.com

Business and Peace-Building
The Role of Natural Resources Companies

Carol Janson Bond

Routledge
Taylor & Francis Group
NEW YORK AND LONDON

First published 2019
by Routledge
605 Third Avenue, New York, NY 10017

and by Routledge
2 Park Square, Milton Park, Abingdon, Oxon, OX14 4RN

First issued in paperback 2020

Routledge is an imprint of the Taylor & Francis Group, an informa business

Library of Congress Cataloging-in-Publication Data
A catalog record for this book has been requested

ISBN 13: 978-0-367-73418-3 (pbk)
ISBN 13: 978-1-138-23638-7 (hbk)

Typeset in Sabon
by Apex CoVantage, LLC

Contents

Acknowledgements

In my work at the University of Queensland, I have had the privilege of speaking with Corporate Social Responsibility (CSR) practitioners from all over the world. They are committed professionals who are earnestly trying to do the right thing for the communities affected by mining, oil and gas, timber, pipelines, hydro-electric dams, windfarms and other large-footprint operations. None of them wakes up in the morning saying, "How can I mess up the lives of people and environments affected by natural resources projects today?"

What I have heard repeatedly is that there is simply too much information to track, too many forms to fill out, insufficient human or financial resources to do the job they know needs to be done and stacks of 'best practice' guidelines—each one saying something slightly different. This surfeit of material leads many to rely, occasionally, on their professional intuition. Professional intuition is the summation of experience, the path of least resistance with either corporate and/or the community, and whatever corporate or international guidance standard is handy at the time. It is clear to this outside observer that CSR professionals are not negligent. On the contrary, they are seeking or developing reliable and innovative shortcuts to making effective and efficient decisions, some with long-lasting consequences. This book is an effort to systematise these shortcuts and make their wisdom more accessible to a wider group of CSR practitioners and communities.

As I hope is evident throughout this book, I fully support the use of best practice guidelines and well-written corporate policy. However, I observe that practitioners who work—consciously or unconsciously—out of a paradigm of peace are successful at working with communities while keeping the social costs of doing business low.

Choosing to work and live within traditions supporting a paradigm of peace takes courage and a great deal of humour. Often, the decisions made within this paradigm seem counter-intuitive or at least puzzling to those unfamiliar with this way of thinking. What does peace have to do with business in the first place or the natural resources industries in particular? I hope that this book will render answers to this question clearly.

Observant readers will also notice that I write out of my commitments to the wisdom and belief in a deep tradition of peace within the oldest interpretations of the Beatitudes within the Gospel of Jesus Christ (Matt 5: 3–12). This wisdom corresponds to similar traditions of peace in Indigenous, Muslim, Buddhist, Sikh, Confucian and other religious or philosophical foundations for peaceful expressions of human society. In appealing to these traditions, it is my hope that CSR practitioners can make their own link to their own traditional sources of wisdom to guide them as they innovate within a Paradigm of Peace towards making efficient, effective decisions beneficial to corporations, communities and the environment.

Finally, I would like to thank the editorial team at Routledge for their care and patience with this manuscript. I am indeed grateful for the many colleagues, students and industry partners who have informed my understanding of the particular challenges faced by natural resources operations and the communities affected by them. I am especially grateful to the CSR practitioners who agreed to interviews vital to the development of the paradigm of peace especially for businesses. My colleagues and the executive leadership team at the UQ Business School have provided a supportive environment in which to complete this manuscript. Of special mention is Joshua Hartmann, who very patiently translated the figures in this manuscript from earlier iterations. I also owe a debt of gratitude to my family for their support and love, most especially to Gilbert, whose own commitment to a life of peace and reconciliation through faith in Jesus Christ is truly inspirational.

Blessed are the peacemakers, for they shall be called children of God.

Matthew 5:9

1 Introduction

Peace or a Pipe Dream?

Businesses around the world have begun putting peace-focused thinking into practice at the local level. This chapter looks at scholarly evidence to explain why. However, the chapter also challenges us to expand peace-focused thinking to include large-scale, heavy industry. After justifying the rationale for this book, the introduction provides an overview of the aims and direction of the book; forecasts conclusions; and positions the reader to think creatively about practical and 'do-able' peace-building activities in the natural resources industries.

1.1 Innovation

This book is innovative in suggesting a paradigm of positive peace as a platform for Corporate Social Responsibility (CSR) practice of natural resources companies (NRCs), particularly in non-war-affected contexts. To date, there has been a gap in the literature in terms of Peace Theory and CSR streams of research and activity. Few researchers have explored them *together* and fewer still within the broader natural resources context. This book uses the literature on business and peace to bridge that gap. By doing so, a contribution to knowledge will be made to the Peace Theory literature related to business activities as well as to the CSR literature. The book considers the gains a paradigm of positive peace might achieve, given the relentless financial and political pressures continuously at play in the natural resources sector. This book is among the first to incorporate key ideas from peace-building to prioritise human thriving, *eudaimonia*, as an outcome from natural resources development.

Insofar as Peace Theory is no longer solely dominated by the (neo)liberal state-building agenda or local capacity-building efforts (Boege, 2012; Richmond, 2009, 2010, 2011; Richmond & Mitchell, 2012), it then becomes increasingly important to locate community-level actors with international profiles, such as NRCs, within the expanding peace-building agenda. In terms of Peace Theory, if NRCs can be viewed and engaged as non-state actors within the sovereign state system, it becomes possible for states, intergovernmental organisations and international NGOs to legitimately address these companies as non-state actors. As the head of an NRC expressed, at the 20th Annual Mining Indaba in South Africa:

> We have to think beyond our historical characterization and eliminate a conversation that talks to us being an 'Extractive Industry'. While we may extract products from rocks—we are overwhelmingly a 'Development Industry' that creates new social possibilities. We should be the 'Development Partner' that supports and catalyses the creation of wealth for all.
>
> (Cutifani, 2013)

Therefore, it may be time to think about a paradigm of positive peace in the natural resources context, creating new socio-economic possibilities for all.

This book proceeds from the assumption that NRCs and the individual CSR practitioners working within them can choose how they will respond to communities and to any conflicts that emerge at the community level. Part of what this book does is examine three influential paradigms informing CSR practice in the natural resources context: Neoliberal Economics, Risk Management and Human Rights. The book explores what these paradigms offer but pays more attention to what they do not. In particular, the book highlights that these three paradigms focus much more on the avoidance of negative consequences rather than on the achievement of productive outcomes resulting from NRC-community interaction.

Focusing on the negative consequences of insufficient community engagement is an understandable corporate response. Stopping or avoiding harm is necessary in situations where a company is trying to stop or prevent rapidly escalating community-level conflict with the potential to cause significant or permanent damage to people, property or the environment. There is a place and a time for such a focus. However, as will be discussed in Chapter 2, this near-exclusive focus on negative consequences coupled with carefully managed public relations campaigns leads to missed opportunities and incorrect analysis of social conflict situations and does not lead to opportunities for conflict transformation. Such an exclusive focus on avoiding negative outcomes or risks can result in the application of ineffective strategies, unaddressed root causes of conflict and worsening NRC-related conflict.

In order to change the focus and sub-optimal outcomes, this book argues there is a place for the paradigm of positive peace. Positive peace can be either an alternate or a complimentary paradigm with the potential to influence CSR responses to communities and community-level conflict. Positive peace neither ignores nor emphasises the negative aspects of conflict. What it does differently is to identify and dismantle structures, situations and relationships that contribute to violence at a social, cultural or physical level and seeks to build structures, situations and relationships that are non-coercive and harmonious in character (Francis, 2010). If NRCs chose to inform their CSR strategies from a paradigm of positive peace, rather than focusing more singularly on negative outcomes of community-level conflict, this choice might engender greater creativity and willingness from both practitioners and communities to achieve mutually beneficial goals.

Publicly addressing the intersection of business and peace often evokes strange looks, even laughter. I have come to recognise that this is an important part of the process. When introducing peace as a universal 'good' into discussions on business, people, at first, do not know how to respond. This moment of not knowing is essential to creating opportunities for innovative solutions to emerge.

1.2 Why This Book? Why Now?

The geo-political world order has changed in ways unimaginable until very recently. Founded on neoliberal, democratic ideals, the geo-political world order that has both enabled and dominated the globalised marketplace is yielding to various new forces. The balance of political and economic power has yet to emerge clearly and may become even more unstable before achieving a new equilibrium. What has become increasingly clear, however, is that significant portions of society in all countries have suffered under free-market-driven, neoliberal values. Those who lack economic vitality, adequate health care, affordable higher education, and who are excluded from networks of power, are entrapped in expanding, intergenerational cycles of poverty, disadvantage and violence.

The geo-political order is changing in response to the rising tide of populations who seek to interrupt these cycles of suffering. People tired of suffering are taking action to either recreate opportunities long denied or lost as a consequence of the global economy. One group of disadvantaged citizens are the low socio-economic status (SES) populations in so-called developed countries. SES populations articulate their dissatisfaction by supporting reactionary politicians and wealthy elites promoting a nationalist agenda. These spokespeople translate the collective anger, fear, intolerance, repression, xenophobia — *Ressentiment* — of low SES populations into regressive, domestic policy populism and aggressive militarism abroad (Fassin, 2013). Another disadvantaged group has become part of the largest population of displaced people since World War II, fleeing war-torn and environmentally degraded regions. Both groups want a better life for themselves and their families. Only a fraction will achieve their goals through massive migration or a political process.

In the West, OECD countries are slowly awakening to the destabilising significance of growing numbers of their impoverished low SES citizens. These 'forgotten' people have been victimised by the same forces of global economic disruption as those from under-developed states in the Global South. Scholars, journalists and Green Party politicians have been warning of the growing gap between rich and poor since early 1980.[1] The political and economic *will* needed to rectify the egregious and growing imbalance, however, has been lacking leadership for almost 40 years. The chasm has yawned so widely that Oxfam presented an alarming report at the 2017 World Economic Forum in Davos: 62 people have control of over half the world's wealth.[2] This statistic is especially troubling because, although these wealthy people do not serve as elected representatives of any government body, they rival voting citizens in their disproportionate power to steer the course of government and shape the fate of social and economic casualties who share insufficiently in the financial benefits accrued from the new global economy.

Meanwhile, governments struggle to respond to 'forgotten', suffering and vulnerable people while also trying to maintain the working and middle class *status quo*. This difficult balancing act of weighing complex needs versus maintaining socio-economic order is vital for the political stability that undergirds social peace. However, shifts in political power have made democratic governments themselves increasingly disordered and searching desperately for some common ground of political and social coherence. In circumstances where democracy fails, other governing structures take their place. Alternate or failed governments stir cauldrons of conflict, as in Syria, North Africa, the former Soviet Union, Afghanistan, North Korea and Central Africa,[3] provoking an uneasy and increasingly worrying military response from the West. Concurrently, the dawning awareness of many that the environmental collapse of our biosphere is a real possibility plunges governments into unknown territories of policy and planning and in some cases into denial.

Governments have no easy response to a wide array of different environmental challenges, whether or not there is consensus on the causes of the looming environmental catastrophe or whose responsibility it is to redress (UNESCO, 1992; United Nations, 2015). Environmental concerns include: escalating greenhouse gas emissions (Zhong et al., 2017); the ongoing Fukushima power plant radiation leak (2011) into the Pacific Ocean (Pvinec, Hirose, & Aoyama, 2013); spills and fugitive emissions from coal mines, gas and petroleum pipelines (Itskos et al., 2016; Ju et al., 2016); melting polar ice caps (Seongsuk & Yu, 2016); deforestation (Golub, Lubowski, & Piris-Cabezas, 2017); droughts (Trenberth et al., 2014); rising sea levels(Carson et al., 2016); and increasing levels of species extinction (Wiens, 2016). Even though some Green groups, Indigenous communities, scientists and industrial companies themselves have made correlations between industrial activity and environmental change, there is absolutely no consensus as to how business should respond, if at all.

While people at all levels of society continue to struggle with threatening environmental challenges, businesses such as multinational corporations (MNCs), Supply Chain firms (SCs) and Small and Medium Enterprises (SMEs) operate within these unpredictable conditions. MNCs, SCs and SMEs, by their persistent efforts to remain economically viable, contribute to conditions of peace both locally and globally while governments of the world utilise varying combinations of hard and soft power to establish what may become a new world order capable of responding to climate and social changes. Consequently, businesses have an unprecedented opportunity to exhibit innovative leadership by creating and maintaining conditions of supportive of a revisioned and stable *status quo* for a significant number of internal and external stakeholders affected by their operations (Gore, 2016).

One international organisation is taking the lead by providing a framework for businesses to rethink how they interact with the communities affected by their operations. The UN Global Compact (UNGC) provides a unifying platform for businesses to contribute to and find resources for a wide range of sustainability initiatives under an umbrella concept of *peace*. While the UNGC acknowledges that governments bear the primary responsibility for peace, they also recognise that businesses of all sizes and all industries can make significant contributions to conditions conducive to peace. The mission statement of the UNGC points to, "Business as a force for good: by committing to sustainability, business can take shared responsibility for achieving a better world". This statement is linked to a larger suite of principles and goals, which include expressions of core values on Human Rights, fair working conditions, environmental responsibility and anti-corruption commitments.[4] The ten principles appear in an expanded format in the 2015 version of the 17 Sustainable Development Goals (SDGs) agreed upon by the governments, businesses, civil society representatives and citizen groups of all 193 UN Member States:

1. No poverty
2. Zero hunger
3. Good health and well-being
4. Quality education
5. Gender equality
6. Clean water and sanitation
7. Affordable and clean energy
8. Decent work and economic growth
9. Industry innovation and infrastructure
10. Reduced inequalities
11. Sustainable cities and communities
12. Responsible consumption and production
13. Climate action
14. Life below water
15. Life on land
16. Peace, justice and strong institutions
17. Partnerships for the goals

The UNGC challenges businesses of all sizes and in all sectors to establish SDGs as a local priority. The Business for Peace (B4P) initiative underscores the importance of businesses working within networks of like-minded organisations, government agencies, NGOs, academics and community groups to implement these goals as integral to doing business.[5] The Global Reporting Initiative (GRI), supported by members of the World Business Council of Sustainable Development (WBCSD), is in the process of developing clusters of metrics around each of the 17 SDGs to measure Economic, Social and Environmental effects.[6]

Although each of the 17 SDGs relates to social conditions of peace, SDG 16 specifically names peace as a desired condition for both conducting business and in which to do business. SDG 16 is also quite specific about the spectrum of activities that are not conducive to peace: human trafficking, underage labour, illicit arms flow, corruption, inadequate representation, expressions of physical violence and inadequate rule of law. This list applies most directly to fragile states, conflict zones, buffer zones and other regions at heightened risk of descending into conflict. In some instances, natural resources industries are implicated in these activities. These conditions, however, are not characteristic of all natural resources projects, some of which actively contribute to conditions of peace where they operate.

The contribution of businesses to conditions of peace in regions where they operate is not entirely new. Some scholars have linked John Locke's *Second Treatise* (1689) and Kant's *Perpetual Peace* (1795) to the early recognition that businesses prosper in peaceful conditions. These two historical texts correlate economic advancement with enhancing peace and development (Doyle, 1986; Miklian, Schouten, & Ganson, 2016). Scholars are more frequently reframing business activities on a spectrum from "peace enhancing" to "peace threatening" and identify innovative opportunities to advance the former. The reasons for advancing aspects of business which enhance and build peace are due to the misinterpretation of the original Brundtland goals for sustainable development. In the last 20 years, the focus upon the principles in *Our Common Future* has shifted from the original intent in two ways. First, environmental priorities have superseded social welfare. Second, the needs of industrialised countries have been prioritised over those of countries most disadvantaged (Barkemeyer, Holt, Preuss, & Tsang, 2014; Brundtland Commission, 1987). These shifting priorities actually undermine the report's original purpose. As a corrective, prioritising practices which create conditions of peace as a result of conducting business would have the effect of renewing emphasis upon the social principles of Sustainable Development that demonstrate genuine care and concern for the more vulnerable.

Prioritising peace responsibilities of business is not a new idea. A watershed moment in the recent scholarly movement to recognise the peace enhancing aspects of business occurred in 2000. With the support of a global NGO, International Alert, renowned scholar Dr Jane Nelson wrote a white paper on how businesses in the private sector could function as agents to resolve and prevent conflict (Nelson, 2000). Dr Nelson was the first in the contemporary era to present practical steps towards making a business case for engaging in peace enhancing behaviour. Shortly thereafter, Fort and Schipani, from the University of Michigan, began writing a series of articles challenging academics, NGOs and businesses to begin thinking more strategically about contributing to peace from within the business sector. While their papers focused more on preventing and responding to violent conflict, it was, nevertheless, the start of a new and robust dialogue. The influential Academy of Management published five papers from a symposium on *Conflict Management and Peace* in 2015. Among the contributions to the still fledgling field of business and peace were the following four observations.

First, scholars in business management are much more willing to engage in research about the political role of businesses enhancing conditions of peace than political scientists (Ford, 2015; Haufler, 2015). In general, international relations scholars are of the view that businesses can cause harm just as much if not more than they can contribute to peace. Political scientists view the role of business as generally neutral to slightly negative in terms of their ability to affect factors such as the 'resource curse', Human Rights, poverty and security. Overall, political scientists have concluded that the contribution of businesses to peace is insignificant when various other political actors set the terms of engagement at the macro level.

Ultimately, this disciplinary divide has deep roots in international relations theory because political scientists adopt a 'pure' approach to analysing geo-political power as though it were exercised only by states and non-state organisations such as the United Nations, the World Bank, the International Monetary Fund and similar entities. This divide, however, has become much more difficult to maintain after the Ruggie Mandate carefully outlined the responsibilities businesses have to protect and respect Human Rights while remediating any violations they may have committed (Ruggie, 2011b). Ruggie maintains that states have responsibility for establishing and upholding internationally enshrined Human Rights standards, but that businesses be accountable within the sphere of their own influence (IHRB, 2011; Knox, 2011; Ruggie, 2011a). This structured way of holding both states and businesses accountable is applicable, theoretically, across the entire suite of 17 Sustainable Development Goals at the micro level, including peace.

Second, government regulation and legislation are no longer sufficient to create the conditions of peace in which human society flourishes especially in weak, impoverished and failing states. Countries in the Global South have neither the revenue base nor the infrastructure to deliver benefits equitably. Often, host governments approve large resource projects specifically because international corporations have both the capacity and the technical knowledge to provide infrastructure, hospitals, and schools. These types of community benefits characterise and constitute conditions of greater peacefulness for both the community and for the company according to the SDGs; and go beyond merely doing no harm to actively contributing to the social welfare (Ford, 2015; Forrer & Katsos, 2015). Although managers of large resources projects repeatedly state that they are not in the development business, it is increasingly difficult for the companies undertaking these large resource projects to resist appeals for developmental assistance.

Third is the movement to include leaders of larger corporations into second- and third-tier diplomatic circles. In these circumstances, government and corporate leaders work collaboratively to design conditions that maximise the benefits of operating a business in a particular context. Ideally, the benefits accrue to the host state, the company and the communities proximate to operation sites. Because of the size of some of the multinationals, however, they may be asked to cover gaps in governance, play a role in reducing conflict and actually creating conditions for peace at the community level (Westermann-Behaylo, Rehbein, & Fort, 2015).

Finally, many businesses have supply chains that encircle the globe. Insofar as it is important for businesses to contribute to conditions of peacefulness throughout their supply chains, employees are the biggest contributors in each location. Therefore, achieving conditions of peace at the local level becomes untenable if employees are afraid of losing their job for speaking up about an injustice or unfairness. Circumstances wherein employees feel free to introduce ideas for improvements to processes and voice concerns about safety, working conditions or terms of employment enhance peacemaking prospects. This micro level of engagement is often where the struggle for making contributions to overall peacefulness is won or lost (Milliken, Schipani, Bishara, & Prado, 2015).

The innovation needed now is for businesses in heavy industrial sectors to understand their activities as 'peace-enhancing' or 'peace-building'. Businesses in the technology (ICT) sector, some financial investment houses, renewable energy firms, and free-trade producers are early adopters of advancing a peace-friendly profile. There are even initiatives such as B-Corp, a voluntary group of enterprises holding themselves and their suppliers to a set of standards designed to leave a responsible environmental and social legacy.[7] Companies in the natural resources sectors, however, are not as familiar with aligning their business practices with peace-building language or principles and in some instances see no need to either adopt peacemaking vocabulary or engage communities in this manner.

Mining, oil and gas, forestry and hydro-power companies are large-footprint industries that all must locate their operations in areas where resources naturally occur. They have no other option. Whether state or privately owned, each operation must contend with reality on the ground at the community level. Consequently, global political-economic pressures, climate change debates and community-level demands are making it less possible for NRCs to escape unprecedented scrutiny of their businesses. Society is calling for transparency, realistic assessment of benefit/risks and accountability over current and historic project legacies.

No matter where they are located, communities affected by natural resources projects share one thing in common: they often do not have a choice about whether or not a project will proceed. At best, communities can negotiate a benefit arrangement with an NRC. Occasionally, communities will halt a project for a time—sometimes for a few months, years or even decades. There are few examples, however, of communities stopping natural resource development from proceeding at all over an extended period of time. Globally, natural resource projects affect traditional, rural and Indigenous communities disproportionately. The well-documented examples are of NRCs precipitating the permanent resettlement of communities away from their traditional lands for mining, hydro-power or forestry projects which render those lands uninhabitable.

Unlike in years past, neither privately held nor state-owned NRCs are legally free to disregard the effect that they have on communities according to international law and various norms enshrined in voluntary codes of practice. Ever since the publication of the Brundtland Commission[8] Report (1987), there has been a concerted effort to mitigate the community level effects of NRC's, including environmental, economic, as well as social aspects. As will be discussed in Chapter 2, a substantial suite of Sustainable Development and Corporate Social Responsibility initiatives developed to help NRC staff, and their counterparts in NGOs and Government, to mitigate the deleterious effects at the community level in a thoughtful and thorough fashion.

The guidance for NRCs at the local, national and even international levels, however, only work when both NRCs and communities cooperate to achieve mutually desired benefits. Successful outcomes are not as well known as the narratives of failure. Community dissatisfaction with the results of NRC engagement endures for the life span of these projects, which at times can extend up to 100 years. Consequently, dissatisfaction with historic and current outcomes leads to cycles of conflict between NRCs and the community at varying levels of intensity. Greater than 85% of NRC-community conflict is not physically violent in nature, but it still can cause environmental damage, emotional and psychological trauma for individuals and groups within the communities.

Although NRCs are not blind to community-level grievances, they do not always have the economic or human resources necessary to redress grievances in line with international, national or even local standards. In some circumstances, the NRCs lack the will to do so. Furthermore, not all communities wish to achieve a mutually agreeable arrangement about either the distribution of benefits or compromises required by the presence of NRC operations. Some communities do not want the NRC there at all and are committed to doing anything in their power to halt development and confound operations through legal, activist or other means. In situations where NRCs are under-resourced and communities are defiant, or even in less contentious situations, where an NRC-community relationship has soured, it is difficult to determine how the parties can find a way forward.

This book explores physically non-violent conflict between NRCs and the communities affected by their development and operations. Why? Because most conflict regarding NRC development and operations is not located in war zones or failed states. Approaching company-community conflict with a peace-focused lens, the book demonstrates the value of peace and conflict theory for the implementation of CSR as a sub-set of the Brundtland-Commission-defined Sustainable Development strategies. The heuristic device from peace and conflict theory on which this book is based is positive peace. Positive peace is defined as an intentional commitment to strengthen non-violent attitudes, behaviours, institutions and structures leading toward "peaceful relationships and processes, economic well-being [and] environmental protection" (Francis, 2010, p. 168). In other words, achieving positive peace means addressing the following core question: if the NRC takes action 'x', does the result encourage or discourage greater conditions of peacefulness at the community level?

The elegant simplicity of this question is that day-to-day operational level staff, technical as well as community-facing, can use it just as effectively as C-suite executives and strategic planners. Of course, simple, elegant questions such as this one need a little more explanation. If the answer to the question is 'yes', then the follow-up series of questions entails a search for 'how to operationalise' action 'x' in innovative ways to maximise the benefits and minimise the compromises or harms. If the answer to the question is 'no', then the follow-up series of questions must include a search for different ways to address the need for action 'x' that do not lead to conditions of less peacefulness at the community level.

Looking at the big picture, NRCs will continue to operate as long as people perceive a need to use the earth's resources at an industrial scale for construction, manufacturing and energy generation purposes, one of the most important considerations to the viability of these industries is to maintain operating conditions of relative peacefulness. Common wisdom in the business community says that it is difficult to run an NRC business in an environment riven with conflict. Consequently, this book discusses how a CSR emphasis on positive peace has potential to support the development of more holistic, productive and longer-term conflict outcomes than those privileging neoliberal economic, Human Rights and risk management considerations.

Towards making this argument, the book undertakes the development of an analytical, conceptual framework to determine the potential for a paradigm of positive peace to influence CSR practice in the natural resources context. The question driving this book is: *what kind of potential is there in applying a paradigm of positive peace to prevent and respond to conflicts in the natural resources context?* The subsidiary question is: *how responsive to using the paradigm of positive peace are the community-facing staff of natural resources companies?* Underlying these questions is the assumption that it is possible to interpret and apply positive peace in a paradigmatic way, as described in Chapters 2 and 4.

The CSR practitioners interviewed in preparation for this book are from the natural resources sector. They represent company employees, independent contractors, government employees, NGO representatives and similar professionals across a range of organisational settings. Their scope of responsibilities includes shaping and delivering CSR policies and outcomes for businesses. The term CSR is variably defined in the literature and examined further in Chapter 2, but is used in this book as follows:

> [CSR] encompass[es] not only what companies do with their profits, but also how they make them. It goes beyond philanthropy and compliance to address the manner in which companies manage their economic, social, and environmental impacts and their stakeholder relationships in all their key spheres of influence: the workplace, the marketplace, the supply chain, the community and the public policy realm.
>
> (Kytle & Ruggie, 2005, p. 9)

The reasons to focus on CSR practitioners as core actors in the natural resources industry are two-fold. The first is that although every employee or contractor of an NRC is potentially an ambassador for site-based operations, it is usually the remit of CSR practitioners to be the primary point of contact and relationship manager between an NRC and affected communities. Secondly, the interaction between individual CSR practitioners[9] and members of the community significantly affects the emergence or diminution of NRC-community conflict (Kemp & Bond, 2009). When conflict does emerge from unaddressed grievances between NRCs and communities, how CSR practitioners handle or are instructed to handle those situations on behalf of an NRC affects the duration and intensity of this conflict.

A key aspect of *positive peace* is that it has transformational potential to reframe conflict as an opportunity for constructive change and assist in communicating those opportunities effectively to internal and external stakeholders. Disputants can then view latent and emergent conflict not as just (1) something to avoid, but (2) as a catalytic opportunity to increase desired outcomes from best-practice CSR strategies. The outcomes of the research underpinning this book show that *positive peace* has traction with CSR professionals working in the natural resources sector. In fact, the research strongly suggests that there is potential to explore further the ways in which CSR professionals could use the paradigm of *positive peace* to frame and address community level conflict. Follow-up research in this direction would focus on how peace-building processes of conflict transformation are both necessary and could be aligned with effective CSR frameworks to accomplish conflict outcomes characteristic of a paradigm of positive peace. This research might usefully incorporate the receptivity of vocational peacebuilders and community leaders responding to conflict-prone NRC operations to apply their knowledge, skills and talents in the natural resources sector.

There are significant limits to the scope of this book. The first limitation is in regard to the number of paradigms reviewed. I chose to focus on paradigms most commonly invoked in the NRC-community space, paradigms with which most CSR practitioners are familiar. Secondly, by focusing on three common paradigms already accepted as part of the CSR space, there is less potential to be imbued with highly charged, emotive content, such as with environmental, Indigenous[10] and human security paradigms. Future research will consider these paradigms, as they are vitally important. The choice to exclude them in this volume reflects the reality that people often conflate social justice aspects of environmental, Indigenous and human security paradigms with aspects of peace and conflict literature. Although social justice is vital, as both an outcome of and condition for peace, the inclusion of social justice-driven paradigms here makes it more difficult to tease apart the unique benefits *positive peace* brings as a paradigm. It is all the more important for preliminary research about paradigms and positive peace in the NRC-community space to avoid emotive overtones as much as possible because anecdotal evidence and media reports strongly indicate that NRCs respond neither swiftly nor satisfactorily to emotional claims by individuals or community groups (Lloyd, 2014).

The second limitation is in the exploratory nature of this research. It was both logistically and economically unfeasible to determine receptivity to positive peace as a paradigm with representative samples from all varieties of NRCs on multiple continents. Nor was it possible to test the research approach with a representative sample of community and local-level stakeholders from Western, non-Western, modern and traditional groups of natural resources-affected peoples. It would be valuable to test the validity of the claims of this book amongst these and other stakeholder groups through a series of comparative studies. After all, the research outcomes of this book are only applicable if the paradigm of positive peace resonates with a broad range of corporate and community stakeholders including but not limited to CSR practitioners. The conclusions of this book are therefore strictly limited to: (1) the views and receptivity of a modest sample of CSR practitioners to the paradigm of positive peace and (2) their evaluation of whether or not a paradigm of positive peace had value for their practice.

A third limitation to this book is that it relies on the experience of practitioners, not the experience of the author. Due to confidentiality agreements, many of the cases mentioned throughout the book are presented in a limited fashion. It would be quite useful if people who have had experience transforming a conflict situation into a peaceful situation could share their examples more freely so others can share in the learnings.

An alternative approach to evaluating the appetite for incorporating peace-focused thinking in the natural resources space would have been to start at the community level. However, during the scoping stage of the research, it was clear that a number of Australian and Canadian research projects were studying the effect of a range of CSR decisions on natural resources-affected communities. Many of these projects relied on, to at least some extent, ethnographic field work in remote corners of Canada, Australia, Brazil, Peru, Viet Nam, Papua New Guinea, Ghana, Mongolia, India, China and Pakistan. As a point of differentiation, the research underpinning this book made the practitioner side of the NRC-community relationship continuum a priority. The book explicitly relies on the views of CSR practitioners working for and with NRCs to approach conflict.

The final limit relates to ownership of large NRCs. In many parts of the world, state governments own all or significant parts of these NRCs. This book does not dig deeply into the state-owned businesses primarily because history shows that states have not done a thorough job in regulating themselves in terms of sustainability practice in natural resources projects. For example, there is very little motivation for a state with a large hydro-power plant to impose limits on social and environmental effects for a small population of affected people when a much larger group of people deeply desire access to electricity. Reports of a similar lack of consultation occur in the construction of petroleum pipelines, the granting of leases or easements through forested land and areas with large mining deposits.

The next sections of this chapter look at what this book does cover. First, I outline the varieties of conflict in the natural resources context that this book seeks to address. Second is a brief sketch of the particular concept of CSR the book uses as the avenue for action on peace-building activities. Third is a summary of particular definitions of 'paradigms', 'positive peace' and 'violence'. Fourth is an explanation of the innovative assumptions underlying this book. Finally, there is the outline of how the book unfolds followed by the explanation of a philosophical world-view that stems from learnings gleaned after the pain of the two great 20th-century global conflicts.

1.3 Context: Natural Resources-Related Conflict

Depending on the context, natural resources activities can either generate or reawaken both sustained and episodic social conflict with communities. It is not difficult to find examples of overt, physically violent conflict between mining companies and communities:

- Tampakan copper mine in the Philippines (Pamfilo, Viña, Perez, & Santos, 2005);
- Panguna gold and copper mine in Bougainville (Boege, 2010);
- Diamond fields of Sierra Leone and Liberia (Custers & Matthysen, 2009); and
- Gold mines in South Africa or the Americas (BICC, 2008; Clark, 2002; Özkaynak et al., 2012; Rustad & Binningsbø, 2012; World Gold Council, 2012)

Forestry-related conflicts include activities such as palm oil production, clearing for grazing and cropping land and timber harvesting. Efforts to stop both environmental harm as well as expressions of physical violence between forest dwellers and corporations have inspired a host of REDD+ initiatives around the world from Cameroon to Brazil to Indonesia (Awono, Somorin, Eba'a Atyi, & Levang, 2014; den Besten, Arts, & Verkooijen, 2014; Sunderlin et al., 2014; Wolosin, 2016). Equally, hydro-power projects (HPP) in South America as well as south and central Asia have conditions of transboundary claims to scarce water resources that create conditions ripe for conflict to develop (Allens Arthur Robinson, 2009; Global Witness, 2015; Ito, El Khatib, & Nakayama, 2016; Schulz & Rachel, 2009; Sternberg, 2008). Importantly, most of the scholarship on NRCs and conflict feature physically violent examples.

Physical violence, however, is not characteristic of most NRC-community conflict, most of which is not linked to large-scale physical violence but still results in negative outcomes for both NRCs and communities (Bond, Shi, & Kirsch, 2013). In situations of violent conflict, formal peacekeeping methods may be necessary to halt behaviours that present barriers to peace, potentially requiring international intervention within the sovereign state system. Extensive scholarship addresses NRCs and conflict zones where war may potentially emerge or has already emerged.

Putting those cases to the side, this book focuses on the majority of NRC-community conflicts where larger-scale physical violence, war or armed insurrection is *not* an emerging issue. Examples of non-warlike conflict include disputes over land and water access/use, compensation, employment, development benefits, infrastructure provision and services such as health care and education. In these instances, it is possible to say that conflict in the natural resources context is changing. The manner in which NRCs and communities currently engage one another has altered with both parties having access to a greater range of engagement mechanisms.

Communities now have more avenues than ever before to 'push back' NRCs or to object to various aspects of their operation. These avenues include: appealing to governments and regulatory bodies; direct protest; social media campaigns; NGO involvement; making presentations to boards of directors at large banks; legal mechanisms; non-judicial grievance mechanisms such as ombudsmen; and appeal to various international organisations (IOs). Communities have successfully delayed or halted the development of natural resources projects in cases where communities experience or anticipate resultant harm. Examples from the mining sector include: the Dongria Kondh in India (Sahu, 2009), the Cajamarca people in Peru (Kemp, Owen, Cervantes, Arbelaez-Ruiz, & Rueda, 2012), the Innu and Inuit people in Canada (Gibson, MacDonald, & O'Faircheallaigh, 2011) and the Aboriginal people in Australia (Kunanayagam & Tomlinson, 2011).

NRCs have the capacity to respond to concerned communities in a more nuanced way than in years past. They do not need to resort to heavy-handed means (e.g., police or military) when conflict arises at the community level, or accept as somehow 'normal' or 'unavoidable' physically violent outcomes from conflict-laden instances of community engagement. There are a broad range of toolkits, guidance notes, voluntary initiatives and regulatory structures (collectively referred to here as 'strategies') that have been developed to help NRCs pro-actively anticipate community concerns and respond appropriately during or after community engagement becomes conflictual. Additionally, natural resources industry leaders have developed internal policies and systems to reflect and address community concerns. To date, however, this broad array of strategies and accumulated wisdom has not been sufficient to adequately reduce or eliminate negative effects of natural resources affiliated with community-level discord and conflict.

Conflict is not a bad thing, *per se*. Non-violent conflict can be an indication that an opportunity for change is emerging. The outcomes from conflict, however, have the potential to be either positive or negative for the parties involved. Extracting natural resources precipitates change and disrupts communities in the competition for land and water. Conflict continues to occur in the NRC-community space as a response to both potential and actual natural resources-related change in environments as well as within/between communities. Negative outcomes from conflict between NRCs and communities can be costly financially and in other ways, such as: damaged property, loss of life, injury, relational rupture, reputational damage, legal complications, lost income and lost development opportunities.

The urgency of addressing conflict in the natural resources context is magnified when looking at the projected intensification of pressures on relationships between NRCs and communities mentioned in the first part of this chapter. These mounting pressures have the potential to increase the amount and intensity of conflict at the community level. An increase in conflict will affect both the quality of community life as well as having the potential to delay or halt natural resources projects and operations in developed and developing contexts around the world. In order to minimise the complex and cumulative impacts of these trends, CSR practice will need to be proactive in its approach.

1.4 Corporate Social Responsibility in the Natural Resources Context

There are already a number of scholars who have written on CSR practice. One of the world's experts in CSR, Archie Carroll, has written extensively on this topic for 40 years and has shaped the business case for CSR in both academic and corporate spheres of influence (Carroll, 1999; Carroll & Shabana, 2010). The 1999 literature review traces the development of CSR from the 1950s forward. It identifies four major themes that became dominant by the 1990s in CSR practice: corporate social performance, stakeholder theory, corporate citizenship and business ethics. Regardless of which of these thematic areas is emphasised or even if new areas of CSR practice are identified, Carroll remains confident of the construct's lasting utility.

> The CSR concept will remain as an essential part of business language and practice, because it is a vital underpinning to many of the other theories and is continually consistent with what the public expects of the business community today.
>
> (Carroll, 1999, p. 292)

In the 2010 article, which reviews subsequent developments in CSR practice, Carroll and Shabana reiterate the relevance for CSR and summarise the various reasons for its continued utility to business from a primarily financial point of view.

> The rationale for the business case for CSR may be categorized under four arguments: (1) reducing cost and risk; (2) strengthening legitimacy and reputation; (3) building competitive advantage; and (4) creating win—win situations through synergistic value creation.
>
> (Carroll & Shabana, 2010, p. 101)

Even though the business case is emphasised in their literature review, social aspects feature prominently. The authors highlight two in particular: (1) people feel better about working for a firm that takes CSR seriously which both reduces staff turnover and attracts higher-quality employees and (2) communities affected by business activities are much less likely to object or protest if CSR is properly addressing society's social concerns. They conclude that not only businesses, but academics and CSR professionals are achieving a mature understanding of CSR practice and the benefits it offers to all stakeholders, boding well for the continued relevance of CSR.

CSR has grown in understanding and acceptance by the natural resources sector since the Brundtland Report introduced the concept of sustainable development as a responsibility of all businesses (1987). Because the extractives industry has operations of such large size, natural resources operations affect whole communities and regions socially, economically and environmentally. These three aspects are the pillars of sustainable development (SD). CSR, although addressing all three, prioritises the social pillar of SD ahead of the economic and environmental pillars. This book does the same by focusing on the social effects of natural resources and subsequently interrogates the implications of positive peace as a paradigm with the potential to increase positive outcomes from CSR practice.

In the literature about natural resources and CSR, there is no shortage of material. Business ethics, social performance, multi-stakeholder engagement and corporate citizenship aspects of CSR are covered by scholars looking at cases of NRC commitments to local communities (Hilson, 2012; Kapelus, 2002; Mutti, Yakovleva, Vazquez-Brust, & Di Marco, 2012; Rees,

Kemp, & Davis, 2012; Wit & Schouten, 2006). However, when corporations emphasise pragmatic (e.g., profit-driven) reasons for engaging in CSR, communities, NGOs and activist groups object that CSR is serving as a public relations campaign rather than a true commitment to doing the right thing (Pendleton, McClenaghan, Melamed, Bunn, & Graymore, 2004; Walker & Howard, 2002). Moreover, the identification of what a 'natural resources-affected community' is becomes increasingly problematic, especially when evaluated by an NRC instead of by the people who consider themselves part of the community (Jenkins, 2004). Finally, CSR seems to have traction with practitioners and NRCs in terms of the Social License to Operate (SLTO) (Thomson & Boutilier, 2011; Wilburn & Wilburn, 2011). Like other aspects of CSR practice, SLTO is contested in terms of its utility to enhance genuine stakeholder engagement with community groups and NGOs (Owen & Kemp, 2013).

As a researcher, I am keenly aware of the complexity of CSR and the tendency for scholars to specialise in particular aspects of CSR. It was appealing to consider an exhaustive review of the aspects of CSR such as stakeholder theory, business ethics, benefits to businesses and their external stakeholders and SLTO. It remains an important task to undertake these comparisons in order to compare their strengths and weaknesses in terms of peace-building and positive peace theories. A comparative review, however, is not the purpose of this chapter.

Instead, I would argue that CSR practitioners in the natural resources industry do not need another 'how to' article, a manual or a suite of imperatives to address natural resources related conflicts emergent at the community level. Anecdotal evidence suggests that CSR practitioners are already overwhelmed with these resources, with sometimes competing ideas of 'what to do' and 'what not to do' in any given situation. What I propose for CSR practitioners is innovative ways of thinking (e.g., a new paradigm) about how to use the current strategies to their fullest potential. Consequently, this book is particularly concerned with which paradigm CSR practitioners use when employing strategies to handle non-warlike conflict in the natural resources context. Chapter 4 explores this idea further.

1.5 Key Terms

There are three concepts central to the development of the book: paradigms, positive peace and violence. They are described briefly below. The relationship between these concepts is expanded on in Chapters 4 and 5.

1.5.1 Paradigms

Chapter 4 of this book explores the concept of paradigms as an organising construct and then looks carefully at three influential paradigms in the CSR space. A paradigm shapes the way we look at the world and guides the way we behave in it. It is a way of looking at and knowing how to behave in the world. More specifically, it is "a generally accepted or widely shared set of concepts, assumptions, values and practices that constitute a way of understanding [. . .], a practical model for how to think through or handle a particular class of problems, rather than as a set of explicit rules we might follow" (de Neufville, 2010, p. 1014). In addition, paradigms have the capacity to "frame language, meanings and relationships" (Wilkinson-Maposa & Fowler, 2009, p. 33) by "guid[ing] acts and behaviour" (Jonker & Pennink, 2010, p. 26). According to Kuhn (1996 [1962]), paradigms govern how groups of people understand and respond to phenomena, making them an important factor in how people behave. This book examines the frameworks CSR practitioners employ within the natural resources context which could be utilised within a paradigm of positive peace to achieve productive outcomes.

Whether or not people are aware of the paradigms in which they operate, paradigms always function in the background of human thought and activity—loosely analogous to the background operating systems of computers or smart phones. The research underpinning this book proposes that the paradigms through which NRCs engage communities on the social aspects of natural resources activities matters significantly in determining: (1) their relationship(s) and (2) the decisions they make. The selection of a particular paradigm also affects the *processes* by which particular outcomes are achieved and the actual *possibilities* for particular outcomes. Consequently, for NRCs, the intentional choice of which paradigms to use in their CSR practices will significantly affect activities and potential outcomes.

1.5.2 Positive Peace

Chapter 3 explores various aspects of peace. In peace-building literature, there are two basic categories of peace: positive peace and negative peace. Positive peace refers to the conditions chosen by people, in relationship with one another, at any level in society from local to national, who are actively working together to generate conditions of peacefulness. It is more than just the absence of violence but the intentional creation and maintenance of conditions of peace and well-being for all. The achievement of positive peace has been referred to by Lederach and his colleagues as the activities of peace-building which affect positive social and cultural change using conversation as the primary means of transforming conflict (Lederach, Neufeldt, & Culbertson, 2007). The objective for positive peace is to resolve deeply rooted causes of conflict so that conditions for violent conflict are removed or resolved (Sandole, 2003). To do so requires carefully addressing identified causes within processes of conflict transformation.

Key to the success of these processes is the intentional inclusion of causal mechanisms that might otherwise be perceived as difficult, inconvenient or in some way 'thorny'. Therefore, the establishment of a strong, long-term, durable, positive peace requires the cooperation of a number of stakeholders over time attending to a wide range of variables on a number of levels, depending on how complex or entrenched the conflict situation is or might become. Ultimately, positive peace refers to "a holistic vision of peace that includes well-being, as well as right and just relationships and structures" (Neufeldt et al., 2006, p. 30). Alternately, negative peace simply means that there is no overt expression of large-scale physical violence (Galtung, 1969). Negative peace relies on the threat of or potential for violence, expressed in Western societies at the hands of the state in the armed forces, the police, the National Guard and the criminal justice system.

Positive peace, according to Francis in *From Pacification to Peacebuilding* (2010), is the opposite of violence. Positive peace is achieved when people see themselves and one another as interconnected and interdependent. Within this paradigm, conflict is viewed as

> [P]otentially constructive and often necessary for changing the things that are unjust. Constructive conflict seeks solutions that address the rights and needs of all who are involved. Violence goes against the value of inclusive respect for people and for life, so nonviolent methods must be used. Coercion, if and when it is used, must be temporary, and must not inflict lasting harm. It should open the way to dialogue.
>
> (Francis, 2010, p. 75)

Francis casts positive peace as activities which are peace-building, using conflict for constructive change, whereas she casts negative peace activities as pacification and subduing by force conflict that develops in response to change. Although violent intervention may halt a particular instance of conflict and restore a semblance of order, it affects the ongoing quality of a relationship between parties (Paffenholz & Spurk, 2010; Pearce, 1997). If this relational quality deteriorates as a result of how the conflict was handled, the prospect for positive peace is reduced, and the motivation for renewed and increasingly violent conflict is escalated (Francis, 2010).

Peace-building strategies, therefore, have five core characteristics that put the quality of the relationship between parties as the primary outcome. First, they focus on improving the quality of the relationship between parties first and particular conflicts within that relationship second (Lederach, 1995). Second, they assume conflict is a natural part of being in a relationship and not necessarily a 'bad' thing; indeed, conflict can be creative and generate productive outcomes (Kreisberg, 2011; Santa Barbara, Dubee, & Galtung, 2009). Third, they emphasise ongoing, dynamic and sustainable or ongoing peace as a process rather than as a goal. Fourth, there is a recognition that peace is a particular manner or condition of relationality between parties which acknowledges and addresses the effects of any historical conflicts that the parties may have experienced together or separately (Reychler & Paffenholz, 2001; Swiss Federal Department of Foreign Affairs & Swisspeace, 2009). The final distinguishing feature is that peace-building practices do not rely upon structural, cultural or physical violence for the creation or maintenance of peace (Francis, 2010; Neufeldt et al., 2006).

People who advocate for a resolution to or avoidance of various types of violence by implementing a paradigm of positive peace function as peacebuilders, whether they would call themselves by that name or not. This is a nuanced term discussed in the *Peace Theory* chapter but here stated in brief: peacebuilders advocate for and apply strategies that result in positive peace for people experiencing the threat or open expression of violence. They apply this through processes of conflict transformation. This application of conflict transformation distinguishes peace-building from stakeholder engagement. The actions they take to achieve a state of peacefulness within a paradigm of positive peace are peace-building strategies, whether badged as such or not, which can be applied before, during and after a related violent conflict of whatever intensity or duration.

If the achievement of positive peace between NRCs and communities can become an explicit goal of NRC's CSR practices within a paradigm of positive peace, it could have the effect of recasting their practices as 'peacebuilding' insofar as they address conflict before, during or after it occurs. As Galtung says, "peacebuilding addressees the underlying causes of conflict and prevents their transformation into violence" (Galtung in Paffenholz, 2010, p. 45). Therefore, to recast CSR activities in the natural resources context as addressing root causes of 'violence' (*see below*), in the broad sense of the term, would mean that CSR practitioners would in effect act as peacebuilders employing peace-building strategies.

1.5.3 Different Forms of Violence

Violence is the opposite of peace. It does not contribute to human wellbeing. Violence, however, is not limited to physical expressions or bellicose behaviour. Violence comes in three forms each of which are found in the natural resources context: structural, cultural or direct. Its onset can be either acute (suddenly) or chronic (cumulative effects over time). Table 1.1 was developed for this book to suggest indicative examples:

As the above table indicates, some forms of violence can be expressed by either or both parties—the NRC or the community members (including NRC workers)—and may implicate host governments. Regardless of who initiates, responds or escalates, when violent action or violent *non*-action is expressed (e.g., some cases of structural violence (Galtung, 1969)), it is an indication that one or more parties have unilaterally decided that there is no other alternative to resolving a conflict.

NRCs may not share the view that communities might perceive their activities as violent, especially when no physical violence is evident. However, complex and intertwined chronic cultural and structural violence, at the company

Table 1.1 Varieties of Violence

Type	*Definition*	*Local Actor*	*Examples in the natural resources context*
Structural Violence (chronic; often long-term and inadvertent)	Unintended harm done to human beings at the structural, or socio-political level (Galtung, 1985, p. 145)	Employees and contractors, sex workers	*The unintended sexual health consequences (e.g., HIV/AIDs) that appear with the in-migration pressures of a natural resources workforce.
		Government	*When governments grant natural resources leases without adequate consultation of and no recourse for people already living on the land.
Cultural Violence (chronic or acute)	Restrictions or prohibitions that affect the welfare and well-being of human beings related to cultural, heritage or religious values (Parlevliet, 2011, p. 380)	Natural resources company	*When NRCs exercise their legal right to excavate an ore body, lay a pipeline or harvest timber without the consent of Indigenous peoples who consider the land sacred or as having traditional value.
Direct/ Physical Violence (acute)	Physical violence or intimidation that results in bodily injury, pain or death (Parlevliet, 2011, p. 383)	Community members	*When community members throw rocks at resource company workers; vandalise property and equipment; and otherwise threaten the physical safety of resource company workers and management.
		Natural resources company, government	*When NRCs call on the assistance of the state via police, military, riot squads or para-military groups to forcibly remove protesters or villagers from a natural resources lease

and/or state level, can drive conflict just as much as acute or episodic physical violence and is sometimes more difficult to handle. Addressing chronic expressions of violence requires a sustained effort from multiple stakeholders and is difficult to maintain. An indicative illustration is the protracted conflict at the Argyle diamond mine in the Kimberley region of Western Australia (ca. 1980–2004) which involved mining giant Rio Tinto, several Indigenous groups and the Western Australian government. In this instance, issues of cultural violence (e.g., physical damage to sacred sites) and structural violence (e.g., the bureaucratic morass caused by the competing claims in the Native Title Act, the conditions of the natural resources lease and an insufficient 'Good Neighbour Agreement') led to chronic conflict between Rio Tinto and the Traditional Owner groups. The latter experienced many aspects of this conflict as deeply injurious and hurtful (i.e. violent) until all parties were satisfied with the Argyle Participation Agreement[11].

Before concluding the discussion of peace and violence, it is worth clarifying two aspects related to the use of the word *violence* in the natural resources context. First, NRCs prefer to reserve the term *violence* for physical confrontation (Bond et al., 2013) and are reluctant to label any of their activities as causing or participating in structural or cultural violence. Alternately, community organisers, news and social media are quick to use the term 'violence' in a colloquial way to characterise a range of natural resources-related conflicts. For example, the aversion to using the term by one party, coupled with usage by others, has a tendency to inflame negative aspects of NRC-community conflict. Second, despite the contested use of the term *violence*, when NRC-community conflict escalates into expressions of violence at the structural, cultural or direct/physical level (Table 1.1), parties can suffer direct or indirect consequences that inhibit well-being. Expressions of violent conflict can last for a few moments or for years, neither of which helps NRCs or communities achieve desired benefits from the activities of natural resources. It is therefore in NRCs' and communities' best interests to develop productive ways to respond to conflict that emerges in the context of their relationship. This is sometimes difficult to do, especially when there is either a legacy of natural resources conflict related to particular sites or historic community conflict that pre-existed the development of a natural resource.

1.6 Coda

Before closing this chapter, I want to point to the bigger frame within which this book sits. The significance of shifting how conflict is viewed in general, and in the natural resources conflict in particular, can be seen as part of a larger dynamic, problematised in Giorgio Agamben's *Homo Sacer: sovereign power and bare life* (1998). Agamben asks very serious questions about the human condition which transcend but remain relevant to specific human activities such as natural resources. Agamben's text examines the following issues very carefully: how or whether societies place a value on human life, which he considers a sacred trust; and who or what is responsible for how human life is protected. The struggle, at its most elemental, is one of priority between meta-value systems: life—the pursuit of human flourishing; or death—the struggle for human survival. Agamben classifies all human activity as trained on one or the other of those teleological[12] goals (e.g., what is the ultimate purpose that can be achieved).

In terms of this book, few people working in any part of the natural resources industry would couch their decisions as a daily teleological choice between life and death. Natural resources activities, however, increasingly occur in areas of the world where the sacredness of life is a daily reality, particularly for Indigenous and traditional peoples. People with explicitly life-affirming, meta-value systems sometimes see the activities of NRCs as a threat at a deep ontological level. In other words, rightly or wrongly, some people perceive natural resources as the harbinger of death and therefore a considerable menace to cultures, social systems and environments. It may be necessary in such instances to address this ontological issue, either directly or indirectly, in order for NRC-community conflicts to result in beneficial outcomes. This includes the very real possibility to decide *not* to 'develop' natural resources. The question is—how can ontological issues be addressed effectively, efficiently and without specialist training?

The difference in meta-value systems (life/death) is largely unarticulated in the natural resources context and efforts to engage that level of discourse are more philosophical than practical. Yet, if one can situate CSR activity within these meta-value systems and engage NRC-community conflict at the paradigmatic level, there may be potential to use CSR strategies in practice in a way that satisfactorily addresses deep ontological concerns. However, it is the prosaic, low-level activities where most of the problems lie and current ways of addressing them are not sufficient to the task. This book is intended as a contribution towards achieving better outcomes at the local level.

Notes

1 *www.ineqalityor/income-inequality/* [accessed 24.03.2017]
2 *www.oxfam.org.uk/media-centre/press-releases/2016/01/62-people-own-same-as-half-world-says-oxfam-inequality-report-davos-world-economic-forum* [accessed 24.03.2017]
3 Static.visionofhumanity.org/#/page/indexes/global-peace-index [accessed 24.03.2017]
4 *www.unglobalcompact.org.au/about/principles/* [Accessed 25.03.2017]
5 *www.unglobalcompact.org/docs/issues_doc/Peace_and_Business/* [Accessed: 25.03.2017]
6 *www.globalreporting.org/information/news-and-press-center/Pages/Leading-global-organizations-welcome-the-new-GRI-Standards.aspx* [Accessed: 27.03.2017]
7 *http://bcorporation.com.au/what-are-b-corps-0* [Accessed: 18.04.2017]
8 *www.un-documents.net/our-common-future.pdf* [accessed: 21.03.2017]
9 CSR practitioners' overall effectiveness is influenced by the level of organisational and departmental support from the corporate level as well as the general manager on site.
10 Insofar as paradigms are considered equivalent to worldviews, it is possible to argue that indigenous worldviews are equivalent to indigenous paradigms (Korhonen, 2002).
11 http://klc.org.au/agreements/argyle-mining-agreement/ [Accessed: 16 May 2013]
12 **Teleology: the doctrine or study of ends or final causes, esp. as related to the evidences of design or purpose in nature (OED, 2013)**

Bibliography

Agamben, G. (1998). *Homo sacer: Sovereign power and bare life*. Stanford, CA: Stanford University Press.

Allens Arthur Robinson. (2009). *Human rights review of hydropower sustainability assessment protocol*. Carlton.

Awono, A., Somorin, O. A., Eba'a Atyi, R., & Levang, P. (2014). Tenure and participation in local REDD+ projects: Insights from southern Cameroon. *Environmental Science & Policy*, *35*, 76–86. doi:10.1016/j.envsci.2013.01.017

Barkemeyer, R., Holt, D., Preuss, L., & Tsang, S. (2014). What happened to the 'Development' in sustainable development? Business guidelines two decades after Brundtland. *Sustainable Development*, *22*(1), 15–32. doi:10.1002/sd.521

BICC. (2008). *Digging for peace: Private companies and emerging economies in zones of conflict*. Paper presented at the Fatal Transactions Conference, Bonn, Germany.

Boege, V. (2010). *In-depth analysis: Bougainville*. Brisbane: The University of Queensland.

Boege, V. (2012). Hybrid forms of peace and order on a South Sea Island: Experiences from Bougainville (Papua New Guinea). In O. Richmond & A. Mitchell (Eds.), *Hybrid forms of peace: From everyday agency to post-liberalism*. Hampshire: Palgrave Macmillan.

Bond, C., Shi, M., & Kirsch, P. (2013). *Violence per Ounce*. Paper presented at the World Mining Congress, Montreal, Canada.

Brundtland Commission. (1987). *Report of the world commission on environment and development: Our common future*. New York, NY.

Carroll, A. B. (1999). Corporate social responsibility: Evolution of a definitional construct. *Business & Society*, *38*(3), 268–295.

Carroll, A. B., & Shabana, K. M. (2010). The business case for corporate social responsibility: A review of concepts, research and practice. *International Journal of Management Reviews*, *12*(1), 85–105. doi:10.1111/j.1468-2370.2009.00275.x

Carroll, C. (2013). *A shared vision for the future*. Paper presented at the South Africa's 20th Annual Mining Indaba, Johannesburg, South Africa.

Carson, M., Köhl, A., Stammer, D., Slangen, A. B. A., Katsman, C. A., van de Wal, R. S. W., . . . White, N. (2016). Coastal sea level changes, observed and projected during the 20th and 21st century. *Climatic Change*, *134*(1), 269–281. doi:10.1007/s10584-015-1520-1

Clark, T. (2002). *Canadian mining companies in Latin America: Community rights and corporate responsibility*. Paper presented at the CERLAC COLLOQUIA PAPERS SERIES, Toronto, Canada.

Custers, R., & Matthysen, K. (2009). *Africa's natural resources in a global context*. Antwerp.

Cutifani, M. (2013). *Mining's contribution to sustainable development*. Paper presented at the South Africa's 20th Annual Mining Indaba, Johannesburg, South Africa.

de Neufville, R. (2010). Paradigm. In M. Bevir (Ed.), *Encyclopedia of political theory* (pp. 1014–1015). Thousand Oaks, CA: Sage.

den Besten, J. W., Arts, B., & Verkooijen, P. (2014). The evolution of REDD+: An analysis of discursive-institutional dynamics. *Environmental Science & Policy*, *35*, 40–48. doi:10.1016/j.envsci.2013.03.009

Doyle, M. (1986). Liberalism and world politics. *American Political Science Review*, *80*(December), 1151–1169.
Fassin, D. (2013). On resentment and ressentiment. *Current Anthropology*, *54*(3), 249–267. doi:10.1086/670390
Ford, J. (2015). Perspectives on the evolving "business and peace" debate. *Academy of Management Perspectives*, *29*(4), 451–460.
Forrer, J., & Katsos, J. (2015). Business and peace in the buffer condition. *Academy of Management Perspectives*, *29*(4), 438–450.
Francis, D. (2010). *From pacification to peacebuilding: A call to global transformation*. New York, NY: Palgrave Macmillan.
Galtung, J. (1969). Violence, peace and peace research. *Journal of Peace Research*, *6*(3), 167–191.
Galtung, J. (1985). Twenty-five years of peace research: Ten challenges and some responses. *Journal of Peace Research*, *22*(2), 141–158.
Gibson, G., MacDonald, A., & O'Faircheallaigh, C. (2011). Cultural considerations for mining and indigenous communities. In P. Darling (Ed.), *SME mining engineering handbook* (3rd ed.). Englewood, CO: Society for Mining, Metallurgy, and Exploraiton, Inc.
Global Witness. (2015). *How many more? 2014's deadly environment: The killing and intimidation of environmental and land activists, with a spotlight on Honduras*.London: Global Witness Publishing.
Golub, A., Lubowski, R., & Piris-Cabezas, P. (2017). Balancing risks from climate policy uncertainties: The role of options and reduced emissions from deforestation and forest degradation. *Ecological Economics*, *138*, 90–98. doi:10.1016/j.ecolecon.2017.03.013
Gore, A. (2016). *The climate reality project*. Retrieved from www.climatereality project.org/
Haufler, V. (2015). Symposium on conflict, management, and peace: Comments from an international relations scholar. *Academy of Management Perspectives*, *29*(4), 461–468.
Hilson, G. (2012). Corporate social responsibility in the extractive industries: Experiences from developing countries. *Resources Policy*, *37*(2), 131–137. doi:10.1016/j.resourpol.2012.01.002
IHRB. (2011). *The UN global compact and human rights: Developing a vision for 2020*.
Ito, S., El Khatib, S., & Nakayama, M. (2016). Conflict over a hydropower plant project between Tajikistan and Uzbekistan. *International Journal of Water Resources Development*, *32*(5), 692–707. doi:10.1080/07900627.2015.1076381
Itskos, G., Nicolopoulos, N., Kourkoumpas, D. S., Koutsianos, A., Violidadkis, I., Drosatos, P. L., & Grammelis, P. (2016). *Energy and the environment and development: Basic principles, human activities, and environmental implications*. New York, NY: Elseveier.
Jenkins, H. (2004). Corporate social responsibility and the mining industry: Conflicts and constructs. *Corporate Social Responsibility and Environmental Management*, *11*, 23–34.
Jonker, J., & Pennink, B. W. (2010). *The essence of methodology. The essence of research methodology: A concise guide for master and PhD students in management science*. London: Springer.

Ju, Y., Sun, Y., Sa, Z., Pan, J., Wang, J., Hou, Q., . . . Liu, J. (2016). A new approach to estimate fugitive methane emissions from coal mining in China. *Science of the Total Environment*, *543*(Pt A), 514–523. doi:10.1016/j.scitotenv.2015.11.024

Kant, I. (1983 [1795]). *Perpetual peace, and other essays on politics, history, and morals* (T. Humphrey, Trans.). Indianapolis, IN: Hackett Pub. Co.

Kapelus, P. (2002). Mining, corporate social responsibility and the "Community": The case of Rio Tinto, Richards Bay Minerals and the Mbonambi. *Journal of Business Ethics*, *39*(3), 275–296.

Kemp, D., & Bond, C. (2009). *Mining industry perspectives on handling community grievances: Summary and analysis of industry interviews*. Brisbane.

Kemp, D., Owen, J., Cervantes, M., Arbelaez-Ruiz, D., & Rueda, J. B. (2012). *Listening to the city of Cajamarca*.Brisbane: Centre for Social Responsibility in Mining.

Knox, J. H. (2011). The Ruggie rules: Applying human rights law to corporations. In R. Mares (Ed.), *The UN guiding principles on business and human rights*. Leiden: BRILL.

Korhonen, J. (2002). The dominant economics paradigm and corporate social responsibility. *Corporate Social Responsibility and Environmental Management*, *9*(1), 66–79. doi:10.1002/csr.7

Kreisberg, L. (2011). The state of the art in conflict transformation. In B. Austin, M. Fischer, & H. J. Giessmann (Eds.), *The Berghoff handbook on conflict transformation*. Framington Hills, MA: Barbara Budrich.

Kuhn, T. A. (1996 [1962]). *The structure of scientific revolutions*. Chicago, IL: University of Chicago Press.

Kunanayagam, R., & Tomlinson, K. (2011). Indigenous peoples and extractive projects: Success factors in compensation and benefit sharing agreements. *Oil, Gas & Energy Law Intelligence*, *9*(4).

Kytle, B., & Ruggie, J. G. (2005). *Corporate social responsibility as risk management: A model for multinationals*.Cambridge, MA: Harvard.

Lederach, J. P. (1995). *Preparing for peace: Conflict transformation across cultures*. Syracuse, NY: Syracuse University Press.

Lederach, J. P., Neufeldt, R., & Culbertson, H. (2007). *Reflective peacebuilding: A planning, monitoring and learning toolkit*. Notre Dame, IN. Retrieved from http://kroc.nd.edu; http://www.crs.org

Lloyd, G. (2014, April 26–27). When rigs turn farmers into radicals. *The Australian*, p. 7.

Locke, J. (1966 [1689]). *The second treatise of government: (An essay concerning the true original, extent and end of civil government), A letter concerning toleration*. Oxford, UK: Blackwell.

Miklian, J., Schouten, P., & Ganson, B. (2016). From boardrooms to battlefields: 5 new ways that businesses claim to build peace. *Harvard International Review*, *37*(2), 1–4. http://hir.harvard.edu/article/?a=13494

Milliken, F., Schipani, C. A., Bishara, N., & Prado, A. (2015). Linking workplace practices to community engagement: The case for encouraging employee voice. *Academy of Management Perspectives*, *15*(29), 405–421.

Mutti, D., Yakovleva, N., Vazquez-Brust, D., & Di Marco, M. H. (2012). Corporate social responsibility in the mining industry: Perspectives from stakeholder groups in Argentina. *Resources Policy*, *37*(2), 212–222. doi:10.1016/j.resourpol.2011.05.001

Nelson, J. (2000). *The business of peace*. London.

Neufeldt, R., Fast, L., Schreiter, F. R., Starken, F. B., MacLaren, D., Cilliers, J., & Lederach, J. P. (2006). *Peacebuilding: A caritas training manual*. Vatican City: Caritas Internationalis.

Owen, J. R., & Kemp, D. (2013). Social licence and mining: A critical perspective. *Resources Policy*. 38(1):29–35.

Özkaynak, B., Rodríguez-Labajos, B., Chicaiza, G., Conde, M., Kohrs, B., Raeva, D., . . . Walter, M. (2012). Mining conflicts around the world: Common grounds from environmental justice perspective, Western Europe. EJOLT Report No. 7, 198 p.Paffenholz, T. (2010). Civil society and peacebuilding. In T. Paffenholz (Ed.), *Civil society and peacebuilding* (pp. 43–64). Boulder, CO: Lynne Reinner.

Paffenholz, T. and C. Spurk (2010). A comprehensive analytical framework. In T. Paffenholz (Ed.), *Civil society and peacebuilding* (pp. 65–76). Boulder, CO: Lynne Reinner.

Pamfilo, J. F. M., Viña, A. G. M. L., Perez, I. E., & Santos, M. G. P. (2005). *Mapping out conflicts in mining areas: Drawing lessons and seeking spaces for building principled consensus towards effective mining governance*. Ateneo.

Parlevliet, M. (2009). *Rethinking conflict transformation from a human rights perspective*. Berlin, Germany: The Berghof Conflict Research Group. Retrieved from https://www.berghof-foundation.org/fileadmin/redaktion/Publications/Handbook/Dialogues/dialogue9_humanrights_complete.pdf

Pearce, J. (1997). Sustainable peace-building in the South. *Development in Practice*, 7(4), 438–455.

Pendleton, A., McClenaghan, S., Melamed, C., Bunn, I., & Graymore, D. (2004). *Behind the mask: The real face of corporate social responsibility*. London.

Pvinec, P., Hirose, K., & Aoyama, M. (2013). *Fukushima accident: Radioactivity impact on the environment*. New York, NY: Newnes (Elsevier).

Rees, C., Kemp, D., & Davis, R. (2012). *Conflict management and corporate culture in extractive industries: A study in Peru*. Cambridge, MA: John F Kennedy School of Government.

Reychler, L., & Paffenholz, T. (Eds.). (2001). *Peacebuilding: A field guide*. Boulder, CO: Lynne Rienner.

Richmond, O. (2009). Becoming liberal, unbecoming liberalism: Liberal-local hybridity via the everyday as a response to the paradoxes of liberal peacebuilding. *Journal of Intervention and Statebuilding*, *3*(3), 324–344.

Richmond, O. (2010). A genealogy of peace and conflict theory. In O. Richmond (Ed.), *Palgrave advances in peacebuilding*.

Richmond, O. (2011). *A post-liberal peace*. London: Routledge.

Richmond, O., & Mitchell, A. (Eds.). (2012). *Hybrid forms of peace: From everyday agency to post-liberalism*. Hampshire: Palgrave Macmillan.

Ruggie, J. (2011a). *Applications of the U.N. "Protect, Respect and Remedy" framework*. New York, NY.

Ruggie, J. (2011b). *Guiding principles on business and human rights: Implementing the United Nations "Protect, Respect and Remedy" framework* (A/HRC/17/31). New York, NY: United Nations.

Rustad, S. A., & Binningsbø, H. M. (2012). A price worth fighting for? Natural resources and conflict recurrence. *Journal of Peace Research*, 49(4), 531–546. doi:10.1177/0022343312444942

Sahu, S. (2009, July 7). Indians protest over mining plans. *BBC News*. Retrieved from http://news.bbc.co.uk/go/pr/fr/-/2/hi/south_asia/7854369.stm
Sandole, D. J. D. (2003). Typology. In S. Cheldelin, D. Druckman, & L. Fast (Eds.), *Conflict: From analysis to intervention*. London, UK: Continuum.
Santa Barbara, J., Dubee, F., & Galtung, J. (2009). *Peace business: People and nature above markets and capital*. Oslo: Transcend University Press.
Schulz, C. N., & Rachel, B. (2009). *Oxfam human rights review of hydropower sustainability assessment protocol*.
Seongsuk, L., & Yu, Y. (2016). Abnormal winter melting of the Arctic Sea Ice Cap observed by the Spaceborne passive microwave sensors. *Journal of Astronomy and Space Sciences*, *33*(4), 305–311.
Sternberg, R. (2008). Hydropower: Dimensions of social and environmental coexistence. *Renewable and Sustainable Energy Reviews*, *12*(6), 1588–1621. doi:10.1016/j.rser.2007.01.027
Sunderlin, W. D., Larson, A. M., Duchelle, A. E., Resosudarmo, I. A. P., Huynh, T. B., Awono, A., & Dokken, T. (2014). How are REDD+ Proponents addressing tenure problems? Evidence from Brazil, Cameroon, Tanzania, Indonesia, and Vietnam. *World Development*, *55*, 37–52. doi:10.1016/j.worlddev.2013.01.013
Swiss Federal Department of Foreign Affairs, & Swisspeace. (2009). *Dealing with the past in peace mediation*. Bern: Government of Switzerland.
Thomson, I., & Boutili er, R. G. (2011). Social license to operate. In P. Darling (Ed.), *SME mining engineering handbook* (3rd ed.). Englewood, CO: Society for Mining Metallurgy and Exploration, Inc.
Trenberth, K. E., Dai, A., Schrier, G. V. D., Jones, P. D., Barichivich, J., Briffa, K. R., & Sheffield, J. (2014). Global warming and changes in drought. *Nature Climate Change*, *4*, 17–22. doi:10.1038/nclimate2067
UNESCO. (1992). *Report of the United Nations conference on environment and development*. Rio de Janiero. Retrieved from www.un.org/documents/ga/conf151/aconf15126-1annex1.htm
United Nations. (2015). *Paris agreement*. Paris. Retrieved from http://unfccc.int/paris_agreement/items/9485.php
Walker, J., & Howard, S. (2002). *Finding the way forward: How could voluntary action move mining towards sustainable development?*
Westermann-Behaylo, M. K., Rehbein, K., & Fort, T. (2015). Enhancing the concept of corporate diplomacy: Encompassing political corporate social responsibility, international relations, and peace through commerce. *Academy of Management Perspectives*, *29*(4), 387–404.
Wiens, J. J. (2016). Climate-related local extinctions are already widespread among plant and animal species. *PLoS Biology*, *14*(12). doi:10.1371/journal.pbio.2001104
Wilburn, K. M., & Wilburn, R. (2011). Achieving a social license to operate using stakeholder theory. *Journal of International Business Ethics*, *4*(2), 3–16, 70.
Wilkinson-Maposa, S., & Fowler, A. (2009). *The poor philanthropist II: New approaches to sustainable development*. Cape Town: UCT Graduate School of Business.
Wit, M. D., & Schouten, E. (2006). CSR in the extractive industry: An integrated approach. In J. Jonker & M. D. Witte (Eds.), *Management models for corporate social responsibility* (pp. 19–27). Berlin: Springer.

Wolosin, M. (2016). *WWF discussion paper: Jurisdictional approaches to zero deforestation commodities.*

World Gold Council. (2012). *Conflict-free gold standard.* London: World Gold Council.

Zhong, Q., Huang, Y., Shen, H., Chen, Y., Chen, H., Huang, T., . . . Tao, S. (2017). Global estimates of carbon monoxide emissions from 1960 to 2013. *Environmental Science and Pollution Research*, *24*(1), 864–873. doi:10.1007/s11356-016-7896-2

2 Business, Peace and Natural Resources

The Case for Peace-Focused Thinking

This chapter examines how peace-focused thinking already exists in the natural resources industries, although it is infrequently labelled as such. The chapter makes the case that because peace is a part of the conversation between communities affected by natural resources industries and local-level operations, there are benefits for all stakeholders when businesses name the use of peace frameworks.

2.1 Overview

One contribution of this book is to reframe NRC-community conflict in terms of the emerging literature on business and peace. This chapter surveys the relevant literature: first, a summary of the foundational scholarship that launched contemporary inquiries into the role business can play in creating societal conditions of peace, followed by a discussion of CSR-relevant publications mentioning peace and conflict in the natural resources context. The limited literature investigating these interfaces is covered in depth, while gaps in the literature featuring peace and/or natural resources are highlighted. The chapter concludes that NRCs, just as much as other businesses, have a meaningful role to play in supporting and contributing to conditions of peace in their operating environments.

2.2 A Business Case for Peace

Discourse about the contribution international businesses can make to global conditions of peace has been gaining momentum in the current millennium and fuelled by the fact that NRCs are beginning to enter this dialogue in partnership with NGOs. Recent publications by natural resources-related organisations such as IISD, International Alert, the Global Compact and the IFC, plus reports by two leading NRCs, have already invoked 'peace' in the natural resources context (Anglo American, 2011; Ballentine & Haufler, 2009 [2005]; Banfield, Barbolet, Goldwyn, & Killick, 2005; Goldcorp, 2011; IFC, 2010; IISD, 2010; International Alert, 2006; Powell & Chung, 2010; Powell, Gardaz, Chung, & Liu, 2010; UN

Global Compact & Deloitte, 2011). However, with the important exceptions of an International Alert Publication, *Conflict-Sensitive Business Practice: Guidance for Extractive Industries* (Banfield et al., 2005), *Forest Resources and Peacebuilding: Preliminary lessons from Liberia and Sierra Leone* (Beevers, 2012) and recent Australian scholarship on peacebuilding and the natural resources sector (Bond, 2014), scholars have been slower to include NRCs in discussions about responsible business practices related to 'business and peace' (Samset, 2009). This absence may be due in part to more scholarly interest in understanding the linkages between natural resources and violent conflict, as in the DRC, Nepal and Cambodia, than in the broader thematic area of natural resources and peace (de Lopez, 2002; Hintjens, 2006; Le Billon & Levin, 2009). In fact, most of the scholarship on peace-building relating to mining, oil and gas, hydropower and forestry focuses on post-conflict rebuilding rather than the role of these projects in conflict prevention. As an alternative to focusing on violent conflict and how natural resources industries contribute to or provoke conflict, this book expands the platform for dialogue about business and peace as specifically related to natural resources operations in contexts not affected by war.

There are two major gaps in this literature on business and peace. The first is that most studies focus primarily on warlike conflict and physical violence. Fewer focus on injurious conflicts that are the result of structural or cultural rather than physical violence. The second is the failure to consider NRCs as the type of business that have a contribution to make in creating and supporting conditions of peace. This chapter suggests expanding the discussion of business and peace to include mining alongside the timber industry, hydro-geological projects and other large-footprint, natural resources-based industries. NRCs are customarily engaged in ongoing relationships with communities over many decades with a need to earn and maintain social approval for their activities. Consequently, there is a potentially substantial incentive to enhance conditions of peace as an intentional outcome of doing business, with short- and long-term benefits for both NRCs and natural resources-affected communities.

This chapter also addresses two aspects of 'conflict' needing clarification. First are conflicts that result from one or more forms of violence, where the paradigm of positive peace has the potential to make the biggest contribution. These are the conflicts referred to in the literature below. Secondly, the literature suggests that natural resources—in and of themselves—do not directly cause conflict. The production of excavated ores, timber products, hydro-electric power and the resultant poorly managed and distributed inflows of cash, however, can amplify social and political conflict in a variety of ways (Aall, 2011). Current thinking in 'Resource Curse' scholarship points out that peoples' use of natural resources, and the use of funds generated through both legal and illegal trade, can cause the kind of insecurity leading to conflict and occasionally one or more forms of violence

(Brunnschweiler & Bulte, 2008; Carbonnier, Wagner, & Brugger, 2010; Lahiri-Dutt, 2006; Lederman & Maloney, 2007).

A further caveat is that this book does not look at NRC-community conflicts that are the result of ideological opposition. For example, when communities and NGOs in Australia oppose the use of coal because burning coal produces the greenhouse gases believed by many to contribute to global warming; or in the United States, where the American Rivers activist group advises communities not to talk to the hydro-power industry at all because dialogue could lead to compromise. When various stakeholders embrace ideological thinking, the complexity and variety of claims make it difficult to enter the kind of dialogue necessary to work towards positive peace with parties who refuse to engage or even listen to another. Although ideologically based conflicts can be just as intense and harmful as those resulting from other root causes of violence, issues championed by ideologically informed groups is outside of the scope of this book.

2.3 The Role of Business in Contributing to Conditions of Peace

The scholarship cited in this section identifies where and how CSR activities could contribute to peace-building practices and outcomes. Scholars invoke the language, practices and concepts related to positive peace and peace-building in service to changing the way businesses think about and act toward achieving their goals. While the paradigm of positive peace is not expressly mentioned by these scholars, their contributions are representative of how the paradigm encourages envisioning the relationship between business and peace.

2.3.1 The Business of Peace

"The business of business is business" (Friedman, 1970) is a commonly used aphorism about any type of commercial activity. Some scholars and businesspeople, however, are suggesting an alternative: "the business of business is peace, which is good for business (and society)". This latter view has its roots in the recent development of literature on business and peace, dated to 2000, when Nelson published a report titled *The Business of Peace*. At the time, Nelson was the Director at the International Business Leaders Forum (IBLF). Her report's central focus is how the private sector can participate in advancing UN agendas as reflected in the Global Compact and other initiatives. This work is particularly important in the context of this book because it has both clearly defined the issues and set the tone for subsequent research on business and peace. A summary of Nelson's key contributions of is below.

One of the primary messages of the report is that businesses are capable of and some are already doing more than aspiring to basic goals of regulatory compliance and the age-old ethical principle of 'do no harm'. Nelson's research was commissioned and led by the Prince of Wales Business Leaders Forum, with key project members also coming from International Alert and the Council on Economic Priorities. Of the 78 UK and Azerbaijani corporations profiled, 13 are from the extractives industry, and four of those are international mining companies. No other types of NRCs are included in this list. The other corporations profiled are large industrial, pharmaceutical, technological, telecommunications, banking and consulting firms. Additionally, of the 71 NGOs, foundations, academic institutions and civil society networks profiled, 12 are explicitly interested in engaging the natural resources sector (Nelson, 2000, pp. 154–155).

> Companies can proactively create positive societal value by optimising the external multipliers of their own business operations and engaging in innovative social investment, stakeholder consultation, policy dialogue, advocacy and civic institution building, including collective action with other companies.
>
> (Nelson, 2000, p. 7)

In other words, businesses can contribute intentionally towards the well-being of the communities affected by their activities.

By advocating that businesses can create positive social value and increase conditions of positive peace, Nelson makes a business case for how to engage conflict situations that result in physical, structural or cultural violence. She then outlines principles for corporate engagement and provides a framework for analysis. This framework allows corporations from different sectors to locate themselves on a risk-responsibility matrix with natural resources MNCs in the quadrant with the highest level of both risk and responsibility.

> [MNCs are] big 'footprint' players with long-term, capital-intensive investments, high profile position and minimal flexibility in terms of location. [They exploit] strategic resources with high potential of creating conflict over control of and access to resources, unfair distribution of revenues and poor management of security arrangements and community relations.
>
> (Nelson, 2000, p. 58)

As corporations consider the direct and indirect business costs of the risks they face, Nelson encourages them to foreground peace as a means of conflict prevention and resolution Foregrounding peace, she argues, will reduce both direct and indirect risks.

There are several aspects to consider as corporations attend to the business risks they face and seek to optimise the "business benefits of peace" (Nelson, 2000, p. 26). She highlights three. The first is that businesses need to be aware of and continue to monitor the affected country's or regional communities' location on a war-peace continuum. Clearly, if a country is at war, the risk of company-community conflict as the result of violence is potentially much higher than during other times. The second is to determine and put in place policies/practices to avoid the different triggers for conflict situations that might exist in any particular location. For example, Nelson advises corporations to be aware of any latent conflicts that their presence might reawaken. They also need to be sensitive to cultural issues that they may want to avoid trespassing. The third is that corporations should map who the various stakeholder groups might be in relation to their business. These include but are not limited to government, legal opposition parties, lawless groups, traditional leaders, NGOs, grassroots organisations, bi- and multi-lateral agencies, religious groups, the media and business associations (Nelson, 2000). This book's chapter on *paradigms* covers the topics of defining conflict and its potential as constructive or destructive opportunity in response to social change.

Finally, Nelson suggests practical steps businesses can take to foreground peace and play a supportive role in addressing, preventing and recovering from conflict situations through their core business activities. These steps include the following:

- Conduct pre-investment conflict impact assessments and follow-up monitoring;
- Engage in meaningful stakeholder consultation;
- Actively promote diversity in the workforce;
- Prioritise local procurement, training and hiring practices;
- Have a 'zero tolerance' policy towards bribery and corruption, both internally and externally;
- Develop policies and management to prevent and address Human Rights abuses linked to business activities and security arrangements; and
- Invest in social development programs (e.g., support capacity building and community empowerment instead of promoting welfare-style or philanthropic programs that encourage dependency).

Businesses can also engage in public policy discourse and civic institution building for the purpose of building peace. However, this high-level engagement is likely to require CSR practitioners to work as part of a larger team of people within a corporation. This team would work towards addressing conflict in the operating environment before, during and after it occurs. Consequently, a corporation needs to carefully consider which functions, at which levels of engagement, are best placed to engage with governments and related stakeholders on public policy discourse and civic institution building.

Towards that end, Nelson points to Killick's adaptation of Lederach's pyramid (Francis, 2010; Lederach, 1997, 2003; Schirch, 2004). This classification system for the business environment shows at what level people can address conflict, at each level of a business, and thereby make a contribution towards the conditions characteristic of a paradigm of positive peace. Lederach's well-known pyramid and Killick's reinterpretation are below in Figures 2.1 and 2.2.

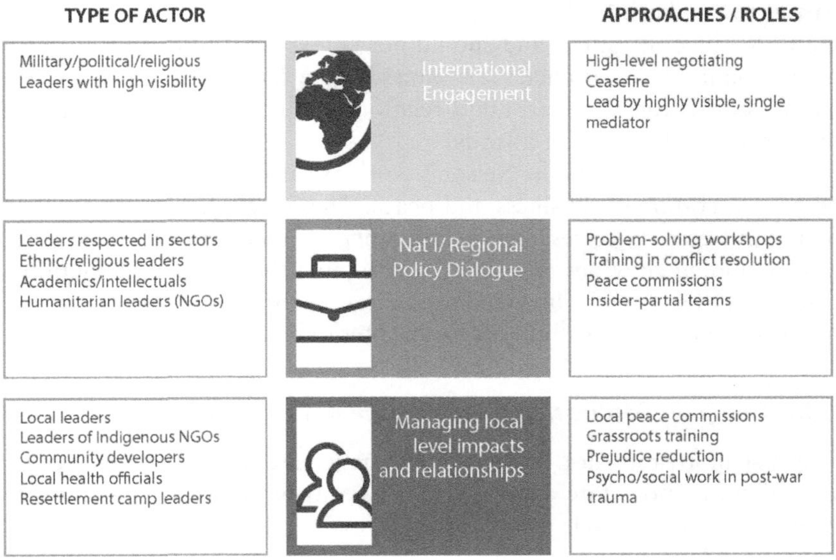

Figure 2.1 Peace-Building Actors/Roles

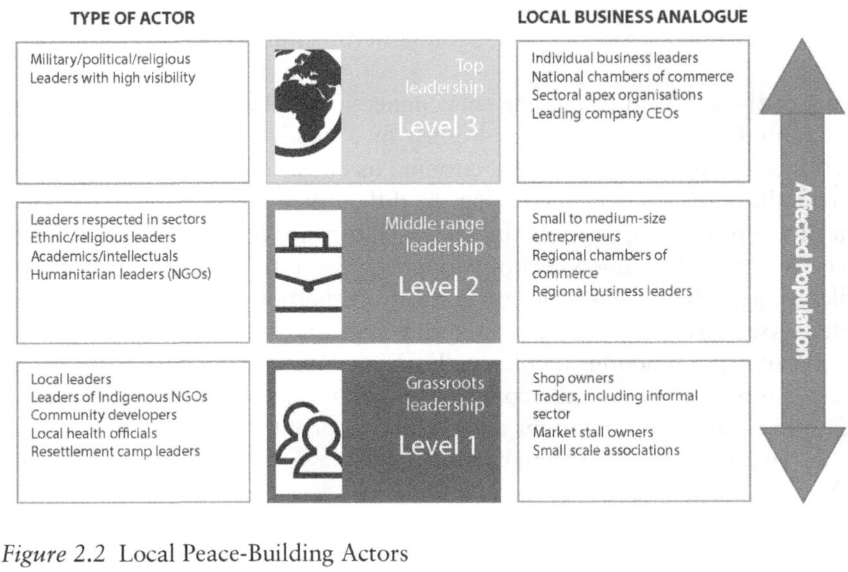

Figure 2.2 Local Peace-Building Actors

Nelson emphasises two things with these frameworks. The first is that in societies, organisations and groups, there are hierarchies of responsibility and authority. People need to work at their level and within their own spheres of influence in order to address conflict and promote peace (Santa Barbara, Dubee, & Galtung, 2009). The second is to show clearly that no one person or function can address the broad range of stakeholders who are parties to conflicts. In the natural resources context, the implication is that the CSR function cannot and should not be expected to handle all aspects of community-level conflict. Companies need a more comprehensive team, cutting across functions, to build relationships necessary to maximise the opportunities that conflict affords.

Several themes present in Nelson's work are also evident in the emerging body of literature on business and peace. These include businesses participating in peace processes, supporting other actors in their own exercise of peace-building activities and actually designing their own contributions to community-level peace. Included are reflections on the moral responsibility of businesses. Key contributions to this literature are below.

2.3.2 Company Motivation to Participate in Peace Processes

The first motivation for businesses to participate in peace processes is to view them as non-state actors with a role to work with or alongside of NGOs at the local level.

> The role of business actors in supporting peace processes remains a novel perspective and approach as little research has been done on their activities. Despite a growing number of practical examples [the role of business actors] is significantly less established than that of NGOs.
>
> (Iff, Sguaitamatti, Alluri, & Kohler, 2010, p. 7)

Part of the problem in making this connection is that businesses, although influential, are often perceived—rightly or wrongly—as acting in their own self-interest and thereby not functioning as consistently trustworthy actors in conflict situations. Exacerbating the difficulty in viewing the role of businesses in promoting peace is the fallacy that peace is the opposite of profit. The reality is that unless a company profits from the business of war, conflict almost always has a negative effect on the bottom line. The fact that businesses have financial and material interests that they explicitly want to protect can function to enhance businesses' credibility as a party with a vested interest in seeing the conflict handled peaceably, even if their role in the peace processes maintains a low external profile.

In 14 cases, local and international businesses (including NRCs) were able to act as mediators in various conflict-ridden scenarios from the Americas, Africa and Asia to the UK (Iff et al., 2010). These businesses successfully supported peace initiatives successfully because of their position as non-state actors with track-two diplomacy functionality.[1] In each case, the parties to the disputes were able to create the relational bridgework necessary to move beyond the impasses at the track-one diplomacy level and encourage the parties to find practical solutions at the track-two level. These activities included arranging neutral mediation space for conflicting parties, resolving disputes between local businesses, encouraging participation in legitimate economic (rather than black or grey market) activities and becoming involved in wider civil society initiatives supportive of peace. Incentives for businesses and individuals working within corporations to participate in these voluntary roles, besides altruism, included: not being implicated in regional conflict, creating a more stable business/trade environment, providing greater security for employees and contractors and maintaining open communication channels with governments.

The second set of reasons for business corporations to participate in peace processes is related to the role or purpose of corporations more generally. The question is whether corporations are a legal entity/fiction, a loosely bound community or an individual. Whichever the answer, corporations can be viewed as moral agents with a degree of accountability to the larger society.

> The corporation . . . is a community of persons situated in a wider community, of which it is part and which it cannot ignore on the grounds of being merely a 'legal entity'.
>
> (Smurthwaite, 2008, p. 19)

And

> Moral responsibility and moral accountability for policies and practices of the corporation rest with the individuals (as individuals and as community) who comprise the corporation.
>
> (Smurthwaite, 2008, p. 24)

These points suggest that simply making a profit (Friedman, 1970) is not a sufficient reason for a corporation to exist.

Corporations have an obligation to contribute to the common good, not as a welfare agency, but in fulfilling their roles as service and product providers within the larger community of which they are an integral, related part. "The purpose of business tends toward the 'profit-plus-extras' view rather than 'profit only' view. Exactly how those 'extras' are defined varies considerably, as do the ways in which such purpose is fulfilled" (Smurthwaite, 2008, p. 29). Some of the categories reflecting the diversity of opinion about 'extras' are: CSR; stakeholder model; corporate governance model; social contract model; and Catholic social thought. What is important to note is that firms have more than one way to conceptualise their obligations to the larger society in which they operate. Out of each conceptualisation, it is possible to make a robust case that a firm has a responsibility and in some circles an obligation to participate in peace processes as part of its moral duty towards society.

Finally, the third reason for businesses to participate in peace processes is because, ultimately, peace is the responsibility of actors at the local level. Local-level communities and businesses often have a "robust expectation of peace" (Lederach, 2008, p. 101) since they are the ones that are most affected on a day-to-day level when peace is compromised. Peace at the community level has a direct effect on the quality of community life, affecting: adequate housing; decent employment; choice of livelihood; access to food, water and sanitation; and a sense of well-being. These basic building-blocks, necessary as a bare minimum for human thriving, are sometimes difficult to achieve given the complex situations, conditions, political and historical histories of communities. Peace is therefore never accomplished by one actor but requires all stakeholders to move, as well as they can, toward the goal of a community's well-being. The only way to achieve this goal is to acknowledge, openly, the interdependent nature of communities—including the role of businesses; this means that businesses need to participate in peace-building processes.

Despite these imperatives reasons for businesses contributing to conditions of peace, the reality is many companies do not adequately participate in peace processes, engage with communities or contribute to the 'common good'. The reasons why they do not participate are not enumerated because most scholars and practitioners with a view towards business and peace write from *outside* the business sector *about* the business sector, rather than from an insider's point of view. This lack of insider perspective from within the natural resources sector points to an area for greater research. Chapter 6 contributes towards filling this gap by canvassing the opinions of CSR professionals on business and peace in the natural resources sector, seeking precisely that 'insider' point of view.

2.3.3 A Framework for Corporate Peace-Building Activities

Some researchers report there is a growing number of scholars who are making linkages between business activities and peace-building (Forrer, Fort, & Gilpin, 2012). Even in circumstances where peace-building efforts are not engaged directly, corporate decisions to behave ethically, with sensitivity to conflict, make it possible for people and groups to engage broader peace-building efforts.

> The argument arising out of the literature is not that businesses should promote peace, but that, given the overlap between nonviolent attributes and consensus ethical actions, ethical businesses are already contributing to peace, and knowing the potential consequences of such behavior provides additional motivation to be ethical . . . [in] five main

> areas: economic activity, rule of law and international standards, corporate citizenship, track-two diplomacy, and unique practices and risk assessment.
>
> (Forrer et al., 2012, p. 3)

Large MNCs in general and NRCs, in particular, have the capacity to institute practices in these areas that result in peace both for the companies and for SMEs in their supply chains. It is a choice whether businesses want to actively promote peace-building themselves. At a minimum, however, they can contribute towards local or regional conditions of peace by being aware of how their direct and indirect actions resonate in their operating contexts and by making appropriate ethical decisions.

On their own, businesses, on their own, are only one part of multi-sectoral, multi-layered processes that lead towards conditions of peace and a reduction of the risks posed by conflict. "The dominant focus for research and policy on private investment and conflict has been business behaviour in fragile environments" (Ganson & Wennmann, 2012, p. 4). However, conflict emerging between companies and communities is not simply a bi-lateral issue. There are larger contexts and more actors implicated than is reflected in research and policy frameworks. Importantly, stakeholders to resource development-based conflict need to identify synergies between peace-building and business imperatives, especially when developing locally grounded responses to conflict or seeking solutions requiring support from international and national actors. As large-scale businesses accelerate their entry into emerging economies, there is a growing need to understand the dynamic relationship between stress factors, large-scale resource development, preventative action and risk mitigation (Ganson & Wennmann, 2012). Business scholarship as well as industry-specific reports demonstrate the need to develop infrastructures for peace. "[Peace infrastructure] facilitates finding internal solutions to disputes through multi-stakeholder dialogue [that are] cooperative, inclusive, problem-solving approaches to conflict based on dialogue and mediation" (Ganson & Wennmann, 2012, p. 7).

The private sector, peace-building practitioners and development agents have the scope to intentionally engage one another collaboratively towards developing local conditions of peace rather than operate on parallel tracks. Whether large-scale businesses operate *in* a particular conflict zone or *on* a particular conflict, they can work within their own sphere of influence to encourage conditions of peace.

> To meet conflict prevention needs where business operates in fragile environments, there is compelling value to situating company-centred frameworks for action within a multi-sectoral, multi-layered action framework that builds on the strengths of business, peacebuilding and local actors.
>
> (2012, p. 15)

A framework, on its own, is not sufficient to achieve conditions of peace for businesses and the communities affected by their operations. There must be willingness and capacity of the various actors to put such a framework into action.

2.3.4 Helping Companies Contribute to Community-Level Peace

Whereas the seminal work by Nelson (2000) with International Alert was part of a first generation of work on business and peace, a second generation of work includes International Alert's *Local Business, Local Peace* (2006). Second-generation work is intended to stimulate thinking about how businesses can creatively contribute to conditions of peace in their operating environments. In the 2006 study cited above, 19 country-specific case studies as illustrations across a range of business profiles and conflict conditions. This richly textured resource focuses on businesses in communities affected by physically violent (armed) conflict. The premise behind the multi-dimensional study is that there should be integration between two parallel tracks of discourse: (1) peace and security and (2) economic growth in conflict-prone societies. This resource does not seek to define how, or the extent to which, businesses assume one or more roles as part of a multi-stakeholder peace-building process. It does, however, focus attention on the relationships between the stakeholders as well as the relationship each stakeholder has to the conflict context. The emphasis of *Local Business, Local Peace* is not so much on businesses operating at the local level but how their efforts can become integrated with the activities of a broad range of actors both at the local and international levels. Working together, rather than discretely, stakeholders in a peace process can create and sustain the structures and relationships that support peace.

The concept of "peace entrepreneur" emerged in this second generation to describe business actors (International Alert, 2006, p. 23). Peace entrepreneurs understand that peace-building practices "encourage the development of the structural conditions, attitudes and modes of political behaviour that may permit peaceful, stable and ultimately prosperous social and economic development" (2006, p. 26). They reframe conflict as an opportunity for productive change and share that vision within their own organisation to influence behaviour, making them catalysts for finding constructive opportunities and partnerships to reduce violent conflict.

To incorporate the idea of peace entrepreneurs at the local level, a third conceptualisation developed. This version takes the three levels of influence from the international stage and business level of influence as in Figures 2.1 and 2.2 and applies it to a hierarchy of influence and responsibility for peace-building at the local level. It indicates a broader range of engagement for businesses of all sectors. Engagement occurs when actors recognise new opportunities for horizontal and vertical linkages with networks and individuals from conflict-affected populations, especially

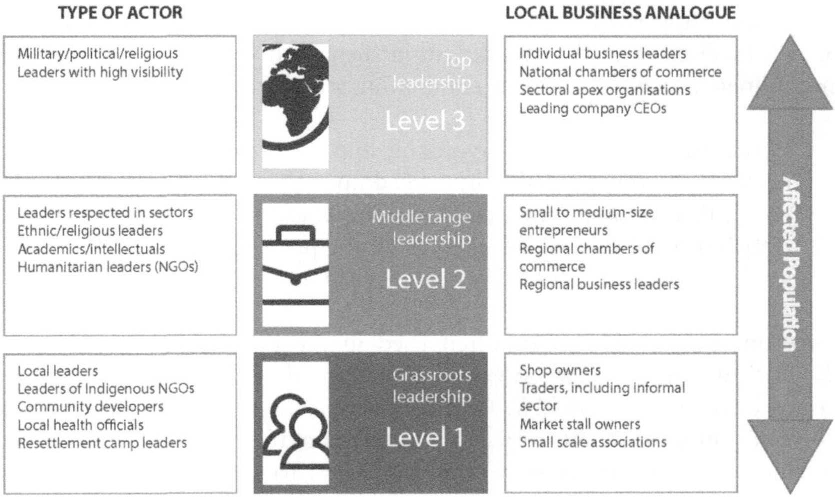

Figure 2.3

women, who have unique and vital roles to play in promoting and sustaining peace processes.

It is possible to make several observations based on this iteration of the framework. The first is that it is not enough to work for peace or establish peace at only one level of influence. International actors, diplomats and high-level politics are necessary to create the overarching structures, but actors at all level of society and in all sectors—including business—must be engaged for positive peace to be established and maintained. Businesses have a great deal of influence in affecting the conditions of economic well-being for local populations through jobs, opportunities and investment. Thoughtful and creative distribution of the economic benefits of a local business, emphasising peace, can reduce instances of resentment and distortion of development. Perceived or actual inequitable distribution of economic benefits can lead to conflict and violence.

Nevertheless, there is some concern about the growing urgency in some quarters for global business to account for human and environmental well-being, not just free markets and economic growth (Santa Barbara et al., 2009). Businesses should support, participate in and design peace processes insofar as they contribute to ecological and social sustainability through products and services, production cycles, organisational culture/structure and innovative investment of business profits. There is a concept called "enlightened self-interest" (Santa Barbara et al., 2009, p. 130) which is more than philanthropy or social responsibility; it is about creating an external enabling environment that allows a business to grow and flourish over the long term by investing in education, capacity building, public goods and services.

The most important topic to cover here is Corporate Structural Violence (CSV). Businesses need to work within their own spheres of responsibility and influence to work towards eliminating structural violence.

> [Structural violence is the] avoidable impairment of fundamental human needs . . . survival, well-being, freedom and identity . . . built into the political, economic and social systems and expressed in the unequal distribution of power and as a result unequal opportunities.
>
> (Santa Barbara et al., 2009, pp. 115–116)

The concept of CSV is not often used in the business sector. However, the critical point is that CSR initiatives—on their own—will not reduce instances or impacts of CSV. CSR focuses on the moral obligations to do 'the right thing', commit to sustainability, maintain a license to operate and enhance corporate reputation; these can serve to emphasise points of tension between communities and corporations. The winner/loser dichotomy that emerges only prolongs conflict cycles between the parties. Instead, a focus on peace can reframe those points of tension as points of interdependence. With this view, instances of CSV can be addressed and reduced more successfully.

The change in how to view corporate-community relationships, and the conflicts that occur within those relationships, needs to start from within a company. Processes of internal change, including a shift in corporate culture, will result in a change in how corporations interact with society. Contributing to social, environmental and economic outcomes in a strategic way is more effectively accomplished if corporations act in the following way, "to shift from [being] a concentrator of wealth to a distributor of value" (Santa Barbara et al., 2009, p. 157). This last point is visionary in nature. It indicates that there is potential to broaden perspectives on the corporate-community relationship in a number of directions by shifting the corporate paradigm to one that prioritises peace as well as profits. This shift is integral to the new paradigm necessary for real change to occur for CSR outcomes at the local level.

2.4 Scholarship Linking Business, Peace and Natural Resources

There is clearly work underway to expand the platform for dialogue about the various roles businesses can take to support, participate in and design processes that contribute to conditions of peace in their operating environments. By comparison, not as much work directly targets the natural resources sector. This section refers to three scholars who have made that connection. It also looks at guidance notes and voluntary initiatives which, although most do not even include the word peace, build on Nelson's (2000) suggestions for practical steps businesses can take towards that end (as in Section 2.3). This section highlights that activities, structures and attitudes that make for peace rather than violence can be put into place to address or prevent conflict, whether or not the word 'peace' is actually used.

A small number of scholars are already exploring the edges of the peacebuilding frontier at the community level by invoking and contextualising 'peace' specifically regarding natural resources (Escobar, 2006; Lowry, 2008; Samset, 2009). These scholars agree that extractive industries have a significant influence on conditions of relative peacefulness for communities affected by their activities. They each emphasise a different aspect of what is important for NRCs to consider regarding creating and supporting conditions of peace. The contributions of each of these scholars are presented in sequence below. None of the scholars features CSR as the professional function with the responsibility to shepherd peace practices and mindsets in this scholarship. Nevertheless, they all highlight factors CSR practitioners need to keep in frame in terms of relationships between NRCs and communities: keep the long-term relationship with local communities in view; learn from and collaborate with traditions of local and Indigenous communities; and support as well as work within good international policy on natural resources. These three factors are all implicated in creating and maintaining relationships and a working environment characteristic of positive peace. Table 2.1 below summarises the key concepts these scholars highlight alongside indicative examples of relevant international frameworks, also referred to in Tables 2.2, 2.3 and 2.5.

The fact is only three scholars have previously linked business-peace-natural resources in non-physically violent conflicts outside of reports and guidance notes. If positive peace is to become a more common outcome of CSR practice in the natural resources sector, much more work is required in this area. The work of each scholar is summarised next.

2.4.1 Natural Resources Projects Have a Long-Term Regional Presence

Lowry is a scholar-practitioner with 15 years' experience working in CSR at major NRCs and makes the following observation about extractive industries.

> The extractive industries most directly affect peace and stability in the developing world. With their massive size and social and environmental impacts, as well as their presence in the least developed areas of the world, the extractives have the potential to positively 'jump-start' the economic and social development of people in remote and underdeveloped areas. Equally, they have the potential to disrupt fragile societies and cause conflict and even civil war.
>
> (Lowry, 2008, p. 134)

Table 2.1 Tying the Literature and the Frameworks Together

Key concept related to positive peace	*Author*	*Strengths*	*Weaknesses*	*Indicative Int'l Frameworks*
Long-term regional presence	Lowry	Jump-start economic and social development	Disrupt traditional cultures Environmental damage	*From Conflict to Peacebuilding: the role of natural resources and the environment (2009)* *Doing business while advancing peace and development (2010)*
Financial effects	Samset	Appropriate policy can lead to responsible investment Support growth of local economy	Purchase of weapons Corruption/graft 'Resource curse' effects	*Minerals and Conflict: a toolkit for intervention (2005)* *Practice note 6: Natural Resource Governance in Conflict-Affected Contexts (2010)*
Interaction with Indigenous populations	Escobar	Learn a more holistic view of 'development' of natural resources with an ethos of environmental and human thriving	Amplification of difference, fear, distrust and exercises of 'power over' which destroy communities	*Akwe: Kon Guidelines (2004)* *IFC Performance Standards on Economic and Social Sustainability (2012)*

He shares lessons from his experience at Freeport's mining operation in Irian Jaya, Indonesia, and identifies five major challenges for NRCs operating in less-developed regions of the world. The first is that these regions frequently deal with states whose "legal and/or moral control over the area in which they are located are in question" (2008, p. 136). The second is that land ownership and land rights in Indigenous areas are murky at best. Often governments do not have control over Indigenous lands and NRCs must try to sort out traditional land ownership structures rarely documented with Western-style real estate deeds. The third is the rapid onset of cultural changes that arrive with the onset of natural resources. These include the transformation of local economies from barter to cash to physical alterations of traditional living situations, resulting in unpredictable changes with the potential to increase conflict between NRCs and

Table 2.2 Guides That Build on Nelson's Work (2000)

Year	*Title*	*Organisation*
2005	*Conflict-Sensitive Business Practice: guidance for extractive industries*	International Alert
2008	*Resources for Peace? Managing revenues from extractive industries in post-conflict environments*	Center on International Cooperation
2008	*Strengthening post-conflict peacebuilding through natural resource management*	UNEP
2009	*From Conflict to Peacebuilding: the role of natural resources and the environment*	UNEP
2009 [2005]	*Enabling Economies of Peace: Public Policy for Conflict-Sensitive Business*	UN Global Compact
2010	*Practice note 6: Natural Resource Governance in Conflict-Affected Contexts*	International Alert
2010	*Oil, Gas and Minerals: The Impact of Resource-Dependence and Governance on Sustainable Development*	The Centre on Conflict, Development and Peacebuilding
2010	*Doing business while advancing peace and development*	UN Global Compact

Table 2.3 Selection of Guides Addressing Conflict and Peace Issues in the Natural Resources Context

Year	*Title*	*Organisation*
2001	*Armed Conflict and Natural Resources: The case of the Minerals Sector*	MMSD
2005	*Minerals and Conflict: a toolkit for intervention*	USAID
2007	*Oil and Natural resources in Violent Places: why voluntary codes for companies don't guarantee Human rights Rights*	Global Witness
2010	*Guidance on Responsible Business in Conflict-Affected and High-Risk Areas*	UN Global Compact
2012	*Collaborative conflict management for enhanced national forest programs*	NFPS—FAO

local communities. The fourth is the environmental changes caused by natural resource development which sometimes result in irreparable damage. With the environmental changes, there is potential for significant, long-term social and cultural disruption. The fifth is that the employment of security forces, whether private or government, often leads to serious Human Rights abuses against artisanal and small-scale miners and women.

Each of these factors contributes to conflict between communities and NRCs. The most important, in Lowry's opinion, is the way NRCs handle security issues. Success in this area has the greatest opportunity to positively affect peace during their long-term presence of a company in a region.

Nevertheless, any of the challenges he mentions are 'hot buttons' when it comes to conflict with traditional cultures. Communities and NRCs need to continuously engage with the implementing the necessary changes.

2.4.2 Policy Affects the Resource-Conflict Nexus

Samset presents a substantial literature review on scholarship that has tried to link natural resources activity to violent conflict (2009). Natural resources projects often exist in unstable regions of the world, and natural resources can exacerbate violent conflict of a variety of forms. Non-renewable resources are more likely to be linked to conflict than renewables. "Countries which are both resource-abundant and resource-dependent are more peaceful than those that are merely resource-dependent" (Samset, 2009, p. 3). In resource-dependent countries, there is a stronger link between violent conflict and rentier state conditions than in regions where warlords or rebel groups are rampant. Samset concludes that "the presumed link between resources and conflict is not automatic and deserves a nuanced understanding" (2009, p. 6). The link between conflict and high-value natural resources has been established in some circumstances. However, the link between conflict and less valuable natural resources is not as clearly drawn. This means that natural resources, in and of themselves, are not related to violent conflict in all or even most circumstances. There is a great need for much more work at the micro level to make those linkages, if indeed they are there.

There remains potential for implementing policy to increase the opportunities for NRCs to contribute to peace rather than violence in five ways. The first is to curb conflict financing. This has already begun to happen at the international level for resources such as gold, diamonds, tin, platinum and rare earth metals. Policies are in place for some minerals (e.g., 'The Kimberley Process' for diamonds and 'The Conflict Free Gold Standard' for gold) and are in development for others so that the sources of these minerals can be traced and consumers in the market can make responsible purchasing decisions. In the forestry sector, the REDD+ initiatives discourage the destruction of forests and encourage the creation of sustainable livelihoods based on forest products (Blundell, Harwell, & Canby, 2015; Fujisaki, Hyakumura, Scheyvens, & Cadman, 2016; Tanzler & Ries, 2012). The second is to transform war economies. This transformation occurs when local populations generate income that does not come from economic activities supplying military needs, find alternate employment for demobilised combatants, formalise informal economic activity and diversify the economic base. The third is fiscal transparency. The Extractives Industry Transparency Initiative is one effort to encourage both extractive companies and host countries to be transparent about the wealth generated and received by extractive and forestry activities. The fourth is for NRCs to engage in conflict-sensitive business practices. This includes doing conflict impact assessments throughout the lifecycle of an operation to prioritise the quality of the relationship between the operation and local communities and "engage with other stakeholders, such as NGOs, UN agencies, and government representatives, to reduce chances that their activities provoke or stoke local tensions" (2009, p. 8). Finally, one of the most important ways natural resources can contribute to conditions of peace is by sharing resource revenues equitably and in a way that helps communities plan for a future when natural resources activities have concluded. She concludes that natural resources would be less implicated in conflict if scholars and policy analysts worked more closely with one another than they have in the past to design a broad, pro-peace policy agenda. It is not enough to have good policy; it is important to also have productive relationships with local people who may or may not operate out of a Western context.

2.4.3 Peace With Justice for Indigenous People

Escobar describes global movements of traditional people who want to participate in the decisions regarding how their resources are developed and used (2006). He develops a political ecology framework of economy-ecology-culture and makes the argument that these aspects have been used, in the past, to gloss over differences in natural resources environments to the disadvantage of traditional people. Instead, natural resource-intensive industries should no longer participate in the structural violence he sees as inherent in processes of neoliberal globalisation that continue to dispossess traditional people from full participation in development processes.

Neoliberal processes of development can amplify difference, fear, distrust and exercise 'power over' which destroy communities and environments and exacerbates the current imbalanced in the global distribution of resources. An alternative is a peace-with-justice approach with a human- and environment-centred ethos, in closer accord with traditional ways of viewing the world and relationships. Traditional cultures have a different understanding of how humans should interact with and appropriate natural resources taking an approach that is more holistic than simply considering technical and economic variables. Traditional cultural approaches do not depend on everybody liking or getting along with one another; instead, they emphasise a shared understanding of humanity's relationship with the earth. With that understanding, the potential to resolve conflict peaceably is increased for businesses and communities wishing to benefit from resource development. Towards that goal, several guidance notes have been developed for use by the natural resources and extractives sectors; these are discussed below.

2.5 Guidance Notes on Operating a Business Without Inflaming Conflict

A number these guidance notes have built on Nelson's (2000) work and her adaptation of Lederach's concept of "conflict as the catalyst for constructive change and peace promotion" (Lederach, 1995) in relationships both between businesses and those affected by their activities. Most of the guides look at the big picture regarding conflict, conditions of peace and opportunities for businesses to address both. The table below highlights some of these guides building specifically on Nelson's work by featuring CSR and related concepts as relevant to business and peace in the extractives sector. Another series of guides addresses conflict and peace in the natural resources sector without citing Nelson's work directly while advocating similar responses from natural resources and other large-scale companies (see Tables 2.2 and 2.3).

While these guides acknowledge that the primary responsibility for maintaining civil order rests with the sovereign state, they also focus on the roles of MNEs in general and large NRCs in particular. The guides map ways to conceptualise how MNEs can encourage economies and conditions that do not promote or fuel conflict but rather contribute to conditions of peace. They provide few technical instructions, but all offer points of reference for companies and stakeholders intent upon developing policies and procedures to improve the conduct of NRCs' conduct and performance in preventing or responding to community-level conflict. Following is a closer examination of how business, peace and are brought together in two publications: one by International Alert (2006) and the other by UN Global Compact (2010). Although International Alert's publication *Local Business, Local Peace* (2006) is mentioned in section 2.3, there is a prior publication that also makes an important and distinct contribution to the business and peace literature specifically regarding natural resources; it is reviewed below.

2.5.1 International Alert

International Alert was one of the earliest organisations to apply and advance the recommendations from Nelson's report specifically to the natural resources industry in a comprehensive way in *Conflict-sensitive business practices: guidance for the extractives industry* (Banfield et al., 2005). This report represents another important contribution to the second generation of work linking business and peace. The report focuses upon pre-existing or latent regional conflicts with the potential to erupt in physical violence. Although NRCs frequently invest in conflict-prone societies, they have little choice regarding where to conduct their business. Companies locate their operations where the natural resources are located. NRCs are inherently conflict averse, as conflict and violence increase the cost of exploiting natural resources and inhibit the ability to both remove them from their location and take them to market. Yet, NRCs often find themselves in the position of first-responder in conflict-prone regions, even though they have neither the skills, the interest nor the official responsibility for doing so. It behooves NRCs, therefore, to be able to conduct both macro and project-level conflict risk and impact assessments to determine the causes of conflict, as summarised in Table 2.4 below:

Table 2.4 Factors Underpinning Violence in the Natural Resources Context

Causes of Conflict	*(1) Definition*	*(2) Banfield's Examples*	*(3) Natural resources Example: Consultation*	*(4) Natural resources Example: ASM Issues*	*(5) Natural resources Example: Employment*
Root causes and type of violence indicated	pervasive factors built into structures, situations and relationships that contribute to violence at a structural (**S**), cultural (**C**) or physical (**P**) level	illegitimate government, lack of equal economic and social opportunity, lack of political participation (S)	failure of government and/or NRC to consult adequately with landholders about footprint of a natural resources lease (S) (C)	NRC hires a security force to patrol the property fence (P); lack of job opportunities at an NRC operation site or elsewhere in the community (S)	during construction and operation an NRC has a finite number of skilled and unskilled positions available; communities have expectations exceeding NRC's capacity to hire (S)
Proximate causes (conflict characteristics)	factors that are symptomatic of the root causes of conflicts or may lead to further escalation	light-weapons proliferation, Human Rights abuse, objectives of political actors, role of diasporas	community-level protests and road blockades	antagonism between security forces and ASM groups who continue to mine on the lease without permission	in-migration of workers from outside the region looking for employment; fly-in/ fly-out skilled workforce
Triggers	single acts, events or the anticipation thereof that set off violent conflict or its escalation	elections, behaviour of political actors, sudden collapse of currency, increased food scarcity	bulldozing of a sacred site (e.g., hilltop, grove of trees, site of a temple)	security personnel or wounds or kills illegal/ unlicensed logger who is deemed to be trespassing	climatic conditions suddenly ruin seasonal crops leaving many community members without employment or means to care for their families

(*Adapted from Banfield et al., 2005, pp. 2–14*)

Banfield's typology can also be mapped against other major issues related to natural resources with categories of conflict, which include: resettlement, Human Rights, Indigenous employment and compensation, security issues, bribery, corruption, transparency, trade and environment (Franks & Davis, 2011; Zandvliet & Anderson, 2009). Covered elsewhere, it is still worth mentioning that NRCs also have choices to make about complicity with violence in war-affected zones in terms of how resources fund violent activity or political regimes suspected of major Human Rights abuses. The examples Banfield uses are obviously on a larger scale than the community-level illustrations offered from the natural resources context. The typology holds even when scaling down the types of conflict for application at the local level.

2.5.2 *Global Compact*

The United Nations Global Compact[2] suggests areas where businesses can make contributions towards addressing a variety of regional, national and international conflicts (Powell & Chung, 2010; Powell et al., 2010). These guides assist businesses in making decisions to address and prevent conflict within their sphere of influence and extend their core business by contributing to conditions of peace. Using examples from both mining and oil contexts as well as other industries that operate in conflict-prone areas of the world, the authors identify four major areas of influence. The first is to pay attention to running one's core business responsibly, lawfully and inclusively. This means paying attention to fair hiring practices at the local level, local procurement where possible, paying taxes (not bribes), establishing a reliable grievance mechanism and contributing to infrastructure development. The second is to make constructive alliances with host country governments, even when those are fragile or in transition. By engaging host country governments rather than withdrawing or refusing to engage, businesses can bolster good governance, clarify the delineation of separate government and company roles and responsibility and encourage a healthier climate in which to do business. The third is local stakeholder engagement. The overall goal is to create relationships based on trust, "fostering positive relationships between conflicting groups and reducing the possibility of violent conflict" (Powell et al., 2010, p. 21). Strategies include stakeholder engagement mechanisms, listening carefully to a full range of stakeholders to build their capacity to become part of decision-making processes and using conflict analysis tools as well as independent third parties. The fourth is strategic social investment. This refers to the ways in which large-resource companies can contribute to the long-term development needs and aspirations of local communities. The guides emphasise the need for a planned, not *ad hoc*, strategy that considers the social impact and mitigates the potential to exacerbate conflict. A further source of metrics and conceptual frameworks on the economic and political incentives for businesses contributing to peace can be found in the *Global Peace Index*, published annually (Institute for Economics & Peace, 2017).

2.6 Voluntary Initiatives Supportive of Natural Resources and Peace

Most of the guidance about how to address thematic areas which initiate or sustain violence in natural resources regions comes from voluntary strategies (Global Witness, 2007). The frameworks, codes, guidelines and toolkits (collectively: strategies) most commonly used in the natural resources context are indicated as follows.[3] The *Corporate Responsibility Code Book* discusses the strengths, weaknesses and application potential of many of these strategies in one anthology (Leipziger, 2014). The book highlights that each business sector is unique, has different drivers and stakeholders and that there is no 'one-size-fits-all' voluntary strategy to encourage good or best practices in CSR work. Instead, the book highlights some of the more effective strategies as well as tracking the evolving CSR dialogue amongst stakeholders to MNEs. The book identifies hallmarks of effective strategies as those which: raise awareness about CSR within a company; help companies set objectives; assist with implantation strategies; minimise risk; and foster dialogue and partnerships between internal and external stakeholders (see Table 2.5).

These strategies are valuable in framing corporate behaviour across a range of conflict scenarios in the natural resources context. Each one of them provides guidance that could lead to conditions of increased peace between NRCs and affected communities without mentioning peace directly. Topics include: increasing dialogue between MNEs and communities; encouraging community consultation on the development or expansion of a natural resources operation; respecting the Human Rights of NRC affected peoples, both workers and community members; eschewing the use of physical force to resolve NRC-community conflict; refusing to participate in practices of bribery; developing and using an effective complaints and grievance mechanism; and honouring local customs.

However, some argue that these voluntary strategies lack mandatory transparency or reporting requirements and therefore do not ensure that corporations are actually putting voluntary policies and procedures into place (Global Witness, 2007). Furthermore, no singular, neutral third party is required to evaluate performance or enforce a change in corporate behaviour. Finally, voluntary initiatives give little guidance on what to do in conflict situations when violence breaks out. This evaluation of voluntary initiatives by Global Witness is not entirely accurate, however, as many of the strategies do require auditing and reporting for certification purposes (e.g., GRI, ISO26000, EITI). The point of contention remains that they are not mandatory, leading to concern that the incentive for putting these

Table 2.5 Strategies Supporting Best-Practice CSR in Natural Resources Contexts

Strategies	*Acronym/Year Instituted*	*Mentions Peace*
Akwe: Kon Guidelines	Secretariat of the Convention on Biological Diversity, 2004	
Conflict Free Gold Standard	World Gold Council, 2012	Yes
REDD+ Program on reducing emissions from deforestation and degradation and	UN-REDD, 2008	
IFC Performance Standards on Economic and Social Sustainability	IFC, 2012	
The Guiding Principles on Business and Human Rights	UNHROHC, 2011	
GRI Sustainability Reporting Guidelines	GRI, 2011	
ISO 26000	ISO, 2010	Yes
Extractive Industries Transparency Initiative (EITI)	EITI, 2006	
The Equator Principles	Equator Principles, 2006	
Responsible Jewellery Council	RJC, 2009	Yes
ICMM Sustainability Principles	ICMM, 2003	
Kimberley Process (Conflict free diamonds)	Kimberley Process, 2002	Yes
The Voluntary Principles on Security and Human Rights	Voluntary Principles, 2000	Yes
UN Global Compact	UNGC, 2000	Yes
OECD Guidelines for Multinational Enterprises	OECD, [1976] 2011	
The Natural Resource Charter	NRC, 2011	

practices in place, when NRC-community relationships become increasingly difficult, has to come from somewhere other than a regulatory body or international agency (Bridgeman & Hunter, 2008).

2.7 Summary

Natural resources-related literature infrequently uses the language of peace or activities related to peace-building. When peace is explicitly mentioned, it is either as an ethical goal (*telos*), a foundational heurism or a desired general state of affairs. Even with contributions by the scholars and international organisations cited in this literature review, the connection between peace and natural resources has not become mainstream in either industry, policy or academic circles. The peace and business agenda remains poorly defined regarding natural resources, even though NRCs must and do engage with communities and have both business and moral imperatives to do so productively. The remainder of this section highlights places where the connection between peace and natural resources could be strengthened.

2.7.1 Gaps

There are several gaps relating to NRCs and peace. The first is in sustainability and the annual reports of large NRCs (2008–2015). When the reports use the word or concept of peace, it is largely in the most general terms; there is no direct linkage between an NRC's activities and the conditions of peacefulness in the surrounding communities. This apparent omission of any discussion or mention of *peace* in the natural resources industry related reports does not mean that companies are opposed to contexts of peace in which to do business or that they are not promoting activities and strategies conducive to peace. Certainly, NRCs try to avoid operating in conflict zones or exacerbating any level of conflict at the community level. Nevertheless, the companies do not make statements of commitment to peaceful business environments, or to peace more generally, in a public way. This omission is problematic because successful CSR strategies depend on a peaceful operating environment. If so, it could be advantageous to state this goal directly in Annual Reports or Sustainability Reports. Many of these reports do cite variable amounts of commitment to enacting strategies supportive of the conditions of peace, as shown in Table 2.4. These commitments are found in the reports under the following customary categories: a definition of sustainability and how that fits into the corporate vision; safety performance; employee attraction, retention and training; environmental performance, including accidental spills or discharge, recycling of water and use of power sources; socio-economic performance, including community development, Human Rights and Indigenous peoples; and a discussion of shareholder and stakeholder concerns. However, peace is not mentioned as one of the possible outcomes by handling these categories of concern effectively. The second gap is that the voluntary initiatives used by the natural resources sector rarely or only briefly mention peace as a context that maximises the effectiveness of the initiatives. This gap is problematic because it points to a lack of connection, at the policy level, that NRCs have a role in contributing towards peaceful conditions in the regions where they operate. There appear to be no scholarly articles or books that discuss either of these absences.

A third gap is evident in the work emerging on conflict engagement in the natural resources contexts by international advocacy groups (e.g., Mining Watch Canada, International Alert, Oxfam Australia), International Institutions (e.g., the United Nations (UN), the World Bank, the CAO, MIGA) and academic research centres (e.g., the Corporate Social Responsibility Initiative at Harvard University, the Centre for Social Responsibility in Mining at the University of Queensland, the Danish Institute for Human Rights, the United States Institute for Peace (USIP)). These organisations publish reports relevant to both the business community involved in natural resources as well as to the project of pursuing peace as an outcome for CSR activities in the natural resources context. However, except for the UN and the USIP, few of the publications mention any form of peace as either a foundational or transcendent value that could be articulated in practical steps in the NRC-community nexus.

Finally, as outlined above, the body of literature on Peace Theory and International Relations rarely mentions mining, forestry or hydro-electric companies in its discussions of non-state actors. Common examples are manufacturing, retail and oil companies, such as Coca Cola, Wal-Mart, Nike and Shell Oil. The significance of this gap is that natural resources have been largely left out of the conversation, the debates and the development of solutions. This is an unfortunate consequence, given the long-term presence in communities, the scale of their operations and the lasting effects of their activities upon a region. Consequently, much stands to be gained by including them in the conversation.

2.7.2 Limits

The scholarship on business, peace and natural resources is limited in scope and breadth. Those writing about the potential for businesses to contribute to local and even global conditions of peace are not writing from a business point of view; they are writing from academic, NGO and policy-oriented perspectives. As sincerely as they try to create a platform for dialogue with business and to create the business case for peace as an outcome of doing business, the voices missing in this dialogue are those of businesspeople themselves. Speculation that businesspeople are not interested in peace or would not understand it is just that: speculation. As indicated in the literature above, peace-building is important to the economic performance of NRCs, and it is important to individuals within those corporations, irrespective of economic performance. This raises the question of whether more needs to be done to outline pragmatic peace-building steps that can be used in the natural resources context.

2.8 Conclusion

Conflict occurs in the context where businesses operate. Conflict is a normal, dynamic feature of human interaction (Switzer, 2001). Conflict in the natural resources context is not fundamentally something to avoid at all costs; it can simply mean that there is an issue to address. There are a variety of conflicts commonly associated with natural resources. Conflict can occur between an NRC and its neighbouring communities; it can be pre-existing or latent in a region, and it can even take the form of military or combatant activity which may implicate government officials or departments. Any of these conflicts may or may not be directly related to natural resources activity, but can either implicate or affect natural resources focused businesses.

When conflicts begin to escalate as a result of inadequately addressed structural or cultural violence that may provoke physically violent conflict, the social, political, environmental and economic costs can become unacceptably high and disruptive across entire regions, as well as inhibit natural resources activity (Carius, Dabelkko, Capistrano, Fell, & Switzer, 2005). This disruption can have enduring consequences for the relationship between NRCs and affected communities.

More research is therefore necessary because the available literature does not provide the answer to the primary question of: in what ways, and to what extent, could a paradigm of positive peace have traction with CSR practitioners working on social aspects of NRC-community relationships? As this chapter has shown, the literature reflects the views of a few scholars, policy makers, research centres and others theorising *about* the role of NRCs. The most substantial absence in this larger conversation about the role of business and peace, however, is the voice of the NRCs themselves.

Notes

1 "Track I diplomacy: Formal discussions typically involving high-level political and military leaders and focusing on cease-fires, peace talks, and treaties and other agreements. Third-party interveners are almost always official—a government or international organisation, for example.

Track II diplomacy: Unofficial dialogue and problem-solving activities aimed at building relationships and encouraging new thinking that can inform the formal process. [A]ctivities typically involve influential academic, religious, and NGO leaders and other civil society actors who can interact more freely than high-ranking officials". Aall, P. 2011. Peace Terms: Glossary of Terms for Conflict Management and Peacebuilding. In D. Snodderly (Ed.). Washington, D.C.: Academy for International Conflict Management and Peacebuilding (USIP).

2 The Global Compact asks companies to embrace universal principles and to partner with the United Nations. It has grown to become a critical platform for the UN to engage effectively with global business. [Accessed: 10 Sept 2013 at www.unglobalcompact.org/]

3 See further discussion of frameworks in the chapter on paradigms. Also see Table 5.1 for further details on the frameworks in Table 2.3.

Bibliography

Aall, P. (2011). *Peace terms: Glossary of terms for conflict management and peacebuilding* (D. Snodderly, Ed.). Washington, DC: Academy for International Conflict Management and Peacebuilding (USIP).

Anglo American. (2011). *Anglo American signs strategic partnership with International Alert.* Retrieved from http://southafrica.angloamerican.com/media/press-releases/2011/21-01-11.aspx

Ballentine, K., & Haufler, V. (2009 [2005]). *Enabling economies of peace: public policy for conflict-sensitive business.* New York, NY: UN Global Compact.

Banfield, J., Barbolet, A., Goldwyn, R., & Killick, N. (2005). *Conflict-sensitive business practice: Guidance for extractive industries.* London: International Alert.

Beevers, M. (2012). Forest resources and peacebuilding: Preliminary lessons from Liberia and Sierra Leone. In P. Lujala & S. A. Rustad (Eds.), *High-value natural resources and post-conflict peacebuilding*. London: Earthscan.

Blundell, A., Harwell, E., & Canby, K. (2015). *REDD+ and post-conflict*. Oslo: Forest Trends.

Bond, C. (2014). Positive peace and sustainability in the mining context: Beyond the triple bottom line. *Journal of Cleaner Production*, *84*(1), 164–173.

Bridgeman, N. L., & Hunter, D. B. (2008). Narrowing the accountability gap: Toward a new foreign investor accountability mechanism. *Georgetown International Environmental Law Review*, *2008*(20), 187–236.

Brunnschweiler, C. N., & Bulte, E. H. (2008). The resource curse revisited and revised: A tale of paradoxes and red herrings. *Journal of Environmental Economics and Management*, *55*, 248–264.

Carbonnier, G., Wagner, N., & Brugger, F. (2010). Oil, gas and minerals: The impact of resource-dependence and governance on sustainable development. *CCDP Working Paper 8*. Geneva: The Centre on Conflict, Development and Peacebuilding.

Carius, A., Dabelkko, G., Capistrano, D., Fell, M., & Switzer, J. (2005). *Minerals and conflict: A toolkit for intervention*. Washington, DC: Office of Conflict Management and Mitigation.

de Lopez, T. T. (2002). Natural resource exploitation in Cambodia: An examination of use, appropriation, and exclusion. *Journal of Environment and Development*, *11*(4), 355–379.

Escobar, A. (2006). Difference and conflict in the struggle over natural resources: A political ecology framework. *Development*, *39*(3), 6–13.

Forrer, J., Fort, T., & Gilpin, R. (2012). *How business can foster peace. Special Report*. Washington, DC: US Institute of Peace.

Francis, D. (2010). *From pacification to peacebuilding: A call to global transformation*. New York, NY: Palgrave Macmillan.

Franks, D. M., & Davis, R. (2011). The costs of conflict with local communities in the extractive industry. Santiago, Chile: SR Mining 2011.

Friedman, M. (1970). The social responsibility of business is to increase its profits. *The New York Times Magazine*. New York, NY: The New York Times Company.

Fujisaki, T., Hyakumura, K., Scheyvens, H., & Cadman, T. (2016). Does REDD+ ensure sectoral coordination and stakeholder participation? A comparative analysis of REDD+ national governance structures in countries of Asia-Pacific region. *Forests*, *7*(195).

Ganson, B., & Wennmann, A. (2012). *Confronting risk, mobilizing action: A framework for conflict prevention in the context of large-scale business investments*. International Policy Analysis. Geneva: Friedrich Ebert Stiftung.

Global Witness. (2007). *Oil and mining in violent places: Why voluntary codes for companies don't guarantee human rights*. London: Global Witness.

Goldcorp. (2011). *Corporate responsibility for peace and prosperity*. Vancouver: Goldcorp.

Hintjens, H. (2006). Conflict and resources in post-genocide Rwanda and the Great Lakes region. *International Journal of Environmental Studies*, *63*(5), 599–615.

IFC. (2010). *Strategic community investment*. Washington, DC: International Finance Corporation.

Iff, A., Sguaitamatti, D., Alluri, R. M., & Kohler, D. (2010). *Money makers as peace makers? Business actors in mediation processes*. Bern: SwissPeace.

IISD. (2010). *Environment, conflict and peacebuilding at IISD*. Geneva: International Institute for Sustainable Development.

Institute for Economics and Peace (2017), *Global Peace Index*, IEP: Sydney.

Banfield, J., Barbolet, A., Goldwyn, R., & Killick, N. (2005). *Conflict-sensitive business practice: Guidance for extractive industries*. London, UK: International Alert.

International Alert. (2006). Introduction. In J. Banfield, C. Gündüz, & N. Killick (Eds.), *Local business, local peace: The peacebuilding potential of the domestic private sector*. London: International Alert.

Lahiri-Dutt, K. (2006). 'May God Give Us Chaos, So That We Can Plunder': A critique of 'resource curse' and conflict theories. *Development*, *49*(3), 14–21.

Le Billon, P., & Levin, E. (2009). Building peace with conflict diamonds? Merging security and development in Sierra Leone. *Development and Change*, *40*(4), 693–715.

Lederach, J. P. (1995). *Preparing for peace: Conflict transformation across cultures*. Syracuse, NY: Syracuse University Press.

Lederach, J. P. (1997). *Building peace: Sustainable reconciliation in divided societies*. Washington, DC: United States Institute for Peace.

Lederach, J. P. (2003). *The little book of conflict transformation*. Intercourse, PA: Good Books.

Lederach, J. P. (2008). The role of corporate actors in peace-building processes. In C. S. C. Oliver & F. Williams (Eds.), *Peace through commerce*. Notre Dame, IN: University of Notre Dame Press.

Lederman, D., & Maloney, W. F. (Eds.). (2007). *Natural resources neither curse nor destiny*. New York, NY: The World Bank.

Leipziger, D. (2010). *The corporate responsibility code book*. Sheffield: Greenleaf.

Lowry, R. D. B. (2008). International concord and intranational discord. In O. Williams (Ed.), *Peace through commerce*. Notre Dame, IN: Notre Dame University Press.

Nelson, J. (2000). *The business of peace*. London: International Alert and Council on Economic Priorities.

Powell, M., & Chung, D. (2010). *Doing business while advancing peace and development*. New York, NY: United Nations Global Compact.

Powell, M., Gardaz, A., Chung, D., & Liu, M. (2010). *Guidance on responsible business in conflict-affected and high-risk areas: A resource for companies and investors*. New York, NY: United Nations Global Compact, PRI.

Samset, I. (2009). *Natural resource wealth, conflict, and peacebuilding*. New York, NY: Program on States and Security (Synthesis Series), Graduate Center, City University of New York.

Santa Barbara, J., Dubee, F., & Galtung, J. (2009). *Peace business: People and nature above markets and capital*. Oslo: Transcend University Press.

Schirch, L. (2004). *The little book of strategic peacebuilding*. Intercourse, PA: Good Books.

Smurthwaite, M. (2008). The purpose of the corporation. In O. Williams (Ed.), *Peace through commerce*. Notre Dame, IN: Notre Dame University Press.

Switzer, J. (2001). *Armed conflict and natural resources: The case of the minerals sector*. Manitoba: MMSD.

Tanzler, D., & Ries, F. (2012). International climate change policies: The potential relevance of REDD+ for peace and stability. In J. Scheffran, M. Brzoska, H. G. Brauch, P. M. Link, & J. Schilling (Eds.), *Climate change, human security and violent conflict* (pp. 695–705). New York, NY: Springer.

United Nations Global Compact. (2010). *A Global Compact for Development*. United Nations: New York, NY.

UN Global Compact, & Deloitte. (2011). *UN global compact management model*. New York, NY: United Nations.

Zandvliet, L., & Anderson, M. B. (2009). *Getting it right: Making corporate-community relations work*. Sheffield: Greenleaf Publishing.

3 Peace Theory and Natural Resources Companies as Non-State Actors

The focus of this chapter is upon academic peace and conflict theory. Although theorists often state that businesses have a role to play in creating local-level conditions of peace, they rarely go into any detail about how that should happen due to disciplinary boundaries. Pushing the envelope of existing peace and conflict theory, this chapter advances the inclusion of businesses, especially MNEs, which rival the social, environmental and economic influence of small nations. The methodology and methods of applying this enhanced theory are also described.

3.1 Multinational Enterprises as Contributors to Societal Peace

Only since 2000 have scholars and policy makers begun to see MNEs as strategic creators and sustainers of peace at the community level (Nelson, 2000). Although international relations scholars are more sceptical then business scholars in seeing the potential for businesses to be agents of peace (Haufler, 2015), there is significant interest in this role in the international business community. Towards a broader understanding of this strategic role, this chapter applies Peace and Conflict Theory to the natural resources context by identifying NRCs companies as non-state actors[1] with the capacity to enhance or diminish conditions of peace to the regions in which they operate. In order to make this claim, one must start with the responsibility of businesses for Human Rights.

There is precedent to identify large companies as non-state actors in the international sphere. Transnational, and to a lesser extent smaller, companies are now formally considered by the United Nations as non-state actors. Due to tireless work by Prof John Ruggie and his team, over the space of six years of consulting with businesses, community groups, scholars and governments, businesses now have specific responsibilities towards the communities affected by their activities under the *Guiding Principles on Business and Human Rights* (Ruggie, 2011).

Briefly, the *Guiding Principles* declares that businesses have a three-pronged moral obligation and potentially legal mandate to people affected by their activities:

- **Protect** the Human Rights of people within their sphere of influence, even in instances where the state is weak in protecting these rights;
- **Respect** the Human Rights of people within their sphere of influence, including employees, contractors, supply chain workers and affected community members;
- **Remedy** any intentional or unintentional Human Rights violations caused by the company's activities.

Scholarship on the topic of Human Rights responsibilities of business has burgeoned since the publication of the *Guiding Principles* (AHRC, ACCST, & GCNA, 2015; Černič & Černič, 2015; Giuliani, 2016; Martin & Bravo, 2015; Nolan, 2015; van der Ploeg & Vanclay, 2016). Consulting firms also abound to assist larger companies in managing risk exposure to potential Human Rights claims. The *Guiding Principles* is therefore proving to be a durable mandate for businesses.

Due to the increasing focus on Human Rights in the business context, multinational as well as national businesses can thus be considered philosophically, although not legally (Ruggie, 2011), as non-state actors with a responsibility to contribute to, or at least not jeopardise, societal conditions of peace. With this recognition of responsibility, it is possible to make the following two extensions to the application of the *Guiding Principles* in the natural resources context. First, the activities of multinational businesses can be seen as sitting under the preamble to the UDHR recognising "the inherent dignity and of the equal and inalienable rights of all members of the human family [as] the foundation of freedom, justice and peace in the world" (UNGA, 1948). Secondly, the *Guiding Principles* can be considered more broadly under the purposes of the United Nations as a whole. Specifically, the purpose (or ends) of the United Nations are stated as "to practice tolerance and live together in peace with one another as good neighbours, and to unite our strength to maintain international peace and security, and . . . to employ international machinery for the promotion of the economic and social advancement of all peoples" (UNGA, 1945, Preamble). The goal of this chapter is therefore to focus specifically on the roles and responsibilities of state and non-state actors in making this contribution to peace.

3.2 Natural Resources Companies as Non-State Actors

Within the discipline of international relations, it is possible to classify large NRCs as non-state actors under the sub-set of transnational actor, rather than as an international organisation (e.g., the United Nations).

A transnational actor is not a government but a "civil society organization from one country that has relations with any actor from another country or with an international organization" (Willetts, 2005, p. 426). Although large NRCs are classified as non-state actors, host communities/local-level actors have been known to expect NRCs to assume some of the roles of either a state or an international organisations in both developing and developed country contexts (Prno & Slocombe, 2012). This is especially true when natural resources-affected communities perceive that the state has failed in delivering public goods and services or when international organisations lack either the will or the capacity to respond to community concerns. For example, companies often respond to community-level requests to build schools, hospitals, swimming pools and recreation facilities, roads, electricity generators, wells and more. In remote and rural regions, the likelihood that the communities will ask companies to fund these projects increases.

NRCs consequently face three business-level challenges. First, shareholders demand from their companies a saleable product, at a handsome profit, from the ores they are excavating. Second, local governments and local development organisations/NGOs demand increasing proportion of the benefits from natural resources be spent at the community level (Anglo American, 2013; ECOSOC, 2010; ICMM, 2011). Finally, communities expect NRCs to make up economic shortfalls where resource policies result in the distribution of natural resources rents/taxes that privilege politicians rather than those directly affected by natural resources (Collier & Hoeffler, 2005).

Companies publish annual reports and sustainable development reports to answer the first two business-level challenges: financial fitness and sustainable community benefits. Sustainable development reports, or sections of annual reports with sustainability goals mentioned, often reflect corporate distributing benefits at the community level. Where appropriate for the situation, companies often tout their support for the following kinds of projects: providing fresh water and sanitation systems, increasing electrical capacity, building roads, funding schools, contributing to community/cultural facilities and establishing or expanding medical centres. In undertaking these projects, NRCs indicate a preference to partner with local governments (state actors) and development organisations (both local and international organisations) by making a financial contribution directly to them. The agreement, then, is for those organisations to develop agreed-upon infrastructure projects, instead of the companies managing the project development. However, outsourcing these projects to other actors is difficult for NRCs when they operate in regions where local governance is weak and development organisations lack the capacity or resources (Hamann, Kapelus, Sonnenberg, Mackenzie, & Hollesen, 2005).

In circumstances of weak government and poorly resourced development organisations, a common observation by CSR professionals is that NRCs are pressured to assume the role of the state or a development agency. These roles are at odds with the company's primary role is in relation to its portfolio of business activities. Nevertheless, since the Brundtland Commission (1987) articulated the sustainable development responsibilities of businesses, NRCs more frequently engage in development and infrastructure projects at the local level. In other words, whether they want to or not, communities are increasingly asking NRCs to assume the responsibilities of non-state actors, even though the CSR and IR literature discussing the role of transnational enterprises as non-state actors has only begun to include NRCs in the last ten years (Idemudia, 2011; Sklair & Miller, 2010; Wilburn & Wilburn, 2011).

International relations scholar Oliver Richmond has devised a conceptual framework that includes the role of civil society or businesses in relation to both the state and the international order (2010). He is one of a few scholars who has made an effort to articulate these relationships. The coherent expression of the role of companies, as non-state actors within the international order, sets appropriate limits for shaping CSR practice in responding to community level demands levelled at companies.

The conceptual Peace Theory framework developed by Oliver Richmond is only one of a number created by scholars to describe the history and the development of several generations of Peace Theory. However, Richmond's work is an appropriate framework for two important reasons. First, the scholarship of many peace and conflict theorists focuses on conditions of peace and conflict at the state and interstate level. These issues include war, genocide, global environmental issues and the plight of special groups such as refugees. As important as these issues are, even in the natural resources context, this book does not engage peace and conflict theory or peace-building at the state or interstate level. In fact, the challenge in framing NRCs as non-state actors has to do more with local-level activity. Richmond's theory discusses Peace Theory at the local level as well as at the macro level, providing an opening to discuss non-state actors' roles in creating and sustaining positive peace. Second, Richmond's work is linked to scholarship published by the Berghof Foundation. What is distinctive about the research emerging from this non-profit NGO is its commitment to applied research. The Foundation states, "In our research work we address the deeply rooted structural causes of conflict, and seek particularly to develop innovative approaches to the peaceful transformation of violent and protracted social conflict".[2] Therefore, Richmond's work seems most appropriate to provide the theoretical framework on peace for this book.

3.3 Peace and Conflict Theory

Peace and Conflict Theory is a sub-discipline of International Relations theory. Peace and Conflict theorists aspire to create and encourage conditions of peace in a world continually beset by conflict. Peace research is inspired by two main streams of thought (Wallensteen, 2011). First, as a critique of the ruthless Machiavellian legacy, peace research studies violence and endeavours to understand conflict in order to prevent both. Second, as a critique of as yet unrealised Utopian ideals, peace research studies the potential of cooperative conditions that make for peace. Towards those ends, Peace and Conflict theorists have traditionally been concerned with conflicts that occur at state and regional levels. However, not all peace and conflict theorists limit their analysis to state and regional levels. Richmond's "Genealogy of Peace and Conflict Theory" in *Advances in Peacebuilding* (2010) identifies four ways of conceptualising peace and conflict which account for the influence of non-state actors such as MNEs, NGOs and other actors capable of influencing the conditions of peacefulness or violence at the regional as well as state levels. In the next section, each of the four ways is explained in greater detail.

3.3.1 First-Generation Peace and Conflict Theory and Realism

First-generation Peace and Conflict Theory is a conflict management approach principally concerned with establishing and maintaining basic order and stopping openly expressed, physically violent conflict. It focuses on preserving the sovereignty of states. Rather than generating peace, first-generation theory seeks to understand conditions that reduce and manage conflict through the use of neutral third parties, typically diplomats. The foundational philosophy underpinning this stream is political Realism.[3]

Realism is the oldest political theory, dating to Thucydides's *History of the Peloponnesian War*, and includes Machiavelli's *The Prince* in the 16th century as well as Hobbes's philosophical discourses in the 17th century. The Realist School became particularly well articulated after the collapse of the League of Nations and the end of WWII. Realist, as well as Neo-Realist (hereafter referred to jointly as Neo/Realist), scholars emphasise different aspects of the theory. Overall, however, Neo/Realism endures as an appealing theory, in part, because it presents a straightforward interpretation of international relations that appears, on the surface, both strictly factual and inevitable. Neo/Realism is characterised by the ethical principle that might is right. Anthropologically, it assumes that people are naturally violent and that civil order requires the threat of physical force. Finally, it does not account for the effects of the agency of either non-state actors or individuals, since Neo/Realists presume that the actions of non-state actors or individuals do not significantly influence the actions of the state.

Given that frame, Neo/Realism concerns itself mainly with the international system of nations as composed of sovereign nation-states (Boucher, 1998). In other eras of human history, feudal systems, princedoms, kingdoms, empires, city-states and other organisational models have characterised the relationships of large groups of otherwise unrelated peoples. Since the Treaty of Westphalia (1648), Western political life has been characterised by the formation and behaviour of sovereign states (Tilly, 2002).

The notion of sovereign states emerging from the Westphalian era is based upon a Roman idea of property where sovereigns are property-owners. "[Sovereigns claim] the right to do what they [want] within their territory without external interference . . . they also [defend] in principle the rights of other property-owners to do what they [want] with *their* property" (Brown, 2002, p. 29). Sovereign states, defined in terms of property, are a system of agents who mutually observe the rights of ownership[4] and, importantly, control material items and land. These sovereign states are classically recognised as:

- territoriality—each has an actual location on a map of the globe;
- the right to have a standing military to defend their borders and their people;
- the right to run their domestic affairs without external interference; the right to make agreements with other states; and importantly,
- recognition by other sovereign states (Brown, 2002).

Of course, some would-be leaders and regimes have challenged these markers of sovereignty since WWII, but a robust discussion of that development is outside the scope of this book.

There are five defining propositions of Realism (Greico, 1988). First, Realism is concerned with the behaviour of nation-states, primarily those that are considered 'big powers', such as the United States, China and Russia in the current age. Second, the primary motivation for the behaviour of these states is to act in a way that will protect their self-interests, the most crucial of which is survival. Third, the international system is anarchic—meaning that there is no 'body' or inter-state government officially regulating the behaviour of states—and anarchy is a force that shapes the choices states make. Fourth, even when pursing mutually held interests, states are primarily competitive and motivated by security concerns. The focus is on relative gains vis-à-vis other states and the security dilemma, whereby the ongoing assumption is that if another state can cheat and hurt others, it will. Fifth, international institutions, such as trans-national corporations, NGOs or even internationally well-known/charismatic individuals, can only marginally affect the cooperative behaviour of states. Given these five assumptions, it is not necessarily the rule that states will not cooperate under the supervision or recommendation of an international institutional body, it just means that the alliances necessary for those cooperative undertakings to succeed are extremely tenuous and highly conditional because of the concerns with relative gains and security.

In sum, the first generation of peace and conflict theory, and its underlying Neo/Realist foundation, is the oldest frame within which non-state actors operate. The form of peace most associated with the Realist school is now called 'negative peace'. The definition of negative peace is "the absence of violence, absence of war" (Galtung, 1964, p. 2) and focuses upon conditions and people who need to be removed to create conditions for peace (Wallensteen, 2011). This definition is sufficient as 'peace' for Realists and related first-generation Peace and Conflict theorists.

NRCs still operating out of this frame of negative peace (e.g., some state-owned NRCs), as non-state actors, have minimal responsibility towards the communities affected by their operations. In this frame, the state not only assumes primary responsibility for communities affected by NRCs, but also remains the primary entity in partnership for these companies. The operational logic of sufficient peace requires the state, rather than non-state actors such as resource companies, to reduce or eliminate the sources of potential violence through regulation and enforcement. Large resource companies, nevertheless (e.g., Vale, CODELCO, Chinalco) have social and environmental responsibilities. The challenge in meeting them is rendered more difficult if the state is not committed to regulating or mandating the behaviour of NRCs in these vital realms.

3.3.2 Second-Generation Peace and Conflict Theory and Cosmopolitanism

Second-generation Peace and Conflict theorists are of the view that it is not sufficient to prevent physical expressions of violence where permanent incapacitation (e.g., killing) is intended by one actor against another. These theorists agree with Galtung, who levels a sharp critique at the Hobbesian Realism of *bellum omnium contra omnes*,[5] which he saw as informing the justification for nuclear proliferation. Galtung's conception of negative peace, mentioned above, matured by 1969 in "Violence, Peace and Peace Research", in which he clearly identifies violence as the opposite of peace. Galtung's definitions of violence and negative peace are summarised below.

Galtung's *meta* definition of violence is that "violence is present when human beings are being influenced so that their actual somatic and mental realisations are below their potential realisations" (Galtung, 1969, p. 168). He gives a medical example. If someone dies of tuberculosis today, when there are plenty of medical interventions to arrest the progression of the disease, the denial of those medical treatments is an expression of violence leading to loss of potential—or life. With the extension of the definition of violence as beyond the strictly physical, he outlines six dimensions of violence that qualify as the absence of peace.

- *Psychological*: indirect personal threats to constrain human action, including: lies, brainwashing, indoctrination or other forms intended by one actor to control the actions or crush the soul of another actor.
- *Influence*: negative efforts by one actor to personally influence another, thereby diminishing the ability of the actor on the receiving end from realising his/her potential (e.g., threaten to or actually punish).

- *Threat*: when an actor demonstrates they have the ability to cause physical violence, whether or not they actually exercise that ability (e.g., stockpiling and testing of weapons).
- *Structural or indirect*: the uneven distribution of resources because of the prevailing social order or structure. For example, if people lack education, food, shelter and other basic needs in situations where avoidable, then they are the victims of structural violence.
- *Intentionality*: whether or not an actor (A) 'intends' not to hurt, harm or incapacitate another actor (B), if actor (B) suffers a lack of potential because of the actions or inactions of actor (A), violence has been committed.
- *Observable or imminent:* manifest violence is observable, and latent violence is an imminent potential for violence to occur at either a structural or personal level.

Galtung's typology of violence strongly suggests that scholarly conceptions of peace and peacefulness need to expand. With an expanded understanding of the forms of violence, it is possible to design peace-filled responses to violence beyond the boundaries of direct, physical, personal, manifest violence. Negative peace, in relation to these six forms of violence, is the exercise or threat to use force or power to prevent these forms of violence from emerging, a particularly salient observation during the height of the Cold War

In response to Galtung's typology of violence and conception of a negative peace through force, a second generation of Peace and Conflict theory developed which focuses on conflict resolution. The main argument is that the first-generation conflict management does not go far enough. The goal of second-generation Peace and Conflict Theory is not to achieve a limited or negative peace, but a 'win-win' or positive peace.

The foundational philosophy underpinning the second generation of Peace and Conflict theory is political cosmopolitanism. Cosmopolitanism is a concept traceable to Socrates, who inspired the Cynic philosopher Diogenes to consider himself "a citizen of the world *kosmopolites*" (Linklater, 2002, p. 136) but is more commonly linked by theorists to Kant's essay *Perpetual Peace* (1983 [1795]). The peace to which Kant refers is between states. He details six features as the basis for international peace, upholding the sovereignty of federated Republican[6] states, while denouncing any and all material and personal expressions of a future intent to wage war (e.g., stockpiling money to purchase munitions, making plans to employ agents to undermine the sovereignty of another state). The maintenance of the state makes peaceful civilisation possible (Pojman, 2005). Cosmopolitanism makes demands of states to treat insiders and outsiders equally because of a set of universal needs people have for food, water, somewhere to live and the right to live a life in relative peace. We have duties to our community first, certainly, but we also have duties to people outside our communities—the *cosmopolis*. This means that states cannot do as they please to other states (Linklater, 2002) because all human beings are equal, and "efforts to solve global problems should promote welfare of the species as a whole" (Linklater, 2006 [2001], p. 721). Analogously, entities within states are not supposed to treat each other as they please either. In other words, an NRC has a duty of care within the state, just as states have a duty of care towards their own citizenry and the citizens of other states.

A sobering limit to the appeal of cosmopolitanism, in the present day, is that states are not always the most influential actors on the global stage.

> The devolution of state authority to the local and global levels, the emergence of private authority in some issue areas, create[s] the political space for non-state actors, including NGOs and multinationals, to participate in governance at both the global and national levels.
>
> (Dashwood, 2007, p. 132)

This has had significant consequences for NRCs because it is now easier for communities and even states to assign responsibility for the provision of infrastructure, discussed in the section on Realism (3.3.1), to non-state actors such as NRCs. This has presented unique challenges because transnational enterprises as non-state actors are not constrained by the state system. Neither are they required to achieve or even consider a cosmopolitan ideal of acting in such a way to address global welfare (Pojman, 2005), although some transnational enterprises, including natural resources majors, do make contributions towards this effort, as reflected in their commitments to a suite of voluntary initiatives.

Second-generation Peace and Conflict theorists propose that underlying any lack of peace, at the local or international level, is the impediment or denial of basic human needs at the individual, group or societal level. Human needs theory begins with Maslow's (1943) universal hierarchy of needs (see Figure 3.1):

Maslow's point is that when people's physiological and safety needs are either unaddressed or are under threat, it is impossible for them to achieve higher-order human thriving such as belongingness, love needs and esteem needs, culminating in full expression of their humanity as self-actualisation. Therefore, to achieve peace—a higher-order expression of human thriving—peoples' basic needs must be met first. From this model, second-generation theorists, while still adopting a statist orientation, developed a framework for understanding conflict and its resolution that highlights *human needs* as central to peace instead of the state's needs.

John Burton constructed his own human needs theory, which is similar to Maslow's, but simpler. For conflicts to be resolved and not re-emerge, Burton contends that basic needs of all parties to a conflict must be met. These needs are "for security, identity and participation [which] . . . underlie the more 'specific' interests of the conflicting parties" (Burton in Francis, 2010, p. 4). These needs are analogous to Maslow's typology (see Figure 3.2):

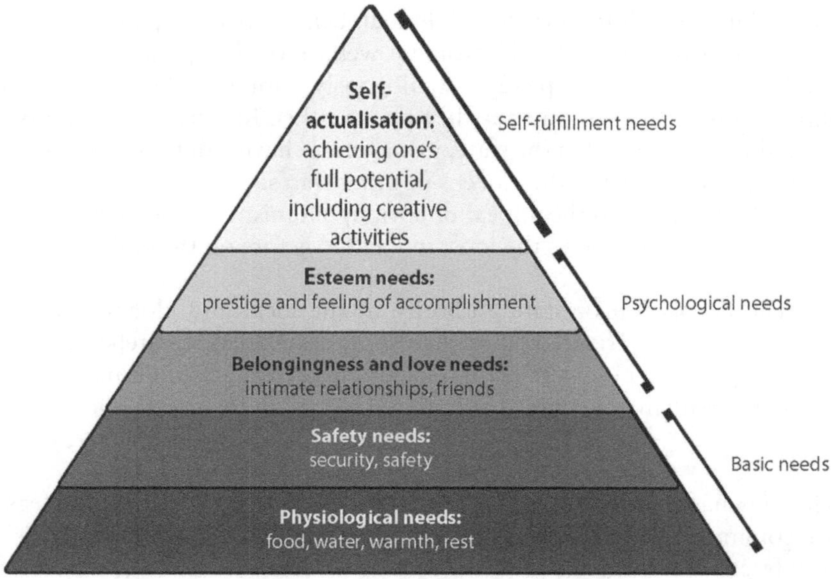

Figure 3.1 Maslow's Hierarchy of Needs

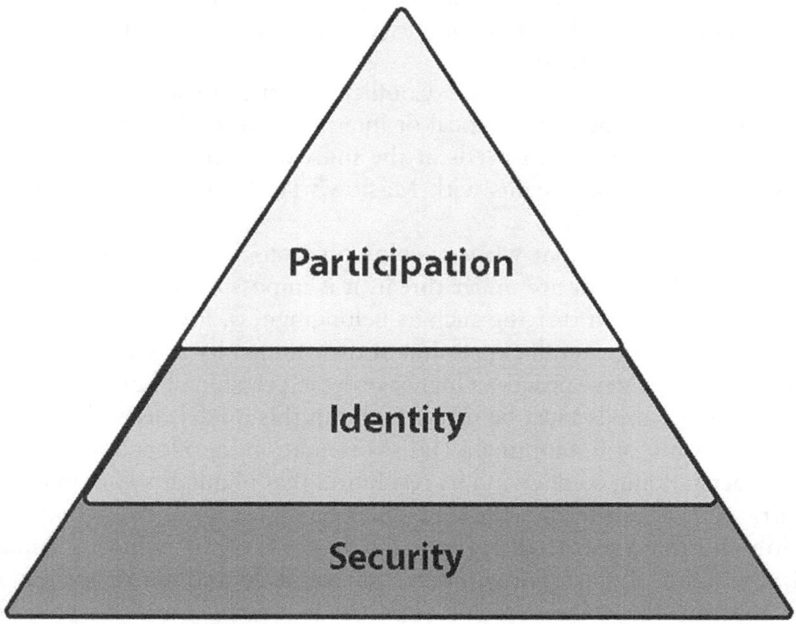

Figure 3.2 Adapted From Burton's Needs Pyramid

The most pressing need is security—physical safety as well as the provision of basic support for human life (e.g., food, water, shelter). The next higher-order need is for identity, which is related to people's role in society as expressed through "occupational, social, political, and economic aspirations" (Burton, 1990, p. 38). Burton links identity to interests as distinct from needs because interests for material items and roles can change, whereas the need for food, water and shelter cannot. However, both needs and interests serve as motivations for action. The denial of either can lead to conflict. The terms of their provision can serve as a subject of negotiation and bargaining. The highest-order need is for participation, since people need to exercise agency in the decisions that affect their lives. Burton argues that peace is more elusive when these needs are not met.

Francis's book *From Pacification to Peacebuilding* (2010) builds on Burton's work, but instead of focusing on needs, she emphasises a particular quality of relationship between people as the primary condition of peace. When relationships are conducive to peace, it means that they are not coercive or violent in nature. They may be intensively persuasive, but there is no underlying or overt use of force to maintain the integrity of the relationship. This is a rather delicate balance to achieve when the notion and importance of basic human needs, and their corresponding Human Rights, differ for various parties to a conflict. Francis illustrates by indicating that warlords, ministers of parliament, presidents, men and women at all levels of society have different sets of needs—including Human Rights, integrity of identity, security as well as perceived needs for wealth or to be in a position of power or domination over others. "The notion of needs can lead us to a greater understanding of what drives different parties to a conflict and what it will take to make them more or less content with any 'solution' "(Francis, 2010, p. 48). Therefore, it is important to proceed carefully with 'needs' and 'rights' language.

Francis is ultimately critical of needs theory for two reasons. The first is that it does not provide any insight on generating sufficient will to resolve conflict. Her other criticism is that needs theory relies too heavily on the idea of disputants recognising the humanity of the 'other/s' with whom they are in conflict—which she sees as more of a spiritual or therapeutic project than a rational exercise. She does not dismiss the value or importance of encountering the 'other' but realises that learning to care about the 'other' does not always lead to a practical or productive solution in situations of scarcity. For example, in the natural resources context, when both parties need access to particular waterways or land parcels, a mutual recognition of humanity may lead to a greater willingness to solve these scarcity problems cooperatively, but it will not produce more water or land to go around. Needs theory therefore has a significant practical importance but is insufficient on its own as the *sole* focus of a desired outcome of positive peace.

The importance of this second generation of Peace and Conflict theory is that it allows both state and non-state actors to work together and exhibit agency in redistributing a wide variety of resources to respond to human needs while honouring the quality of the relationships between actors. In this frame, NRCs are seen as agents who can participate in the redistribution of these resources in cooperation with the state, NGOs and local actors. Second-generation Peace and Conflict Theory is not content with negative peace but encourages agency towards a higher set of goals that is achieved by including the participation of all actors affected by a situation. It also highlights the need to root out structural violence by "social, political and economic engineering on the part of third party interveners to remove the conditions that create violence" (Richmond, 2010, p. 20).

Galtung's concept of positive piece correlates with this higher set of goals as an alternative to negative peace and violence. Positive peace, which Galtung links to social justice, is not simply the absence or reduction of personal or structural violence. It is also about dealing with conflict constructively and attending to participatory human development (Galtung, 1969). In contrast to negative peace, positive peace looks at what needs to be added to a situation to create the conditions necessary for peace (Wallensteen, 2011). Positive peace has also been described by John Burton as "provention" (Burton, 1990, p. 5). It actively seeks to eliminate the social injustices created by structural violence, especially in situations where there is a power imbalance and a minority group with less power is involuntarily dominated by a more powerful majority or mainstream group (Sandole, 2003).

The objective for positive peace, according to Burton, is to resolve deeply rooted causes of conflict so that actors remove or resolve conditions for. Therefore, the establishment of a strong, long-term, durable, positive peace requires the cooperation of number of stakeholders attending to a wide range of variables on a range of levels, depending on how complex or entrenched the conflict situation is or might become. John Paul Lederach and his colleagues refer to the achievement of positive peace as the activities of peace-building which affect positive social and cultural change using conversation as the primary means of transforming conflict (Lederach, Neufeldt, & Culbertson, 2007). Lederach states that positive peace refers to "a holistic vision of peace that includes well-being, as well as right and just relationships and structures" (Neufeldt et al., 2006, p. 30).

There are limits to the effectiveness of this second-generation, bottom-up approach. Firstly, the political Realists, with their continued countervailing emphasis on state power and liberal institutional frameworks, diminish the possibility of fully expressing a positive peace. Secondly, the vision of a liberal positive peace in this theoretical stream depends upon agency benevolently exercised by individuals, civil society and non-state actors as a complement to efforts made at the state and inter-state levels (Richmond, 2010). For that to happen, anthropologically, it assumes that individuals and non-state actors will agree on a common cultural expression of peace and agree to eschew violent means of addressing conflict and that they will not act in their own self-interests at the expense of other actors (*see also*

6.4). This is not always the case. In the natural resources context, there are numerous examples of NRCs that have stated a benevolent commitment to high ideals commensurate with the conditions of positive peace but have not followed through in practice (Gillin & Moseley, 2005; Michaels, 2011). This split between verbal commitment and corporate *praxis* has left a legacy of polluted rivers, toxic tailings dams, burnt forests, disease clusters, cultural fragmentation and scarred landscapes across a wide variety of natural resources projects in the timber, mining, agriculture, hydro-power and unconventional gas projects. Nevertheless, the vision of peace in the second generation is one that develops from the bottom up, not the top down, empowering non-state actors and individuals.

3.3.3 Third-Generation Peace and Conflict Theory and Liberalism

Third-generation Peace and Conflict Theory is an effort to blend the top-down and bottom-up approaches from the first two generations. Within this discourse, a vision for 'universal peace' emerged which depended on democracy as expressed in the *Agenda for Peace* (Boutros-Ghali, 1992). In this vision, states remain the principal actors, but the UN or its designees could intervene if a state was unable or unwilling to attend to internal governance issues. The expression of this theoretical development in support of the liberal peace-building project has therefore been essentially a liberal state-building enterprise in the post-Cold War era (e.g., Eastern Europe, Sierra Leone, Liberia, East Timor) (Richmond, 2010). State-building relies on engaging specialists with particular knowledge about how to create a liberal state. Knowledge streams considered necessary include the following: development, free-market economics, rule of law, justice and Human Rights (Richmond, 2010). This kind of peace-building is particularly relevant to NRCs who have close relationships (whether positive or contentious) with professionals from the large, international NGOs and transnational advocacy networks. They consider themselves part of the class of liberal, state-building specialists with particular knowledge and the ability to direct the spending of NRCs' CSR funds towards those ends (Keck & Sikkink, 1998).

The definition of a liberal order is a source of debate in International Relations theory. Dunne's overview in *Liberalism* (2006 [2001]) summarises several key points in the debate. Liberalism seeks to define the relationship between states, as Realism does. However, Liberalism also looks at the relationship governments have with their own citizens. Core Liberal values include liberty, order, justice and tolerance between states and within states. The debate concerns how to best promote those values. One camp supports a robust interventionist position that requires strong international institutions. An example is the UN, which is called on to assist states when they are not able to fulfil their responsibilities towards their citizens. The other camp prefers a more remote approach, which is non-interventionist and tolerant of diverse and independent ways of promoting these values. An example of this kind of thinking is to encourage states to be democratic because it is rare for democratic states to go to war with one another. Instead, they will engage through economic and cultural avenues which do not need to be monitored by large international institutions. Nevertheless, a Liberal peace is one characterised by "individual liberty, free trade, prosperity, interdependence, national self-determinism, open governments responsive to public opinion, and collective security" (Dunne, 2006 [2001], p. 187). Many of the large, international NGOs that both criticise and work with natural resources operate within this liberal frame and take an interventionist stance.

The foundational philosophy underpinning this stream is political cosmopolitanism, as described in the second generation. However, primary agency is no longer seen to rest only with international state and non-state actors such as International Organisations (IOs), IFIs and larger NGOs. They must work together, with the multi-lateral consent of *local* actors, to create conditions of peace. This vision of peace allows for a broad range of actors who are empowered to address the causes of conflicts through the creation of liberal institutions and a robust civil society. Importantly, civil society's needs are the centrepiece of peace-building efforts while a liberal state is being organised in service to those needs.

It is clear that this approach has not had the success originally hoped for on an international scale, particularly at the local level. There is a tendency for international agencies to take ownership of peace-building projects characterised by the neo-liberal development agenda and free market economics, rather than to empower local-level people to participate in a culturally appropriate way. This tendency can result in an endless series of renegotiations between international, institutional, national and (to a much lesser extent) local actors about whose vision of peace is preferred, what the objectives of particular peace-building activities ought to be and who should be the beneficiaries or recipients of the peace-building activities (Richmond, 2010). In other words, third-generation approaches to peace and conflict still have too much emphasis on top-down and interventionist approaches. As well, the institutional and policy structures linked to the liberal, democratic, free-market activities of non-state actors are too often experienced as structurally and culturally violent by local-level communities (Barnett & Finnemore, 1999; Paris, 2002). This is relevant to NRCs as well insofar as they consider themselves as contributing to development. When companies adopt or take this top-down approach, they risk exacerbating community-based conflict.

This third generation of Peace and Conflict Theory is appealing in its efforts to blend top-down and bottom-up approaches to creating conditions of peace. It has the potential to lead towards a vibrant civil society, robust market activity and legal/law enforcement structures that are compatible with notions of social justice. The reality of achieving these goals is more tenuous, and the third generation of Peace and Conflict Theory has not succeeded in developing a reliable process by which to achieve them. Furthermore, the roles of non-state actors towards contributing to conditions of peace are not clearly defined, especially since the actors responsible for sharing knowledge, creating state institutions and developing a liberal state are continually renegotiating their responsibilities and not actually including the local-level communities they claim to support.

3.3.4 Fourth-Generation Peace and Conflict Theory and Post-Structuralism

The fourth generation of Peace and Conflict Theory, therefore, emerged as a response to the third generation. The key attribute of fourth-generation Peace and Conflict Theory is the desire to move beyond replicating Western, liberal notions of peace and sovereignty to create more culturally specific governance and practices that genuinely respond to the interests, identities and needs of the specific actors. The fourth generation of theorists criticises the third on the basis of: "universal claims, cultural assumptions, top-down institutional, neo-liberal and neo-colonial tones" (Richmond, 2010, p. 26). Habermas has inspired fourth-generation critical theory. "[Habermas] implies an emancipatory form of peace that reflects the interests, identities, and needs of all actors, state and non-state, and aims at the creation of a discursive framework of mutual accommodation and social justice which recognises difference" (Richmond, 2010, p. 26). This iteration of peace-building theory is relevant to the natural resources sector, given the emphasis in recent CSR scholarship and guidance reports that stresses the empowerment of communities as partners to NRCs rather than as strictly beneficiaries.

The political theory underpinning this stream relies on both critical and post-structuralist theories. Marxism is the inspiration for the underlying critical theory. In contrast to Marxism's focus on economics, however, critical theory is primarily concerned with superstructural issues, "questions relating to culture, bureaucracy, the social bias and nature of authoritarianism, the structure of the family . . . and analysing the role of the media" (Hobden & Jones, 2006 [2001], p. 240). Post-structuralism, on the other hand, takes inspiration from Foucault's work, which emphasises binary issues related to identity, sovereignty, hybridity and culture (Richmond, 2010). Because of the differences between critical and post-structural theories, the fourth generation of Peace and Conflict Theory remains divided on governance issues. Post-structural theorists argue that governments produce peace in a top-down fashion, whereas critical theorists emphasise the non-state actors operating at the local level. This divergence of opinion on which actors should have primacy in governance issues has the potential to create confusion, especially for non-state actors in terms of where they sit as socio-economic actors in relation to both the government stakeholders and to local-level stakeholders.

Another defining aspect of the fourth generation is that even the non-state actors addressing local participation at the grass-roots level are encouraged to aspire towards the liberal peace within their sphere of activity. As mentioned in the preceding section, NGOs who operate at the international level do so with the understanding that they are part of this larger project to construct a liberal peace in cooperation with states, other agencies and with the consent/participation of the local-level people they are tasked with helping. Because the NGOs are dependent upon donor institutions for funds, they also need to fulfil conditions in the dispersal of those funds towards human security concerns. NGO involvement usually means that the NGOs become agents of creating or even "foisting" (Richmond, 2010, p. 28) conditions of a liberal peace which, as stated above, is not always the ideal sought by the local-level communities. They can even impose this agenda on NRCs as non-state actors.

The neo-liberal approach can become problematic, especially when working with Indigenous, traditional or culturally conservative Islamic communities. These groups possess tribal or culturally distinct views of peace do not incorporate Western conceptions of Human Rights, democracy or institutional-level dynamics (e.g., the United Nations, the World Bank, the IFC). The biggest objections to the liberal peace project by people from non-Western cultures are the following: it does not accommodate or consider the dynamics of everyday life—essential considerations to create the conditions necessary for positive peace; it does not allow communities to represent themselves; and it negates cultural and identity dynamics including the communities' relationship with the environment. As well, the democracy in which non-Western cultures are being required to participate can be co-opted by elites within their own social systems. Co-option in the forms of bribery, corruption and nepotism means that individuals and groups experience structural violence when required to vote, pay taxes and participate in free-market structures while living with the reality that they may never see any local benefit from participating (Richmond, 2010). When remote and non-Western peoples have not seen any benefit from democracy as interpreted in their cultures, they may expect NRCs to take on the role of the absentee state structures. If NRCs do not or are not able to take on this role, communities can feel betrayed and assign their suffering, the result of structural violence, to an NRC. So when NRCs as non-state actors come into contact with non-Western peoples, as they frequently do in operations throughout the world, their intentional or un-intentional adoption of liberal ideals and strategies may lay the groundwork for increased community-based conflict. It is therefore critically important to address the paradigm of positive peace and the CSR strategies it informs in a way that is not dependent on liberal ideals and strategies.

Richmond (2010) concludes his overview of the four streams of Peace and Conflict Theory by introducing an indicative direction for a fifth generation of theory and praxis. He elaborates further on this idea in *A Post Liberal Peace* (2011). The fifth generation remains a fledgling theoretical construct. Worth briefly stating, however, is a key concern that the fifth generation must link state-building projects with local-level benefits in the everyday lives of people who are non-liberal entities (Richmond, 2009). Local-level people need to develop their own vision of what peace looks like on the ground, day in and day out. Significantly, local visions of peace may not conform to Western, neo-liberal, state-building sensibilities. Richmond calls this a local-liberal hybrid and offers that to move peace-building in this direction allows for benefits from development to actually result in peace rather than sowing the seeds of more conflict. Allowing local interpretations of a sustainable positive peace requires that people who have seen themselves as professional peacebuilders (whether as diplomats, development agents or aid workers) stop treating people on the ground as "guinea pigs in international engineering projects" (Richmond, 2010, p. 32). Instead, Richmond argues that peacebuilders need to engage people at the local level in unscripted conversations about what peace might look like to them, on their terms, and how or whether they would like that peace facilitated. For NRCs, then, it means that that any local-level engagement may need to occur outside of but not conflicting with the liberal vision of peace championed by actors who operate within the frames of the first three generations of Peace and Conflict Theory.

3.4 Implications of Peace and Conflict Theory for the Natural Resources Sector

The evolution of IR theory towards a more neo-liberal, non-state actor scenario emphasises the changing role of the natural resources industry, too. In the current context, NRCs are well placed and active as non-state actors with the capacity to engage the paradigm of positive peace as a foundation for their CSR strategies. When viewing natural resources activities particularly through the fourth generation of Peace and Conflict Theory, the role of an NRC takes on particular significance as non-state actors with varying levels of influence in the contexts in which they operate. This suggests that their highest level of *national* influence occurs at the beginning of a project cycle, when NRCs are negotiating the terms of their lease (Zandvliet, 2005). Meanwhile, their highest level of *local* influence occurs during the active stages of a project cycle. Ultimately, no NRC wants or aspires to take on the sovereign role of a state in meeting the needs of civil society or the role of local governments in terms of championing development projects, providing infrastructure and utilities, amongst other public goods. Neither do they want to be in a position of administering resource rents amongst the various regions and societal sectors claiming a right to the royalties generated by natural resources. In principal, then, NRCs support the states in which they operate to fulfil a governance role for their citizenry so that they can go about the business of natural resources.

The four generations of peace and conflict research are clear about the different ways in which the state is responsible for its citizenry and whether different non-state actors may share the burden of care for civil society in particular ways. However, all four streams of peace and conflict research operate concurrently in the international arena. The porosity of these different streams of peace and conflict theory contributes to the confusion about roles of and relationships between state and non-state actors. Additionally, there is no consensus about which perspective should be dominant, although the common consensus amongst scholars is that Realism is technically dominant in International Affairs literature. The disadvantage of this position is that Realism does not account for the role of non-state actors such as NRCs. This omission is an issue when many of the largest companies have as much financial and political influence as small states with fewer restrictions on their activities.

Putting aside the first generation of Peace and Conflict Theory as insufficient to articulating the roles of state and non-state actors in relation to peace in the natural resources context, there appears more room for choices about how to view the role of non-state actors in the other three generations of theory. The second stream, although focusing on bottom-up visions of how to create peace, does not offer much guidance on how the bottom-up actors are supposed to interact with the inter-state level actors. This may not be much of a problem at all for the bottom-up/grassroots actors, but may pose a problem to NRC personnel who are unsure how to respond to these actors. Furthermore, the second stream still prefers peace-building as a state-building enterprise, which is not the role of an NRC. The third stream accounts for both top-down and bottom-up approaches. It relies on specialists to intervene in particular ways to manage the development of states while taking into account the needs of its citizenry. This is a space in which NRCs have been engaged, especially in developing country contexts in the Global South (e.g., Sub-Saharan Africa, South America, Melanesia). Whether the companies like it or not, local-level communities have enrolled them as local actors to take on the roles of NGOs and development organisations especially, in countries where there is a weak government. Because communities tend to conflate the roles of companies and NGOs in these contexts, companies must recognise that the third stream approach, preferred by NGOs and development organisations, is rightly or wrongly associated to NRCs. The third stream has given rise to wide-spread criticism of promoting neo-liberal, neo-colonial attitudes (Banerjee, 2000). Consequently, criticism also flows to NRCs. The fourth stream, although trying to empower local-level communities as the principal actors responsible for sustaining peace at their own level, finds community participation threatening. In other words, the international and multilateral actors still want to recognise the international vision of peace expressed locally, whether that vision of peace is functional at the local level or not, most notably in Indigenous and non-Western communities. NRCs attracted to the Western values of "human rights and self-determination" (Richmond, 2010, p. 29) in the rhetoric of the fourth generation must be aware of becoming embroiled in the debate whether the responsibility for enacting these values belongs at the state or local level.

NRCs have potential to make their greatest contribution of creating a local level peace if national and international attempts at state-building agenda can be disaggregated at the local level. This does not mean that NRCs should act completely independently of governments, or that they cannot participate in capacity building for weak and otherwise struggling states. What I am suggesting here is that state-building needs to be disaggregated from peace-building. It is possible to participate in peace-building activities at the local level without state-building being the ultimate goal. Furthermore, NRCs do not need to declare that they are supporting a peace-building agenda in order to act in a way that is conducive to just that goal, especially in circumstances where other international actors (e.g. the World Bank, IMF) have a history of conflating peace-building and state-building. Perhaps NRCs could understand their interactions with local communities as having a positive *influence* on the dynamic between local-level communities and the state. From that stance, they could make an intentional decision to contribute to a locally peaceful living and working environment for employees and local communities that would result in benefits such as increased peace, greater stability and reduced violence for all stakeholders.

Whereas this chapter looked at NRCs as non-state actors with a role to play in supporting local-level peace, the next chapter looks at paradigms. Paradigms are a practical tool with the potential to shape and provide the foundation for CSR strategies in the natural resources sector. NRCs, as non-state actors, the choice of the paradigm out of which they operate matters. Paradigms privilege in particular the choice of processes and therefore the outcomes achieved. Processes and outcomes significantly affect both communities proximate to natural resources projects as well as the business outcomes for natural resources operations. The next chapter looks at three established, influential CSR paradigms, neoliberal economics, risk management and Human Rights and introduces positive peace.

Notes

1 States own some natural resources projects (e.g., Codelco in Chile, Three Gorges Dam in China) either partially or wholly. However, even in those instances, the natural resources company is run as a business, not as a government office or bureau with policy-making or governance capacity.

2 www.berghof-foundation.org/ [Accessed: 17 March 2017].

3 Arguably, the development of natural resources, throughout much of recorded human history, has occurred within a Realist frame of reference which has very clear distinctions between the roles of state and non-state actors. It simplifies and streamlines which entities have responsibility for which public goods. In the Realist system, the state builds the hospitals, the libraries, the schools and the infrastructure and is responsible for security, water, sanitation and electricity provision. The natural resources companies go about the business of natural resources and make their contribution to these public goods by paying taxes and providing jobs.

4 This conceptualisation of ownership and property has other consequences, too. The commodifiable understanding of territoriality and ownership of land is a particularly Western concept that has travelled hand in hand with natural resources all over the globe. Consequently, Western natural resources companies expect states to grant leases that will not be challenged by local communities. Proceeding according to this expectation has created a host of issues related to ownership and consent for societies impacted by natural resources who have traditional and matri- or patrilineal ways of understanding human relationships with the land (Boydell, 2010; Macintyre, 2007).

5 A war of all against all, where "everybody uses whatever kind of violence he knows to destroy whomever he wants. Hobbes had the vision, nuclear physics has perfected the means" Galtung (1964, p. 1)

6 "A republic is a term used to describe a secular state in which there is a separation of powers in government and in which citizens are ruled by law and have some constitutional rights" (Steans, Pettiford, & Diez, 2001)

Bibliography

AHRC, ACCST, & GCNA. (2015). *Human rights in the supply chains: Promoting positive practice.*Melbourne: Australian Human Rights Council.

Anglo American. (2013). *Creating value with the future in mind: Sustainable development report 2012.*London: Anglo American.

Banerjee, S. B. (2000). Whose land is it anyway? National interest, indigenous stakeholders, and colonial discourses: The case of the Jabiluka Uranium mine. *Organization Environment, 13*(3), 3–38.

Barnett, M. N., & Finnemore, M. (1999). The politics, power, and pathologies of international organizations. *International Organization, 53*(4), 699–732. doi:10.1162/002081899551048

Boucher, D. (1998). *Political theories of international relations.* Oxford: Oxford University Press.

Boutros-Ghali, B. (1992). *An agenda for peace preventive diplomacy, peacemaking and peace-keeping.* New York, NY. Retrieved from http://globalpolicy.org/component/content/article/226/32313.html

Boydell, S. (2010). South Pacific land: An alternative perspective on tenure traditions, business, and conflict. *Georgetown Journal of International Affairs, 11*(1), 17–25.

Brown, C. (2002). *Sovereignty, rights and justice: International political theory today.* Boston, MA: Polity.

Brundtland Commission. (1987). *Report of the world commission on environment and development: Our common future.* New York, NY.

Burton, J. (1990). *Conflict: Resolution and provention.* London: Palgrave Macmillan.

Černič, J. L., & Černič, J. L. (2015). Corporate accountability for human rights: From a top-down to a bottom-up approach. In J. Martin & K. E. Bravo (Eds.), *The business and human rights landscape*. Cambridge: Cambridge University Press.

Collier, P., & Hoeffler, A. (2005). Resource rents, governance and conflict. *The Journal of Conflict Resolution*, *49*(4), 625–633.

Dashwood, H. S. (2007). Canadian mining companies and corporate social responsibility: Weighing the impact of global norms. *Canadian Journal of Political Science*, *40*(1), 129–156.

Dunne, T. (2006 [2001]). Liberalism. In J. Baylis & S. Smith (Eds.), *The globalization of world politics*. Oxford: Oxford University Press.

ECOSOC. (2010). *Commission on sustainable development report on the eighteenth session*. New York, NY: United Nations.

Francis, D. (2010). *From pacification to peacebuilding: A call to global transformation*. New York, NY: Palgrave Macmillan.

Galtung, J. (1964). An editorial. *Journal of Peace Research*, *1*(1), 1–4.

Galtung, J. (1969). Violence, peace and peace research. *Journal of Peace Research*, *6*(3), 167–191.

Gillin, K., & Moseley, B. (2005). For bread and dignity: Complicating the Bougainville "Resource Conflict". In *Midwestern undergraduate geography symposium*. Minnesota: Midwestern Undergraduate Geography Symposium.

Giuliani, E. (2016). Human rights and corporate social responsibility in developing countries' industrial clusters. *Journal of Business Ethics*, *133*(1), 39–54. doi:10.1007/s10551-014-2375-5

Greico, J. (1988). Anarchy and the limits of cooperation. *International Organization*, *42*(3), 484–507.

Hamann, R., Kapelus, P., Sonnenberg, D., Mackenzie, A., & Hollesen, P. (2005). Local governance as a complex system lessons from mining in South Africa, Mali and Zambia. *Journal of Corporate Citizenship*, *18*, 31–73.

Haufler, V. (2015). Symposium on conflict, management, and peace: Comments from an international relations scholar. *Academy of Management Perspectives*, *29*(4), 461–468.

Hobden, S., & Jones, R. W. (2006 [2001]). Liberalism. In J. Baylis & S. Smith (Eds.), *The globalization of world politics*. Oxford: Oxford University Press.

ICMM. (2011). *Utilizing mining and mineral resources to foster the sustainable development of the Lao PDR*. London: ICMM.

Idemudia, U. (2011). Corporate social responsibility and developing countries: Moving the critical CSR research agenda in Africa forward. *Progress in Development Studies*, *11*(1), 1–18.

Kant, I. (1983 [1795]). *Perpetual peace, and other essays on politics, history, and morals* (T. Humphrey, Trans.). Indianapolis, IN: Hackett Pub. Co.

Keck, M., & Sikkink, K. (1998). Transnational advocacy networks in international politics. In *Activists beyond borders: Advocacy networks in international politics*. Ithaca, NY: Cornell University Press.

Lederach, J. P., Neufeldt, R., & Culbertson, H. (2007). *Reflective peacebuilding: A planning, monitoring and learning toolkit*. Notre Dame, IN. Retrieved from http://kroc.nd.edu www.crs.org

Linklater, A. (2002). Cosmopolitan political communities in international relations. *International Relations*, *16*(1), 135–150.

Linklater, A. (2006 [2001]). Globalization and the transformation of political community. In J. Baylis & S. Smith (Eds.), *The globalization of world politics*. Oxford: Oxford University Press.
Macintyre, M. (2007). Informed consent and mining projects: A view from Papua New Guinea. *Pacific Affairs*, *80*(1), 49–65.
Martin, J., & Bravo, K. E. (2015). *The business and human rights landscape*. Cambridge: Cambridge University Press.
Maslow, A. (1943). A theory of human motivation. *Psychological Review*, *50*, 370–396.
Michaels, S. (2011, November 29). Is a U.S. mining company funding violent crackdown in Indonesia? *The Atlantic*. Retrieved from www.theatlantic.com website: www.theatlantic.com/international/archive/2011/11/is-a-us-mining-company-funding-a-violent-crackdown-in-indonesia/249164/?single_page=true
Nelson, J. (2000). *The business of peace*. London.
Neufeldt, R., Fast, L., Schreiter, F. R., Starken, F. B., MacLaren, D., Cilliers, J., & Lederach, J. P. (2006). *Peacebuilding: A Caritas training manual*. Vatican City.
Nolan, J. (2015). From principles to practice: Implementing corporate responsibility for human rights. In J. Martin & K. E. Bravo (Eds.), *The business and human rights landscape* (pp. 387–413). Cambridge: Cambridge University Press.
Paris, R. (2002). International peacebuilding and the 'mission civilisatrice'. *Review of International Studies*, *28*, 637–656.
Pojman, L. (2005). Kant's perpetual peace and cosmopolitanism. *Journal of Social Philosophy*, *36*(1), 62–71.
Prno, J., & Slocombe, S. (2012). Exploring the origins of 'social license to operate' in the mining sector: Perspectives from governance and sustainability theories. *Resources Policy*, *37*(3), 346–357. doi:10.1016/j.resourpol.2012.04.002
Richmond, O. (2009). A post-liberal peace: Eirenism and the everyday. *Review of International Studies*, *35*(3), 557–580. doi:10.1017/s0260210509008651
Richmond, O. (2010). A genealogy of peace and conflict theory. In O. Richmond (Ed.), *Palgrave advances in peacebuilding*. New York: Palgrave.
Richmond, O. (2011). *A post-liberal peace*. London: Routledge.
Ruggie, J. (2011). *Guiding principles on business and human rights: Implementing the United Nations "Protect, Respect and Remedy" Framework* (A/HRC/17/31). New York, NY: United Nations.
Sandole, D. J. D. (2003). Typology. In S. Cheldelin, D. Druckman, & L. Fast (Eds.), *Conflict: From analysis to intervention*. London: Continuum.
Sklair, L., & Miller, D. (2010). Capitalist globalization, corporate social responsibility and social policy. *Critical Social Policy*, *30*(4), 472–495.
Steans, J., Pettiford, L., & Diez, T. (2001). *Introduction to international relations*. London: Pearson Longman.
Tilly, C. (2002). Cities and states in world history. In A. Linklater (Ed.), *International relations: Critical concepts in political science*. London: Routledge.
UNGA. (1945). *Charter of the United Nations*. San Francisco, CA: United Nations. Retrieved from www.un.org/en/documents/charter/preamble.shtml
UNGA. (1948). *The universal declaration of human rights (UDHR)*. (Resolution 217 A(III) of 10). New York, NY: United Nations.
van der Ploeg, L., & Vanclay, F. (2016). A tool for improving the management of social and human rights risks at project sites: The human rights sphere. *Journal of Cleaner Production*. doi:http://dx.doi.org/10.1016/j.jclepro.2016.10.028

Wallensteen, P. (2011). The origins of contemporary peace research. In K. Hoglund & M. Oberg (Eds.), *Understanding peace research: Methods and challenges*. Hoboken, NJ: Routledge.

Wilburn, K. M., & Wilburn, R. (2011). Achieving a social license to operate using stakeholder theory. *Journal of International Business Ethics*, 4(2), 3–16, 70.

Willetts, P. (2005). Transnational actors and international organizations in global politics. In J. Baylis & S. Smith (Eds.), *The globalization of world politics* (3rd ed.). London: Oxford University Press.

Zandvliet, L. (2005). *Opportunities for synergy*. Berlin.

4 Paradigms

In the age of climate change, global unrest and greater connectivity due to mobile phones, the internet and the media, scholars, politicians and practitioners in the NGO sector use the term 'paradigm shift' to indicate large-scale changes in perception and interpretation. The use of the term in most articles, books and the popular press, however, is both imprecise and misleading. Drawing on Thomas Kuhn's original work, which developed the modern use of the term, this chapter describes what a paradigm actually is and how the term can be used to describe shifts in understanding at an organisational and societal level. Paradigm shifting is then suggested to reframe decision-making on social and environmental issues at the local level, where operations have the most immediate impact.

4.1 Overview

Whether people are aware of the paradigm(s) within which they operate, or would even use the term 'paradigm', paradigms are always functioning in the background of human thought and activity. This chapter explains that the paradigms NRCs use to shape and implement their CSR activities are of crucial significance in how they deal with community-level conflict. The starting point for this research is that NRCs can choose how they will respond to community-level conflict. This chapter focuses on the use of CSR strategies to address these conflicts with a foundation in one or more of the following paradigms: Neoliberal Economic, Risk Management and Human Rights. What the Neoliberal Economic and Risk Management paradigms share is a preference to focus on the avoidance of negative outcomes and try to control a potential or actual conflict to the benefit of one party more than the other (usually the company). Human Rights, as a paradigm, focuses on avoiding negative effects upon people as individuals and in groups, including the most vulnerable. When the exercise of the Human Rights of *some* occurs at the expense of the Human Rights of *others*, this imbalance can bring into question issues of the distribution of benefits from natural resources, which can lead to violence and create ongoing conditions of conflict. In this chapter, the discussion of paradigms and the development of a conceptual framework provide ways to look at how these three CSR paradigms are different from a paradigm of positive peace. Certainly, there are other paradigms at play in the natural resources context such as Environmental, Technical, Engineering and Security. However, these paradigms are not discussed within the scope of this book.

4.2 What Is a Paradigm and What Does It Offer?

Paradigms have significantly influenced the evolution and revolution of ideas, scientific thought and human development. Ancient philosophers from antiquity, including Socrates, Plato and Aristotle, argued passionately that the way in which people approach the world—i.e., the paradigm they use to order and organise ideas, as well as respond to events, decisions and people—matters. China's dominant Confucian paradigm is related to its dynastic history, with its rich philosophical, political and cultural heritage; this paradigm continues to exert a strong influence across Asia and, increasingly, the West. Islamic philosopher-scientists from the early Middle Ages operated out of a paradigm pairing philosophical systems with scientific discovery which shaped the trajectory of modern mathematics and physics. From the Enlightenment, both Jewish and Christian philosopher-theologians have made their own highly nuanced contributions, based on paradigms reflecting systems of belief, which have shaped Western socio-economic and political development. Throughout human existence, Indigenous peoples have preserved entire, pre-written history cosmologies that account for both human behaviour and everything that occurs in the natural and supernatural worlds. These traditional cosmologies—when viewed as paradigms—are gathering renewed interest both within and outside Indigenous communities. In the current era, there is increasing academic and disciplinary specialisation—some would say fragmentation (*vis* Max Weber, Thoreau and Schopenhauer)—which allows people to narrowly focus on areas of interest or expertise. These discrete silos of specialist knowledge can also function as paradigms.

4.2.1 Thomas Kuhn's Influence

Thomas Kuhn inspired a vigorous debate about paradigms and paradigm shifts amongst scholars in a broad range of scientific and social disciplines (Argyrous, 1992; Cedarbaum, 1983; Masterman, 1970; Percival, 1979). Paradigms, for Kuhn, exist within discrete natural, rather than social, scientific communities. Natural science, for Kuhn, includes traditional science disciplines (e.g., physics, chemistry, biology) rather than social sciences, which he initially considers immature because they "disagree among themselves about the nature of legitimate scientific problems and methods" (Percival, 1979, p. 29). This is ironic because social scientists, such as sociologists and economists, have been more enthusiastic about Kuhn's work on paradigms than natural scientists (Fine, 2002; Percival, 1979). Whether used by natural or social scientists, Kuhn's paradigms communicate shared meaning through the distinctive use of language about the following: embodied theory, 'legitimate' research problems related to that theory and 'acceptable solutions' to those research problems (Cedarbaum, 1983). Although Kuhn does not focus on the normative or ethical aspect of paradigms, preferring to use them as analytical tools, he does emphasise that the choice of which paradigm one uses governs one's behaviour; this affects the range of resultant outcomes.

In his original text, *The Structure of Scientific Revolutions*, Kuhn argues that paradigms do not overlap; they are both discrete and bounded. Consequentially, "[when] two scientific schools disagree about what is a problem and what is a solution, they will inevitably talk through each other when debating the relative merits of their respective paradigms" (Kuhn, 1996 [1962], p. 109). For example, when asking chemists and physicists to describe and classify a helium atom, both groups have a quick and sure response. However, their responses differ from one another because the paradigm in which they perceive the phenomenon of the helium atom is radically different even though the phenomenon is empirically the same. (Kuhn, 1996 [1962]). Alternately, "a physicist and a biologist can each use the term 'nucleus' unproblematically, although they refer to entirely different entities" (Cedarbaum, 1983, p. 204).

Lest it appear that this inability to traverse paradigms is a function of either (ir)rationality,[1] relativism or disciplinary myopia, Cedarbaum (1983) highlights the evolution of Kuhn's thought on how scientists use paradigms in *The Essential Tension* (Kuhn, 1977). In this text, Kuhn acknowledges that any one scientist can belong to several different scientific communities, much the way people are capable of learning more than one language. Therefore, it is possible for an individual scientist to understand and operate out of more than one paradigm. However, much as a German speaker would not use her native language in Japan and expect to be understood by a native Japanese speaker, a physicist could not expect to be understood by a chemist by using linguistically specific terms from the physics paradigm. The German speaker would need to speak Japanese; the physicist would need to use linguistically specific terms from the chemistry paradigm. Kuhn points out that the German would not be able to completely understand all the nuances in Japanese because the basic paradigm out of which the German learned language is German. The analogy holds for the scientists. Therefore, there are "barriers to communication [which] are most difficult to overcome for groups committed to competing paradigms in a field" (Cedarbaum, 1983, p. 205). To make an analogy, Kuhn appears to consider paradigms in some way analogous to physical objects that cannot occupy the same space at the same time. Instead, when two paradigms compete for dominance, the selection of one over the other can result in a 'revolution', which Kuhn names a 'paradigm shift'.

Paradigm shifts occur at times of crises when a particular paradigm no longer serves as a valid foundation for further practice. At these moments, new paradigms emerge to solve the problems or puzzles that the old paradigm cannot. Kuhn describes a paradigm shift as a "conversion experience . . . a transfer of allegiance from paradigm to paradigm . . . which cannot be forced" (Kuhn, 1996 [1962], p. 151). People must see for themselves that the new paradigm is solid and it is worth making the conversion. Kuhn acknowledges that when people have been functioning within one paradigm for a long time, it can be difficult to persuade them that another paradigm might help them approach or solve intellectual or practical puzzles. In many ways, the first people to make a paradigm shift make that philosophical decision "on faith" (Kuhn, 1996 [1962], p. 158), especially when a new paradigm does not yet have a demonstrable track record. As a paradigm gains a community of supporters, they will advance both theoretical development and practical applications of the paradigm, strengthening multiple arguments to make a paradigm shift for others. As the newer paradigm gains converts, the older paradigm loses its hold on a group or a community until eventually, a group is operating out of the newer paradigm. For example, Einstein's discovery of the theory of relativity shifted the paradigm in physics from classical Newtonian principles.

Masterman (1970), who self-identifies as pro-Kuhn, cautions fellow scholars to be careful when using the term 'paradigm' and to articulate what one means when invoking it. She points out that even Kuhn uses the term 'paradigm' 21 different ways; a paradigm can be classified as either metaphysical (existing prior to theory), sociological (an established or known achievement) or an artefact/construct (an exemplar or something that helps solve puzzles) (Bird, 2002; Masterman, 1970; Wray, 2011). Of the three classifications, Masterman prefers to conceive of a paradigm as construct, but also allows for the metaphysical classification. With that clarification, she advances Kuhn's work by observing that multiple paradigms can operate at once especially in "psychological, social and information sciences" (Masterman, 1970, p. 74). However, multiple paradigms operating at once have the unfortunate potential to confuse a situation and thwart problem-solving processes within any one paradigm as "an accepted model" or a "foundation for further practice" (Kuhn, 1996 [1962], pp. 23, 10). What Masterman suggests as a remedy is to adopt a *deeper* paradigm "which gives more central insight into the nature of the field [. . .] causing rival, more shallow paradigms to collapse, or alternatively . . . triumphs over the rest so that advanced . . . work can set in, with only one total paradigm" (Masterman, 1970, p. 74). Within this deeper paradigm, different disciplinary groups can even co-exist and achieve additional "insight into the real nature of their own [disciplines]" (Masterman, 1970, p. 88). Because of the potential of paradigms to mould understanding, increase (or decrease) communication and shape relationships between people operating out of different or similar paradigms, the choice of which paradigm(s) is used and applied in discrete contexts is consequential and worth examining. The choice of which paradigm to use is particularly significant in the natural resources context because of the way conflict can affect communication, relationships and outcomes from the macro all the way to the local level.

Although Kuhn and even Masterman, to some extent, train their attention on paradigms and paradigm shifts within the scientific community (e.g., the revolutionary changes in scientific understanding that transcended Newtonian physics and paved the way for the development of relativity theory), both have been able to see the application of paradigms to the social sciences. Wray summarises Kuhn's later thoughts in this regard. "[Kuhn] claims to have invoked the notion of a paradigm to account for the consensus necessary amongst scientists in a specialty in order for them to pursue their research goals effectively" (Wray, 2011, p. 381). Therefore, it no longer mattered whether there was consensus on which *problems* were addressed and which *answers* considered acceptable. Rather, *shared examples of successful practice* could provide the coherence necessary for a group to solve puzzles or problems within one paradigm (Kuhn, 1977).

Paradigms provide a basis to "focus narrowly" (Wray, 2011, p. 393) within the boundaries of a particular discipline (Argyrous, 1992). Consequently, Masterman's interpretation of Kuhn's concepts of paradigms and paradigm shifts are used to articulate paradigms influencing CSR practice in the natural resources context. Like the lone scientist who belongs to several different scientific communities with discrete paradigmatic perspectives, it is possible to conceptualise the phenomenon of NRC-community relationships from several different paradigms. This book identifies three paradigms influencing CSR practice in the natural resources sector that affect how community-level conflicts are handled. Following Masterman, in addition to articulating the differences between these paradigms, the book will also consider whether it is possible to articulate a *deeper* paradigm to increase understanding of influential paradigms so that problems can be more productively solved within them.

4.2.2 *Differentiating Between Classifying Concepts*

There are a few ways to utilise paradigms. Some paradigms have the function of setting a normative component or deontological ethical priority (e.g., prescribing what *ought* to be done), while others are analytical in nature. One of the findings of digging more deeply into the paradigm debate, described above, is a disconnection between that debate and more contemporary scholarship.

Contemporary scholars tend to use the term 'paradigm' without explaining what they mean by it. This has led to usage lacking precision and consistency, which obscures the concept's analytical utility. For example, Jenkins (2004) refers in passing to (1) CSR, (2) Environment and (3) SD as paradigms constructed by scholars and policy makers in the developed world without explaining why she considers them as such. She even suggests that mechanisms shaped by these so-called paradigms are used to "control communities" (2004, p. 32). Nothing that Kuhn or Masterman has written points to the use of paradigms in this way. Esteves and Vanclay (2009) suggest that SD is a paradigm that shapes social development 'needs analyses' capable of reconciling business needs with community needs. Their point is well made about the merit of "embed[ding] concepts of sustainability and social development into core business strategies by linking the future of the company with the future of the local community" (Esteves & Vanclay, 2009, p. 137). It may even be related to SD. However, the case for why they call SD a paradigm is not made here. Finally, Prno and Slocombe (Prno & Slocombe, 2012) refer to SD as a paradigm with an ability to bring about change in governance and to affect balances of power from governments to non-state actors. Paradigms do have an ability to affect outcomes from activities occurring within them. Yet, how SD is (1) a paradigm or (2) capable of accomplishing power shifts remains unclear. Therefore, the case to refer to SD, CSR or environmental concerns as paradigms is not made explicit in these examples.

Paradigms, therefore, must be distinguished from other classifying concepts such as values, perspectives and frameworks. A conceptual model has been developed for this book to simplify and clarify the relationship between these classifying concepts. There are two benefits to using this conceptual model. The first is to improve comparative analysis and dialogue about the various bundles of community-level concern in the CSR space (e.g., Free Prior and Informed Consent, Social License to Operate, Gender, Indigenous Employment). The second is to reduce the confusion that arises when variously and inconsistently referring to these bundles of concern as paradigms, values, perspectives and frameworks. Improved clarity about how these concepts and concerns are related to one another has potential to positively affect NRC-community communication. With clearer communication, the ability to address conflict is strengthened. Consequently, the possibility for violence to emerge from NRC-community conflict can be reduced or eliminated, and the conditions characteristic of positive peace can be advanced. Importantly, greater clarity in and of itself will not reduce conflict, but greater clarity can aid both practitioners and researchers. The relationship between the classifying concepts is illustrated with the following diagram and explained further below in Figure 4.1:

The first classifying concept is values. Values are reflections of ethical principles or moral standards (Oxford University Press, 2012b) that have the ability to influence decision-making within a paradigm (Fine, 2002). It is possible to argue the inverse: that paradigms determine the values by which one chooses to operate. However, rather than entertaining the 'chicken-or-egg' discussion, this book focuses on paradigms as representative of values. Values are both shared and culturally embedded (Shubert, 2010); they reflect what is important to a person or to groups (Avruch, 1998). Values reflect

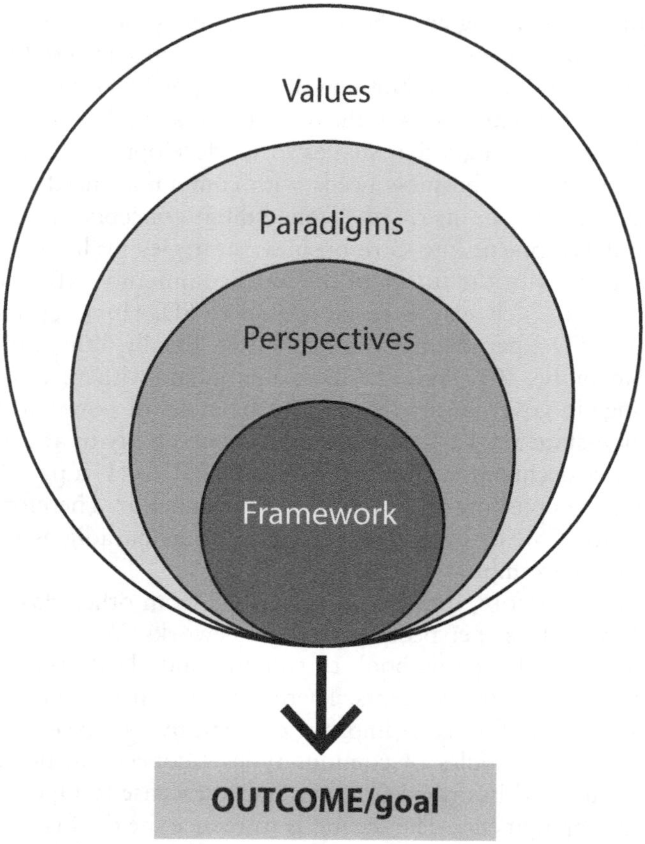

Figure 4.1 Relationship of Classifying Concepts to Outcomes

and are determined by the experiences of individuals and groups (Lambert, Elix, & Priest, 2005). According to Kuhn, discussed earlier, each paradigm has a set of values that informs it (the outer circle in the figure above). An exploration of the values informing CSR paradigms would be a useful exercise to undertake with further research.

The second classifying concept is paradigms. Paradigms define parameters about sets of concepts using specific language, thereby shaping relationships among people who operate or act within them. Considering Kuhn's seminal work (1996 [1962]) this book defines a paradigm as:

> a generally accepted or widely shared set of concepts, assumptions, values and practices that constitute a way of understanding [. . .], a practical model for how to think through or handle a particular class of problems, rather than as a set of explicit rules we might follow.
>
> (de Neufville, 2010, p. 1014)

De Neufville's definition, however, is not entirely sufficient to incorporate the social ramifications of paradigms. This book, therefore, expands de Neufville's definition to acknowledge that paradigms also have the capacity to "*frame language, meanings and relationships*" (Wilkinson-Maposa & Fowler, 2009, p. 33) by "*guid[ing] acts and behaviour*" (Jonker & Pennink, 2010, p. 26). The reason is that paradigms govern how groups of people understand phenomena (Kuhn, 1996 [1962]).

The third classifying concept is perspectives. A perspective prioritises a way of looking at a situation, highlighting a particular point of view as important (Oxford University Press, 2012a). Perspectives do not offer a framework of analysis (Gond & Crane, 2010); neither do they provide scaffolding for analysis, nor do they provide concrete, practical application guidance. For example, Boutilier (2005) develops a typology of perspectives following the work of Castell. The perspectives he emphasises are traditional, modern and post-modern societies. He demonstrates that each of these perspectives prioritise how people living in each of these societies view the relationship between nature and humanity. Boutilier argues that the perspective these societies have on this relationship informs how they interpret the concept of SD. By extension, someone trained as a lawyer and someone trained as an engineer will have discipline-specific perspectives. Their perspectives would also inform how they would interpret a concept such as SD.

The fourth classifying concept is frameworks. Structural, regulatory, policy and even voluntary frameworks are organisational constructions. They assist governments, businesses and civil society organisations to promote and implement initiatives. In the natural resources sector, there are several different issues identified by standards that are developed into frameworks. These frameworks are operationalised to achieve outcomes, as discussed in the next section.

4.2.3 The CSR Perspective and Relevant Frameworks

This book concentrates on the paradigmatic level at which choices about how to approach CSR are made. The reason is that paradigms inform perspectives and guide which practical frameworks are chosen to achieve certain outcomes or goals. Before examining the three influential paradigms informing CSR practice, it is necessary to locate CSR and CSR frameworks within the conceptual model.

CSR is a *perspective*, not a paradigm. CSR does not offer a framework of analysis (Gond & Crane, 2010); neither does it provide scaffolding for analysis, nor does it provide concrete, practical application guidance. Finally, statements of commitment to CSR outcomes do not offer a "widely shared set of concepts, assumptions, values and practices that constitute a way of understanding" (de Neufville, 2010, p. 1014). This last point is especially important given the multiple debates about what CSR is, how to accomplish it and what the outcomes are supposed to be.[2]

At the broadest level, CSR generally is understood as "maximising the positive and minimising the negative social and environmental impacts of natural resources, while maintaining profits" (Hamann & Acutt, 2003, p. 237), with a focus on "enhancing a firm's profitability" (Calvano, 2008, p. 796) in a way that demonstrates "commitment to the local communities in which [a firm] operates" (Kapelus, 2002). Carroll and Shabana (2010) follow Dahlsrud (2008) and earlier work by Carroll (1979, 1999) to demonstrate that CSR is related to "competing, complementary and overlapping concepts such as corporate citizenship, business ethics, stakeholder management, sustainability . . . and corporate social performance" (Carroll & Shabana, 2010, p. 86). CSR is a perspective for which "it is important to consider the basic paradigmatic foundation on which it rests" (Korhonen, 2002, p. 78), both to clarify what it means to various stakeholders as well as to achieve the "overarching integration" (Schwartz & Carroll, 2008, p. 178) necessary to improve CSR outcomes for businesses and communities.

CSR is a way of approaching Community Relations (CR) practice and the concept of SD and its principles (Boutilier, 2005; Dashwood, 2012) by prioritising particular points of view as important. Specifically, CSR is concerned with the societal consequences of business decisions, which often are related to environmental, social and economic impacts (Kytle & Ruggie, 2005). CSR goes beyond philanthropy and legal requirements and points to responsibilities or obligations that "resonate with societal norms and values" (Dashwood, 2012, p. 9). Dahlsrud (2008) summarises that there are 37 definitions of CSR but that they are congruent around five key dimensions: interactions between internal and external stakeholder; commitment to some form of environmental stewardship; willingness to consider community/social impacts; contribution to economic development; and adherence to voluntary (non-judicial) frameworks.

CSR is a *perspective* informing the choice of which frameworks to use in the natural resources context with the potential to facilitate environmental, social and environmental outcomes. The CSR perspective includes sub-themes such as stakeholder theory, business ethics, corporate citizenship, SLTO and corporate social performance (Carroll, 1999; Thomson & Boutilier, 2011). Related frameworks have been developed by third parties and industry bodies through multi-stakeholder consultation processes. All are relevant to handling aspects of issues implicated in conflict between NRCs and communities. Not all were developed specifically for natural resources, but the ones cited here are broadly used in the natural resources context. Indicative examples include the following (see Table 4.1):

It is outside the scope of this book to explore and compare these and related frameworks to one another, although it would be a useful exercise especially to look at the practices recommended and compared to peacebuilding processes of conflict transformation. Nevertheless, it is important to point out that each is flexible enough to be adapted to both in-country contexts and corporate cultures. Frameworks address particular concerns

Table 4.1 Frameworks Applicable to the Natural Resources Context

Year	*Framework*	*Explanation*
1976 (rev. 2011)	OECD Guidelines for Multinational Enterprises	The *OECD Guidelines for Multinational Enterprises* are recommendations addressed by governments to multinational enterprises operating in or from 42 adhering countries. They provide non-binding principles and standards for responsible business conduct in a global context consistent with applicable laws and internationally recognised standards. The *Guidelines* aim to promote positive contributions by enterprises to economic, environmental and social progress worldwide, including: Human Rights, supply chain management, employment, environment, anti-corruption and fiscal transparency (OECD, 2011).
2000 (rev. 2008)	Global Compact	The UN Global Compact is a framework for businesses that are committed to aligning their operations and strategies with ten universally accepted principles in the areas of Human Rights, labour, environment and anti-corruption. It emphasises that business, as a primary driver of globalisation, can help ensure markets, commerce, technology and finance advance in ways benefitting economies and societies around the globe (United Nations Global Compact, 2008; Hall, 2010)
2000	Voluntary Principles on Security and Human Rights	The voluntary principles provide a guide for companies in maintaining the safety and security of their operations within an operating framework that ensures respect for Human Rights and fundamental freedoms. (Voluntary Principles, 2000).
2003	ICMM Sustainable Development Framework	All ICMM members are required to implement its Sustainable Development (SD) Framework. They must: • Implement and maintain ethical business practices and sound systems of corporate governance. • Integrate sustainable development considerations within the corporate decision-making process. • Uphold fundamental Human Rights and respect cultures, customs and values in dealings with employees and others who are affected by our activities. • Implement risk management strategies based on valid data and sound science. • Seek continual improvement of health and safety performance. • Seek continual improvement of environmental performance. • Contribute to conservation of biodiversity and integrated approaches to land use planning. • Facilitate and encourage responsible product design, use, re-use, recycling and disposal of our products. • Contribute to the social, economic and institutional development of the communities in which they operate. • Implement effective and transparent engagement, communication and independently verified reporting arrangements with stakeholders. (ICMM, 2008).

(*Continued*)

Table 4.1 (Continued)

Year	*Framework*	*Explanation*
2003	EITI	Countries rich in natural resources such as oil, gas and mining have tended to under-perform economically, have a higher incidence of conflict and suffer from poor governance. To mitigate these effects, the EITI encourages revenue transparency and accountability by both resource companies and host governments (EITI, 2008)
2004 (rev. 2011)	GRI for Mining and Minerals	The GRI framework includes guidelines or protocols on how to report against specific indicators. It covers issues such as: • The control, use and management of land • The contribution to national economic and social development • Community and stakeholder engagement • Labour relations • Environmental management • Relationships with artisanal and small-scale mining • An integrated approach to minerals use (GRI, 2011)
2006 (rev. 2011)	IFC Performance Standards	IFC's Performance Standards define clients' responsibilities for assessing and managing: • Environmental and Social Risks and Impacts • Labour and working conditions • Community health, safety and security • Land acquisition and involuntary resettlement • Biodiversity Conservation and Management • Indigenous Peoples • Cultural Heritage (IFC, 2011)
2010	Natural Resource Charter	The Natural Resource Charter is a set of principles to guide governments' and societies' use of natural resources so these economic opportunities result in maximum and sustained returns for a country's citizens. It outlines tools and policy options designed to avoid the mismanagement of diminishing natural riches and ensure their ongoing benefits. The Charter contains 12 Precepts. Ten of these offer guidance on core decisions that governments face, beginning with the decision to extract the resources and ending with decisions about using the revenues generated. The remaining two Precepts are addressed to other important actors and their responsibilities (NRC, 2011)

relevant to CSR in the natural resources context to varying degrees including: FPIC, SLTO, Gender issues and Indigenous employment issues.

This book reflects the view that the CSR perspectives and related frameworks are distinct from and operate within paradigms. It is possible to look specifically at the paradigmatic level in the literature. This is especially salient for the natural resources sector where several concepts (e.g., perspectives, frameworks and concerns) float within the CSR space. It is often difficult to determine what underpins how they are used and how they relate to one another or establish what might constitute best practice for dealing with related community concerns. Towards achieving some clarity in these areas, the remainder of this chapter surveys the three influential paradigms foundationally influencing CSR practice in the natural resources context. There are other paradigms influencing the behaviour of NRCs (e.g., engineering, environmental, human security, development), a discussion of which is outside the scope of this book.

4.3 Paradigms Influencing CSR Practice

Having established that CSR is a *perspective*, this section identifies the major paradigms operating in the natural resources sector regarding CR. Building on Masterman (1970), paradigms foundational to achieving CSR goals can be employed either discretely or in overlapping ways to influence both the trajectory of NRC-community relationships as well as possible outcomes emerging from community-level interactions. NRCs' CSR departments primarily use Neoliberal Economic and Risk Management (e.g., reduction or mitigation) paradigms. Human Rights is also emerging as a significant paradigm. It bears mentioning that Environmental, Technical, Human Development, Human Security and other paradigms can also be present in the CSR perspective. However, the three explored were chosen because they are the most commonly used paradigms. A further reason for focusing on these paradigms is because they can be differentiated relatively clearly from each other and the paradigm of positive peace. Clarity on these initial three influential paradigms may assist in describing more accurately distinctions and comparisons in subsequent research into paradigms featuring environment, Indigenous and human security concerns; in developed and developing contexts; as well as for operations of varying sizes and stages an NRC operation's life.

The three paradigms chosen for this book each underpin verbal/written expressions of intention and practical outcomes from CSR commitments made by NRCs, sometimes labelled 'good corporate citizenship' (Palacios, 2004). However, these existing paradigms have not proven entirely sufficient for achieving CSR goals, since aggrieved communities around the world continue to object to aspects of natural resources activities, sometimes violently. This violent reaction is not necessarily due to a failure of paradigm, but because of unaddressed structural factors that contribute to conflict. If these paradigms, either individually or in combination, are insufficient or become ineffective foundations by which to achieve CSR goals, following Kuhn and Masterman, it is time for a paradigm shift or to bring in use another paradigm. Below in Table 4.2 is a summary of the characteristics of the three CSR paradigms; they will be discussed in greater detail in this chapter. The Positive Peace paradigm is discussed in Chapter 6.

Before discussing the three paradigms discretely, it is important to make a distinction between the use of the terms 'neoliberal economics', 'Human Rights' and 'risk management' and the paradigms with the same names. The terms and the paradigms are related but not equivalent. For example, the terms 'economics' and 'Human Rights' are sometimes presented together as in the UDHR articles 4, 17 and (especially) 23 (UNGA, 1948). Within the articles, economic considerations are identified as Human Rights. However, the mere mention of economics within the UDHR does not necessarily mean that the economic paradigm has been invoked. Conversely, even though the UDHR does not classify Human Rights as a paradigm, the UDHR fairly

Table 4.2 Paradigm Characteristics

Paradigm	*Neoliberal Economics*	*Human Rights*	*Risk Management*	*Positive Peace*
Priority beneficiary	Company	Community	Company	Relationship
Requires use of specialist language	Yes	Moderate	Yes	Minimal
Primary Value and Preferred Outcomes	Increase in financial value of the business	Treating each human life as equally valuable *per* the UDHR	Reduce/eliminate threats: economic, social, legal, physical	Reduce/ eliminate all forms of cultural, structural and physical violence
Primary focus	Focus on differentials of money and power	Focus on human beings who are marginalised and mistreated	Focus on probability of risk events both for prevention and remediation	Focus on building trust, finding creative solutions
Has a legal valence (threat of force)	Yes	Yes	Yes	No
Preference for non-violent methods of conflict resolution	Sometimes	Sometimes	Sometimes	Yes

well describes the values informing the Human Rights paradigm. As well, the mere mention of the word 'risk' does not necessarily invoke a Risk Management paradigm.

4.3.1 Neoliberal Economic Paradigm

The late Nobel laureate, Milton Friedman, famously wrote in *Capitalism and Freedom:*

> there is one and only one social responsibility of business—to use its resources and engage in activities designed to increase its profits . . . . Few trends could so thoroughly undermine the very foundations of our free society as the acceptance by corporate officials of a social responsibility other than to make as much money for their stockholders as possible.
>
> (Friedman, 2002 [1962], p. 133)

This rallying cry has been the cornerstone of business strategies around the world, and, until recently, it has been the dominant paradigm informing business decisions in the natural resources sector (Bessire, 2008; Korhonen, 2002). The neoliberal paradigm resolutely privileges economic growth, sometimes at the expense of environmental or social considerations (IISD, 2011; Walker & Howard, 2002).

The appeal of this exclusively economic paradigm is alluring to people who see human activity in terms of its financial benefits and costs. "Economic growth is said to increase our wealth, to eliminate poverty and to provide us with the resources to respect the environment" (Santa Barbara, Dubee, & Galtung, 2009, p. 43). The underlying assumptions of this paradigm according to Santa Barbara et al. assume an inexhaustible supply of resources to excavate from the earth, to manufacture products and, when finished, to dispose of in whatever way is seen as fit. The consequences of poor economic performance are also defined within the paradigm. For the natural resources sector, several of the natural resources majors removed their CEOs and fired large numbers of their staff in late 2012 and early 2013, partly because of poor financial performance (e.g. Rio Tinto, Anglo American, BHP Billiton, VALE, Newmont, Barrick Gold).

It may not be possible or even desirable to ask businesses to consider operating outside an economic paradigm. However, at its most extreme, the highest 'good' of the neoliberal economic paradigm is a robust financial balance sheet and profit maximisation over and above any other consideration. The elevation of these values, in the past, has led to decisions resulting in Human Rights abuses (e.g., forced labour and mistreatment of workers) and environmental disasters (e.g., direct riverine or oceanic tailings disposal of untreated waste from NRC development). The achievement of the highest economic good may be achieved using legal means and or physical force.

These tools belong properly to the negative peace paradigm and are not effective towards creating conditions of positive peace in a non-violent way (Barash & Webel, 2002; Galtung, 1969)

Despite the fact that the Neoliberal Economic paradigm can have an outcome characterised by human and environmental disregard, "the current paradigm for natural resources, espoused almost universally by commentators and international agencies, is that natural resources is performed by private industry for profit" (Southalan, 2011, p. 223). International Alert, in *Local Business and the economic dimensions of peacebuilding*, echoes the point more broadly and comments, "the primacy of free market economics and private sector led growth as a route to economic development . . . is a widespread paradigm and has been articulated in a large number of contemporary policy notes and papers" (2006, p. 17). Finnish economist Korhonen specifically cites Kuhn's use of paradigms to express his view on the limits of economics as indeed the dominant paradigm both for business and for society: "Economics has some serious difficulties in the light of corporate social responsibility. The development of the field of corporate social responsibility needs a new paradigmatic foundation" (Korhonen, 2002, p. 68). In other words, there are difficulties in supposing that all manner of social issues can be addressed either with an economic solution or at least without diminishing high economic profits, despite evidence to the contrary. For example, some say that when natural resources privileges the Neoliberal Economic paradigm, poverty will be alleviated (Bridge, 2004; Fine, 2002). However, poverty alleviation is a core value of the Human Rights paradigm, and, although some scholars flag an uneasy reliance of measuring development by economic prosperity (Fijn, Keen, Lloyd, & Pickering, 2012; Minorities Rights Group International, 2012), it is better addressed within a paradigm prioritising human factors (e.g., the Human Rights paradigm) (University for Peace, 2009).

The point here is to note that some scholars, policy makers and business professionals assert that when CSR practices are used within a Neoliberal Economic paradigm, the outcomes will somehow have Human Rights or Risk Management benefits rather than solely economic benefits (*vis* the work of economists Amartya Sen and Martha Nussbaum). Furthermore, some suppose that CSR activities should demonstrate economic outcomes/benefits to be viable. For example,

> There is no reason to expect that CSR will result in any activity that seriously threatens long-term profitability. Rather, all we can reasonably expect are win—win situations starting with the assumption that [a given CSR activity] makes good business sense and enhances shareholder value.
>
> (Sabadoz, 2011, p. 80)

The equation of a Neoliberal Economic *paradigm* with Human Rights or risk management *outcomes* does not hold. The Neoliberal Economic paradigm will result in economic outcomes. There are scholars who argue instead that "CSR has been viewed as being incompatible with the dominant economics paradigm" (Parsons, 2008, p. 102). Even more strongly, some scholars have made the case that market forces and the Economic paradigm have done nothing to address the Human Rights needs of Indigenous peoples (Minorities Rights Group International, 2012) or the Human Rights concerns of workers or communities (Pendleton, McClenaghan, Melamed, Bunn, & Graymore, 2004). This is because, according to Kuhn and Masterman, although paradigms may overlap and contribute towards complex outcomes, they do not lose their essential nature. A physics paradigm cannot morph into a chemistry paradigm; a German paradigm will never be transformed into a Japanese paradigm. Consequently, a Neoliberal Economic paradigm, informed by economic values, will privilege economic outcomes from CSR frameworks.

Thus, even though an economic solution may positively affect Human Rights or risk management goals and outcomes, Human Rights and risk outcomes are secondary to economic outcomes within the Neoliberal Economic paradigm. With its prioritisation of money, followed closely by power (over), the Economic paradigm may therefore not be very effective towards responding to or reducing structural, cultural or physical violence within the NRC-community interface. Finally, with its focus on mitigating threats to economic viability, it is difficult to use this paradigm to reach outcomes focusing on opportunities for development.

4.3.2 Risk Management Paradigm

Almost as strong a driver as the Neoliberal Economic paradigm is to the operation of NRCs is the Risk Management paradigm. Indeed, "natural resources company decision-making is motivated by profit maximisation and control of risk" (Owen & Kemp, 2012, p. 6). Risk in the natural resources context is defined as "the combination of the probability (or likelihood) and consequence of an event (or outcome or result of exposure). This gives rise to the widely used concept of risk: Risk = Probability x Consequence" (DRET, 2008). In other words, the equation refers risk as the probability of exposure to a hazard that will lead to a negative consequence. Another way of conceptualising risk is the effect of uncertainty on objectives caused by variability and specific uncertain events whereby the priority of a risk is often determined by evaluating a combination of its likelihood and consequence (Hancock, 2010; Klinke & Renn, 2002).

Risks are often categorised in terms of their severity (high, medium, low) and addressed accordingly. Typically, social risks are not factored into risk management strategies. They rely on a safety-based approach linked to discrete events (Kirsch, Goater, Harris, Sprott, & Joy, 2012). For example, risk strategies have been developed to prevent or handle the aftermath of specific events, such as: unplanned ordnance detonation, a burst tyre on an ore hauling truck, electrical engineering issues, slip/trip/fall hazards and severe weather events.

Risk management is different than risk *perception*, a subjective judgement about the likelihood and severity of a risk based on the following being intertwined: physiological response, emotion, and cognitive evaluation. Risk perception is more likely to arise in a heterogeneous way from communities than from companies (Garvin, McGee, Smoyer-Tomic, & Aubynn, 2009). These characteristically emotionally charged responses to perceived risks related to NRC activities, whether at the group level or as rumour and innuendo on the individual level, are referred to as 'social risk amplification' (Kasperson et al., 1988).

Risk management addresses a wide range of issues, including those related to: strategy, governance, the market, finance, stakeholders, technical and operations, human resources, HSEC and security, business services, land and water access and security. Australia's Department of Resources, Environment and Tourism (DRET) guide, *Risk Assessment and Management* (2008), focuses on NRCs' economic, environmental and social performance as SD practices. The emphasis is on how NRCs need to manage an array of risk at all stages of an NRC operation's life by using "well-credentialed risk management frameworks" (DRET, 2008, p. 2). Another example comes from the IFC, which specifically requires NRCs to manage an array of social risks alongside of environmental risks in a "structured way on an ongoing basis" (IFC, 2012, p. 5). There has been a proliferation of frameworks, with tools and mechanisms, as a result of NRCs' and regulators' reliance on the Risk Management paradigm (MMSD, 2009).

Corporate-focused (rather than community-focused) risk frameworks, tools and mechanisms have some common characteristics. First, they emphasise that risks need to be identified and analysed to determine causes. Then, measures can be put in place to mitigate and prevent the risks (Evans, Brereton, & Joy, 2007; Kirsch et al., 2012). Additionally, risk management is increasingly about identifying opportunities to realise potential gains as well as avoid potential losses (Committee OB-007, 2001). Furthermore, "strategic and value-based responses . . . can arise out of the successful management of . . . risks" (IHRB, 2011, p. 20). In terms of CSR risks, this means "recognising the range of stakeholders involved and incorporating their viewpoints into the process in some form" (Evans et al., 2007, p. 615). In the natural resources context, external stakeholders can include a wide variety of interested people and groups, including regulators, government, other industry partners, NGOs and civil society groups (MCA, 2005), while internal stakeholders are NRC employees.

When privileging a Risk paradigm, some NRCs refer to community opposition or protest to natural resources as a social risk (e.g., Newmont's cautionary statement).[3] This term is most often applied to describe the behaviour of external stakeholders who (1) object in some way to the way a natural resources operation is operating and (2) who are seeking a change in corporate behaviour. One common way to articulate social risk is through SLTO concepts. SLTO is a contested term, debated in the literature as to its actual utility (Aloi, 2007; Boutilier & Thomson, 2011; Owen & Kemp, 2012; Prno & Slocombe, 2012; Wilburn & Wilburn, 2011). In this literature, the management of social risk is situated in the portfolio of CSR practitioners.

> CSR programs are a necessary element of risk management for global companies because they provide the framework and principles for stakeholder engagement and can supply a wealth of intelligence on emerging and current social issues/groups to support the corporate risk agenda, and ultimately serve as a countermeasure for social risk.
>
> (Kytle & Ruggie, 2005, p. 1)

Social risk is also defined by NRCs as a reputational risk with financial consequences. One natural resources major offers this explanation of social risk:

> a range of threats or opportunities for business that may result from how [a] business impacts upon and interacts with communities and stakeholders. Social Risks can both directly and indirectly cause lost or enhanced production, affect development timelines and impact capital expenditure . . . . Social risks can also have non-economic consequences [such as affecting] 'social license to operate' with local communities and impact on relationships with government authorities and other stakeholders.
>
> (Rio Tinto, 2011, p. 3)

There is a wide range of examples of the hazards of ignoring social risk (both to companies and to communities) in the natural resources environment which are captured in the SLTO literature as a key expression of the risk-based approach. Two challenges unique to social risk are that first, they are not always understood, especially by the technical departments of NRCs, until or unless a social conflict emerges between a NRC and a community. The second is that to consider social aspects of community engagement 'risky' has the unfortunate potential to underline communities as a 'hazard' or a 'negative impact' on operations.

The Risk paradigm lends itself to being used in a compatible way with other paradigms with its emphasis on identifying and mitigating a wide variety of threats to business, life and property. Nevertheless, like the Economic paradigm, it has the tendency to be used in a "dominant" (Evans et al., 2007, p. 3) way, thus eclipsing the values within and the outcomes possible from other paradigms. This has the effect of limiting the CSR outcomes possible when it is employed as a foundation for CSR practice. Additionally, like the Neoliberal Economic paradigm, there is no disincentive to using legal means or physical force to mitigate or prevent a risk from occurring. As mentioned previously, these methods belong to a negative peace paradigm and are not conducive to reducing or eliminating root causes of violence.

It can be problematic, however, to use 'social risk' as an aspect of the Risk Management paradigm to frame CSR strategies. In practice, 'social risk' only refers to risk to companies from the social domain rather than to consider aspects of the social impact companies have on communities. If a company sees natural resources-affected communities as a risk—a threat to doing business—then there is an inherent lack of trust and cooperation already embedded in an NRC's relationship with those communities. In other words, trying to avoid a negative outcome is very different from trying to achieve a positive outcome. Consequently, it becomes very difficult to view communities as collaborative partners towards achieving CSR goals. It also becomes more difficult for CSR practitioners and the companies they work for to appreciate the social impact their operations have on the communities. For the concept of social risk to be more effective, it should work both ways, reflecting risks to both the company and the community, but, to date, it does not appear to have been used in that flexible way. Therefore, the Risk Management paradigm in the CSR space may only have limited utility for responding to or reducing the effects of conflict between NRCs and communities.

4.3.3 Human Rights Paradigm

The development of Human Rights as a paradigm for businesses began in the legal literature at the turn of the millennium. One example comes from the *Yale Law Journal*, in which Ratner (2001) develops a lengthy argument about the relationship between governments (state actors) and businesses (non-state actors). Ratner explains how the responsibilities of these actors for their own and each other's Human Rights records are linked but separate (e.g., South African mining companies which participated in the government-tolerated Human Rights abuses during the era of Apartheid). He draws the following conclusion about how businesses, in general, need to take responsibility for the consequences of their own activity in relation to Human Rights:

> Building upon the traditional paradigm whereby international law generally places duties on states and, more recently, individuals . . . international law should and can provide for Human Rights obligations, and that the scope of these obligations must be determined in light of the characteristics of corporate activity.
>
> (Ratner, 2001, p. 449)

Other examples exploring this theme include legal analysis of corporate responsibility for Human Rights by Wood and Scharffs (2002) and an exploration of the limits of the Voluntary Principles by the American Society of International Law (ASIL, 2001).

The Human Rights paradigm is based on the values encapsulated in the Universal Declaration of Human Rights (UDHR), a series of 30 articles comprising an international commitment to the freedoms and opportunities expected to be enjoyed equally by all persons. The foundational principle of the UDHR is:

> [R]ecognition of the inherent dignity and of the equal and inalienable rights of all members of the human family is the foundation of freedom, justice and peace in the world.
>
> (UNGA, 1948)

The UDHR is now well established and applies specifically to state actors. There is a suite of conventions, covenants and resolutions that have developed to highlight certain sets of rights:

- *Convention on the Elimination of all forms of Racial Discrimination*, 1965
- *The International Covenant on Civil and Political Rights*, 1966
- *The International Covenant on Economic, Social and Cultural Rights (ECOSOC)*, 1966
- *Convention on the Elimination of all forms of Discrimination Against Women (CEDAW)*, 1979
- *Covenant on Rights of the Child*, 1989
- *Recognition of the Human Right to Water and Sanitation*, 2010

The two international covenants and the UDHR comprise the *International Bill of Human Rights*, which came into force in 1976. Additional support for the observance of Human Rights of workers comes from the ILO with its *Declaration of Fundamental Principles and Rights at Work* in 1989. However, given the increasingly global spread of MNEs, with power, influence and resources that in some instances outstrip those of member nations of the UN,[4] it increasingly has become necessary to expand the sphere of responsibility for upholding the UDHR to businesses as non-state actors.

Support for the idea that MNEs should take responsibility for their impact on Human Rights issues gathered momentum throughout the late 2000s, led by SRSG John Ruggie and his research team. They shouldered an initiative to clearly define businesses' responsibility for Human Rights. Their work began in 2008 and culminated in both a report and a UN resolution, the *Guiding Principles on Business and Human Rights (UNGP)* (Ruggie, 2011b). The UNGP articulates the following:

(*a*) *States' existing obligations to respect, protect and fulfil human rights and fundamental freedoms;*

(*b*) *The role of business enterprises as specialized organs of society performing specialized functions, required to comply with all applicable laws and to respect human rights;*

(*c*) *[There is a] need for rights and obligations to be matched to appropriate and effective remedies [by both states and businesses] when breached* (UNHROHC, 2011, p. 1).

The UNGP, coupled with the guidance document *Applications of the U.N. "Protect, Respect and Remedy" Framework* (Ruggie, 2011a), provides practical advice, not instructions, towards the implementation of the principles of protection, respect and remediation of Human Rights, in theory at least.

In the natural resources context, there are several principal frameworks used to protect Human Rights: the Voluntary Principles on Security and Human Rights (2000); the Kimberley Process Diamond Certification scheme (2002); the OECD Guidelines for Multinational Enterprises (2008); and the Global Compact (2011). In addition, there is a web-based resource called the *Business & Human Rights Resource Centre* which makes a wealth of information available about the relationship between businesses' Human Rights obligations, including those of NRCs (www.business-humanrights.org/Home).

The overarching effectiveness of the Human Rights paradigm in the natural resources sector has yet to be comprehensively evaluated, since in many ways it is still developing. Worth noting is the amount of attention Human Rights are currently receiving as a foundation for CSR activity in the sector is substantial, due to its uptake at the policy level. As well, Human Rights Impact Assessments are being designed and delivered in order for NRCs to "undertake comprehensive due diligence process[es] that consider whether a business causes, contributes to, or is linked to adverse Human Rights impacts through its business relationships" (Kemp & Vanclay, 2013, p. 90). A discussion of these aspects is undertaken in detail elsewhere (Kallman & Karmel, 2012; Kemp, Gronow, Zimmerman, & Kim, 2013; Knox, 2011; Salcito et al., 2013; Umlas, 2009).

The Human Rights paradigm has emphasised the human and social effects of natural resources. Although the natural resources industry's peak bodies and many of the CSR frameworks now prioritise diligence about Human Rights, there five significant barriers limiting its use as a paradigm. The first is that technical departments and general managers find it challenging to operate out of this paradigm, as they "fear human rights would entail extra work" (UN Global Compact, 2009, p. 15). As well, they also resist seeing issues in terms of rights outside of a very narrow frame, not considering the larger sweep and implications of the full range of rights enumerated in the UDHR. These two factors make it all the more difficult for CSR practitioners to build inter-departmental cooperation around community issues (Kemp & Vanclay, 2013).

The second is that to frame conflict issues in terms of 'rights' can make it more difficult to find a durable solution to a conflict and may even escalate it. Using a simplified example, if a timber-bearing truck vehicle runs over a chicken as it drives a load of felled trees for processing, the owner of the chicken could simply lodge a grievance with the NRC and ask the NRC to (1) replace the chicken and (2) take precautions to make sure that incidents of this nature did not happen in the future. Framed as a Human Rights issue, however unlikely, the owner of the chicken could claim its loss as an abridgement of his or her right to a livelihood, complicating matters significantly.

Third, the Human Rights paradigm has not yet crystallised in terms of which rights are encompassed and how corporations are supposed to respect them. Currently, the observation of the 'Protect, Respect, Remedy' framework (*aka* 'The Ruggie Principles') by companies is somewhat of a moveable feast with a multiple-choice element. This lack of consistency about which Human Rights are more likely to need addressing by NRCs is reflected in comparing Sustainability and Annual reports. Many natural resources majors will state a commitment to Human Rights, but then they will focus on the Human Rights of their workers, such as the right to join a union, and not address rights belonging to communities as such, for example, the right to water and sanitation (Kemp, Bond, Cote, & Franks, 2010).

Fourth, when respecting the Human Rights of one individual or group, it is quite possible to violate the Human Rights of another individual or group. This conundrum is not limited to the natural resources sector, but can problematise finding mutually agreeable solutions to conflicts when looked at primarily from a Human Rights paradigm. This challenge can be made even more vexing when individuals or groups hire lawyers to impress upon the other party the importance of respecting their rights—perhaps at the expense of another's. One example is when First Nations communities in Canada begin vigorously prosecute natural resources exploration companies for violating their cultural rights, especially during the exploration phase of an operation (Coates & Poelzer, 2010; Gibson & O'Faircheallaigh, 2010). Likewise, there are situations, such as the case of Human Rights violations at the Porgera mine, where armed force needs to be threatened to stop rogue policemen and NRC security officers from violating the Human Rights of female, artisanal miners (Amnesty International, 2010; Human Rights Watch, 2010; Manjoo, 2013). Although the violence against the women must be stopped, and perhaps the only way to do that is by use of counterforce in the short term, this strategy remains within the paradigm of negative—not positive—peace. Finally, the overall nature of the Human Rights paradigm effectiveness as a CSR foundation is inconclusive—especially in the non-Western contexts in which NRCs are increasingly operating. In these areas of the world, Human Rights are understood in alternate ways (e.g., traditional, Indigenous, tribal) to the current international norm. For example, traditional peoples often claim a right to live on and preserve an ancestral parcel of land, as the Dongria Kondh tribe in India has done (Sahu, 2009) or the Standing Rock Water Protectors have done when protesting the development of the Dakota Access Pipeline (2016-2017). When NRCs, in these two instances a bauxite company and a petroleum company, say they have a counter claim—a right to commercially use the land due to a lease granted them by the government—the adjudication of whose rights should be prioritised becomes murky at best. Consequently, as important as this development is, it remains to be seen how effective the Human Rights paradigm will be towards resolving conflicts between NRCs and communities.

4.4 Conclusion

This chapter has shown that the choice of paradigm one employs has the potential to prioritise and lead to particular outcomes. Despite efforts to achieve productive conflict outcomes using these paradigms, they have not provided consistent or reliable methods to do so. This is especially true in circumstances where structural, cultural and physical violence is implicated in those conflicts. As a consequence, the current paradigms—Neoliberal Economic, Risk Management and Human Rights—are coming under increasing scrutiny in terms of their viability, their contribution to CSR practice and their ability to adequately reflect growing environmental and social concerns (IISD, 2010; Walker & Howard, 2002).

Instead, business and policy leaders are re-thinking the environmental, economic and social viability of the economic growth paradigm in the face of a burgeoning world population requiring more materials and products at lower prices from a diminishing amount of resources. Within the natural resources sector, both the former CEO and the firm's Head of Innovation for Rio Tinto considered the future of the natural resources industry, saying that, "The old ways will not be good or fast enough. Change is essential" (Albanese & McGagh, 2011, p. 21). Natural resources industry scholar Shankleman makes a similar comment.

> We need a new paradigm for developing petroleum and mineral resources in poor countries that builds on, but takes further, the initiatives concerning conflict, transparency, security and human rights and social/environmental risk mitigation. The new paradigm should also explicitly link resource exploitation with development.
>
> (2008, p. 210)

Albanese, McGagh and Shankleman are referring to the need for a new paradigm that will incorporate the realities of community-based development pressure plus the realities of "increasing energy costs, the threat of climate change, the higher cost of natural resources deeper ore bodies and lower grade ores, possibly in more challenging geopolitical environments" (Albanese & McGagh, 2011, p. 22).

The consequences of continuing to use the three established paradigms will be severe, as mentioned in Chapter 1, if there are alternative paradigms that better meet the challenges facing the natural resources industry and communities affected by their operations. If NRCs are not able to stay at the front edge of the rapidly changing[5] and escalating demands of the communities near which they conduct their business and position themselves not just as partners in development, but as partners in leaving a positive long-term legacy, they stand to have both their reputations and their ability to do business hampered. This could put NRCs and communities on a real collision course of misunderstanding, unrealistic expectations (on both sides) and increasing the number and severity of violence-related conflicts between the parties. An increasingly conflictual situation creates a material challenge for CSR practitioners to do their job of facilitating maximum benefits for both communities and NRCs from (1) their relationship and (2) the activities of natural resources.

This chapter has suggested that neither the Neoliberal Economic nor Risk Management nor Human Rights paradigms can fulfil the mandate of providing an adequate foundational CSR platform for dialogue leading to durable, peaceful relationships between stakeholders in the NRC-community space. A key problem with each of these paradigms is that they will tend to preference either the company or the community, each one at the expense of the other. Each of these paradigms for CSR might only exacerbate the tendency to use legal means or physical force to resolve community-level conflict. This will worsen rather than address the root causes of structural, cultural or physical violence between NRCs and communities. Additionally, these three influential paradigms are limited in dealing constructively with structural issues (root causes) as well as legacies of mistrust. Multiple factors contribute to these two conflict drivers. As explained above, these influential paradigms have significant gaps which lead to missed opportunities and incorrect analysis of situations. This can result in the wrong strategies being applied and NRC-community conflict worsening as a result.

Perhaps it is worth considering a different paradigm, then, to either provide (1) a unifying paradigm within which they operate more coherently or (2) an alternate paradigm that operates at the same time as one or more of the other dominant paradigms (Kuhn, 1977; Masterman, 1970). "The Earth Charter's inclusive ethical vision recognizes that environmental protection and sustainability, Human Rights, equitable human development, and peace are interdependent and indivisible" (Brenes, 2009, p. 314). If that is true, this book proposes that the paradigm of positive peace could be explored further as the basis for a paradigm shift in how NRCs shape and implement their CSR activities in the natural resources context contributing to a durable, sustainable, positive peace at the local level. A paradigm of positive peace has potential to animate creative and innovative thinking towards developing conflict responses that contribute to a durable, sustainable, positive peace at the local level. The next chapter explores this idea in greater depth.

Notes

1 There is an academic skirmish about this point which is called the 'incommensurability thesis'. It is about the rationality or absurdity of whether Kuhn is correct in saying, "the difference between successive paradigms are both necessary and irreconcilable" (Kuhn, 1996 [1962], p. 103). Malone traces the debate about the incommensurability of paradigms and concludes that it does not contribute much towards a clearer understanding of Kuhn's work on paradigms. Consequently, incommensurability is acknowledged as a particularly thorny point of disagreement but will neither be discussed in nor resolved by this book, as it is thoroughly covered elsewhere (Malone, 1992).

2 A complete discussion on the broad range of CSR streams of academic inquiry is outside of the scope of this book.

3 www.newmont.com/legal/ [Accessed: 20 September 2017].

4 For an indicative list from 2016, see the following compilation from the *World Economic Forum www.weforum.org/agenda/2016/10/corporations-not-countries-dominate-the-list-of-the-world-s-biggest-economic-entities/* [Accessed: 5 October 2017].

5 The effect of social and electronic media is a factor in the rapidity of change in how communities respond to natural resources. However, a discussion about that development is outside the scope of this book.

Bibliography

Albanese, T., & McGagh, J. (2011). Future trends in mining. In P. Darling (Ed.), *SME mining engineering handbook* (3rd ed.). Englewood, CO: Society for Mining Metallurgy and Exploration, Inc.

Aloi, D. M. (2007). *Reducing social risk and impact by engaging local communities*. Paper presented at the Iron Ore Conference, Perth, Australia.

Amnesty International. (2010). *Undermining rights: Forced evictions and police brutality around the Porgera gold mine, Papua New Guinea*. London.

Argyrous, G. (1992). Kuhn's paradigms and neoclassical economics. *Economics and Philosophy*, *8*(2), 231–248. doi:10.1017/S0266267100003059

ASIL. (2001). Voluntary human rights principles for extractive and energy companies. *The American Journal of International Law*, *95*(3), 636–637.

Avruch, K. (1998). *Culture & conflict resolution*. Washington, DC: United States Institute of Peace Press.

Barash, D. P., & Webel, C. (2002). *Peace and conflict studies*. Thousand Oaks, CA: Sage.

Bessire, D. (2008). Corporate social responsibility: From transparency to 'Constructive Conflict'. In D. Crowther & N. Capaldi (Eds.), *The Ashgate research companion to corporate social responsibility*. Burlington, VT: Ashgate.

Bird, A. (2002). Kuhn's wrong turning. *Studies in History and Philosophy of Science Part A*, *33*(3), 443–463. doi:10.1016/s0039-3681(02)00028-00026

Boutilier, R. (2005). Views of sustainable development: A typology of stakeholders' conflicting perspectives. In *New horizons in research on sustainable organisations*. Sheffeild: Greenleaf Publishing.

Boutilier, R., & Thomson, I. (2011). *Modelling and measuring the social license to operate: Fruits of a dialogue between theory and practice*. Cuernavaca: Boutilier and Associates.

Brenes, A. (2009). Personal transformations needed for cultures of peace. In J. de Rivera (Ed.), *Handbook on building cultures of peace*. New York, NY: Springer.

Bridge, G. (2004). Contested terrain: Mining and the environment. *Annual Review of Environmental Resources*, *29*, 205–259.

Calvano, L. (2008). Multinational corporations and local communities: A critical analysis of conflict. *Journal of Business Ethics*, *82*, 793–805.

Carroll, A. B. (1979). A three-dimensional conceptual model of social performance. *Academy of Management Review*, *4*(4), 497–505.

Carroll, A. B. (1999). Corporate social responsibility: Evolution of a definitional construct. *Business & Society*, *38*(3), 268–295.

Carroll, A. B., & Shabana, K. M. (2010). The business case for corporate social responsibility: A review of concepts, research and practice. *International Journal of Management Reviews*, *12*(1), 85–105. doi:10.1111/j.1468–2370.2009.00275.x

Cedarbaum, D. G. (1983). Paradigms. *Studies in History and Philosophy of Science Part A*, *14*(3), 173–213. doi:10.1016/0039–3681(83)90012–90012

Coates, K., & Poelzer, G. (2010). Defining indigenous space: The constitutional development of aboriginal property and resource rights in Canada. *Georgetown Journal of International Affairs*, *11*(1), 7–15.

Committee OB-007. (2001). *Risk management: AS/NZAS 4360:2004*. Sydney.

Dahlsrud, A. (2008). How corporate social responsibility is defined: An analysis of 37 definitions. *Corporate Social Responsibility and Environmental Management*, *15*(1), 1–13. doi:10.1002/csr.132

Dashwood, H. S. (2012). *The rise of global corporate social responsibility: Mining and the spread of global norms*. Retrieved from http://UQL.eblib.com.au/patron/FullRecord.aspx?p=989175

de Neufville, R. (2010). Paradigm. In M. Bevir (Ed.), *Encyclopedia of political theory* (pp. 1014–1015). Thousand Oaks, CA: Sage.

DRET. (2008). *Risk assessment and management*. Canberra.

EITI. (2008). *Implementing the EITI*. New York, NY. Retrieved from www.eiti.org

Esteves, A. M., & Vanclay, F. (2009). Social development needs analysis as a tool for SIA to guide corporate-community investment: Applications in the minerals industry. *Environmental Impact Assessment Review*, *29*(2), 137–145. doi:10.1016/j.eiar.2008.08.004

Evans, R., Brereton, D., & Joy, J. (2007). Risk assessment as a tool to explore sustainable development issues: Lessons from the Australian coal industry. *International Journal of Risk Assessment and Management*, *7*(5), 607–619.

Fijn, N., Keen, I., Lloyd, C., & Pickering, M. (Eds.). (2012). *Indigenous participation in Australian economies II*. Canberra: Australian National University.

Fine, B. (2002). Economics imperialism and the new development economics as Kuhnian paradigm shift? *World Development*, *30*(12), 2057–2070.

Friedman, M. (2002 [1962]). *Capitalism and freedom*. Chicago, IL: University of Chicago Press.

Galtung, J. (1969). Violence, peace and peace research. *Journal of Peace Research*, *6*(3), 167–191.

Garvin, T., McGee, T. K., Smoyer-Tomic, K. E., & Aubynn, E. A. (2009). Community company relations in gold mining in Ghana. *Journal of Environmental Management*, *90*, 571–586.

Gibson, G., & O'Faircheallaigh, C. (2010). *IBA Community Toolkit: Negotiation and implementation of impact and benefit agreements*. Toronto.

Gond, J-P., & Crane, A. (2010). Corporate social performance disoriented: Saving the lost paradigm? *Business & Society*, *49*(4), 677–703.

GRI. (2011). *Sustainability reporting guidelines & mining and metals sector supplement*.

Hall, C. (2011). *United Nations global compact annual review 2010*. New York, NY: United Nations.

Hamann, R., & Acutt, N. (2003). How should civil society (and the government) respond to 'corproate social responsibility'? A critique of business motivations and the potential for partnerships. *Development Southern Africa*, *20*(2), 255–270.

Hancock, M. G. (2010). *Risk management systems for communicable diseases in the Papua New Guinean Mining Industry: Maturity models—paths for development* (PhD Doctoral), The University of Queensland, Brisbane, Australia.

Human Rights Watch. (2010). *Gold's costly dividend: The Porgera joint venture*. New York, NY: Human Rights Watch.

ICMM. (2008). *Ten principles*. Retrieved from www.icmm.com/our-work/sustainable-development-framework/

IFC. (2011). *Update of IFC's policy and performance standards on environmental and social sustainability, and access to information policy*. New York, NY: IFC.

IFC. (2012). *IFC performance standards on environmental and social sustainability*. IFC: Washington, DC.

IHRB. (2011). *The "State of Play" of human rights due diligence: Anticipating the next five years*. London: IHRB.

IISD. (2010). *Environment, conflict and peace-building at IISD*. IISD: Geneva.

IISD. (2011). *2010–2011 IISD annual report*.Winnipeg: IISD.

International Alert. (2006). *Introduction*.London: International Alert.

Jenkins, H. (2004). Corporate social responsibility and the mining industry: Conflicts and constructs. *Corporate Social Responsibility and Environmental Management*, *11*, 23–34.

Jonker, J., & Pennink, B. W. (2010). The essence of methodology. In *The essence of research methodology: A concise guide for master and PhD students in management science*. London: Springer.

Kallman, J., & Karmel, R. (2012). *Human rights in the mining industry*. London: Mazars.

Kapelus, P. (2002). Mining, corporate social responsibility and the "Community": The case of Rio Tinto, Richards Bay Minerals and the Mbonambi. *Journal of Business Ethics*, *39*(3), 275–296.

Kasperson, R. E., Renn, O., Slovic, P., Brown, H. S., Emel, J., Goble, R., . . . Ratick, S. (1988). The social amplification of risk: A conceptual framework. *Risk Analysis*, *8*(2), 177–187.

Kemp, D., Bond, C., Cote, C., & Franks, D. (2010). Mining, water and human rights: Making the connection. *Journal of Cleaner Production*, *18*(15), 1553–1562.

Kemp, D., Gronow, J., Zimmerman, V., & Kim, J. (2013). *Why human rights matter*. London: Rio Tinto.

Kemp, D., & Vanclay, F. (2013). Human rights and impact assessment: Clarifying the connections in practice. *Impact Assessment and Project Appraisal*, *31*(2), 86–96.

Kimberley Process. (2002). *Kimberley process certification scheme*. Retrieved from www.kimberleyprocess.com/web/kimberley-process/home

Kirsch, P., Goater, S., Harris, J., Sprott, D., & Joy, J. (2012). *RISKGATE: Promoting and redefining best practice for risk management in the Australian Coal Industry*. Brisbane, Australia: MISHC at the University of Queensland.

Klinke, A., & Renn, O. (2002). A new approach to risk evaluation and management: Risk-based, precaution-based, and discourse-based strategies. *Risk Analysis*, *22*(6), 1071–1094. doi:10.1111/1539–6924.00274

Knox, J. H. (2011). The Ruggie rules: Applying human rights law to corporations. In R. Mares (Ed.), *The UN guiding principles on business and human rights*. Leiden: BRILL.

Korhonen, J. (2002). The dominant economics paradigm and corporate social responsibility. *Corporate Social Responsibility and Environmental Management*, 9(1), 66–79. doi:10.1002/csr.7

Kuhn, T. A. (1977). Second thoughts. In *The essential tension*. Chicago, IL: University of Chicago Press.

Kuhn, T. A. (1996 [1962]). *The structure of scientific revolutions*. Chicago, IL: University of Chicago Press.

Kytle, B., & Ruggie, J. G. (2005). *Corporate social responsibility as risk management: A model for multinationals*. Cambridge, MA.

Lambert, J., Elix, J., & Priest, B. (2005). *Values mapping: A flexible tool for building sustainability partnerships*. Sydney: World Wildlife Fund.

Malone, M. (1992). Kuhn reconstructed: Incommensurability without relativism. *Studies in History and Philosophy of Science*, *24*(1), 69–93.

Manjoo, R. (2013). *Report of the special rapporteur on violence against women, its causes and consequences*. New York, NY: United Nations.

Masterman, M. (1970). The nature of a paradigm. In I. Lakatos & A. Musgrave (Eds.), *Criticism and the growth of knowledge*. Cambridge: Cambridge University Press.

MCA. (2005). *Enduring value: The Australian minerals industry framework for sustainable development*. Kingston.

Minorities Rights Group International. (2012). *State of the world's minorities and indigenous peoples 2012: Focus on land rights and natural resources*.

MMSD. (2009). *Breaking new ground*.London: Earthscan.

NRC. (2011). *The natural resource charter*. Natural Resource Governance Institute: Oxford.

OECD. (2008). *OECD guidelines for multinational enterprises*. Paris: OECD.

OECD. (2011). *OECD guidelines for multinational enterprises*. Paris: OECD.

Owen, J. R., & Kemp, D. (2012). Social licence and mining: A critical perspective. *Resources Policy*, *39*(1): 29–35.

Oxford University Press. (2012a). *perspective, n*. OED Online: Oxford University Press. Retrieved from www.oed.com/view/Entry/141520?rskey=C11saO&result=1&isAdvanced=false

Oxford University Press. (2012b). *value, n*. OED Online: Oxford University Press. Retrieved from www.oed.com/view/Entry/141520?rskey=C11saO&result=1&isAdvanced=false

Palacios, J. J. (2004). Corporate citizenship and social responsibility in a globalized world. *Citizenship Studies*, *8*(4), 383–402.

Parsons, R. (2008). We are all stakeholders now: The influence of western discourses of 'community engagement' in an Australian Aboriginal community. *Critical Perspectives on International Business*, 4(2/3), 99–126.

Pendleton, A., McClenaghan, S., Melamed, C., Bunn, I., & Graymore, D. (2004). *Behind the mask: The real face of corporate social responsibility*.London: Christian Aid.

Percival, W. K. (1979). The applicability of Kuhn's paradigms to the social sciences. *The American Sociologist*, *14*(1), 28–31.

Prno, J., & Slocombe, S. (2012). Exploring the origins of 'social license to operate' in the mining sector: Perspectives from governance and sustainability theories. *Resources Policy*, *37*(3), 346–357. doi:10.1016/j.resourpol.2012.04.002

Ratner, S. R. (2001). Corporations and human rights: A theory of legal responsibility. *The Yale Law Journal*, *111*, 443–545.

Rio Tinto. (2011). *Social risk analysis guidance note*.London: Rio Tinto.

Ruggie, J. (2011a). *Applications of the U.N. "Protect, Respect and Remedy" framework*. New York, NY: United Nations.

Ruggie, J. (2011b). *Human rights and transnational corporations and other business enterprises* (A/HRC/RES/17/4).New York, NY: United Nations.

Sabadoz, C. (2011). Between profit-seeking and prosociality: Corporate social responsibility as derridean supplement. *Journal of Business Ethics*, *104*(1), 77–91.

Sahu, S. (2009, 2009/01/07). Indians protest over mining plans. *BBC News*. Retrieved from http://news.bbc.co.uk/go/pr/fr/-/2/hi/south_asia/7854369.stm

Salcito, K., Utzinger, J., Weiss, M. G., Münch, A. K., Singer, B. H., Krieger, G. R., & Wielga, M. (2013). Assessing human rights impacts in corporate development projects. *Environmental Impact Assessment Review*, *42*, 39–50. doi:10.1016/j.eiar.2013.03.002

Santa Barbara, J., Dubee, F., & Galtung, J. (2009). *Peace business: People and nature above markets and capital*. Oslo: Transcend University Press.

Schwartz, M. S., & Carroll, A. B. (2008). Integrating and unifying competing and complementary frameworks: The search for a common core in the business and society field. *Business & Society*, *47*(2), 148–186. doi:10.1177/0007650306297942

Shankleman, J. (2008). Imagine there's no 'Resource Curse'. *Environmental Policy and Law*, *38*(4), 205–211.

Shubert, N. E. (2010). *No farm, no food: Organizing Appalachian family farms around the politics of 'Good Food'*. (Doctor of Philosophy), Ohio University, Athens, OH.

Southalan, J. (2011). What are the implications of human rights for minerals taxation? *Resources Policy*, *36*(3), 214–226.

Thomson, I., & Boutilier, R. G. (2011). Social license to operate. In P. Darling (Ed.), *SME mining engineering handbook* (3rd ed.). Englewood, CO: Society for Mining Metallurgy and Exploration, Inc.

Umlas, E. (2009). *Corporate human rights reporting: An analysis of current trends*. New York, NY: United Nations.

UN Global Compact. (2009). *Embedding rights in business practice*. New York, NY: United Nations.

UNGA. (1948). *The universal declaration of human rights (UDHR)* (Resolution 217 A(III) of 10). New York, NY: United Nations.

UNHROHC. (2011). *Guiding principles on business and human rights*. New York, NY: United Nations.

United Nations Global Compact. (2008). Welcome to the United Nations Global Compact. Retrieved from www.unglobalcompact.org/

University for Peace. (2009). *Development, peace & security: Curriculum manual for South Asia and South-East Asia*. United Nations: New York, NY.

Voluntary Principles. (2000). *Voluntary principles on security and human rights*. Retrieved from www.voluntaryprinciples.org/

Walker, J., & Howard, S. (2002). *Finding the way forward: How could voluntary action move mining towards sustainable development?*

Wilburn, K. M., & Wilburn, R. (2011). Achieving a social license to operate using stakeholder theory. *Journal of International Business Ethics*, *4*(2), 3–16, 70.

Wilkinson-Maposa, S., & Fowler, A. (2009). *The poor philanthropist II: New approaches to sustainable development*. Cape Town: UCT Press.

Wood, S. G., & Scharff, B. G. (2002). Applicability of human rights standards to private corporations: An American perspective. *The American Journal of Comparative Law*, *50*(Autumn 2002), 531–566.

Wray, B. (2011). Kuhn and the discovery of paradigms. *Philosophy of the Social Sciences*, *41*(3), 380–397. doi:10.1177/0048393109359778

5 Paradigm of Positive Peace

This chapter drills down to a more granular level on how the paradigm of Peace—especially Positive Peace—functions conceptually. Positive peace is a distinct concept indicating that violence of any kind is not used to achieve or maintain it. Three other dominant paradigms are also explored: Economic, Risk and Human Rights. Each of these paradigms already operates as a decision-making framework when MNEs and their employees make social and environmental business decisions. Although they are useful in making certain business decisions (e.g., health and safety, worker well-being, HR practices), they limit and preclude certain types of lateral thinking leading to innovative solutions to community-based social and environmental issues. Considered together with the paradigm of Positive Peace, this chapter demonstrates the advantages and disadvantages of each of the three dominant paradigms.

5.1 Overview

'Positive Peace' has only begun to emerge as a paradigm in the natural resources context. It has the potential to be a unifying paradigm to maximise outcomes, or it could be used alongside CSR paradigms, as defined in Chapter 4, in the NRC-community space. This chapter endeavours to show how and why positive peace could be conceptualised. First, 'peace' is described at the philosophical level. Next, peace-building is described and differentiated from positive peace and conflict transformation. Finally, positive peace is described paradigmtically with the potential to structure CSR strategies designed to handle community-level conflict in the natural resources context.

5.2 Peace

Peace and Conflict Theorists have a variety of ways of understanding 'peace'. Despite the fact that philosophers, theologians, analysts and statespersons have long researched, written and orated passionately about the virtues of peace, a coherent and systematic "philosophy of peace" is still in its infancy

(Webel, 2007, p. 4). Nevertheless, peace is as ubiquitous as conflict in everyday life (Boulding, 1987). Most people know what it is and what it is not in their own contexts and cultures.

The first task is to address the question: what does 'peace' mean? Peace is a concept that is culturally couched and notoriously difficult to define in a universal way. Galtung's essay *Social Cosmology and the Concept of Peace (1981)* surveys both Oriental and Occidental conceptions of peace: Judaism, Christianity, Islam, ancient Greece, ancient Rome, the modern period, Jainism, Hinduism, Buddhism, Japanese traditional religion and Chinese Confucian. The essay advocates for dialogue about 'peace' towards developing a richer understanding about what the term means. The essay acknowledges traditional cultures' views of peace and invites those groups into the larger dialogue, but does not attempt to capture their views here. Notably, the essay emphasises the following idea: "the world is dynamic, so are peace concepts" (Galtung, 1981, p. 194). In other words, it is neither possible nor desirable to attempt the achievement of one universal, static definition of peace. The essay cautions occidental scholars and policy makers not to be content with 'peace' as equivalent to the bare minimum definition of the absence of war or violence (negative peace). Instead, occidental views should return to Aristotelian values where peace represents privileging the things that make for human thriving (*Eudaimonia*), such as adequate food, water, shelter, access to livelihoods and education (Biskowski, 1998; Brenes, 2009). Peace in this way is also a commitment to increased well-being, but not at the expense of the 'other'. Peace highlights a focus on the combination of justice, prosperity, harmonious co-existence with your cultural reference group as well as with those external to it, peace of mind and a compassionate commitment to non-injury. It is not a system, concept or a program exported onto another as a form of 'idea colonialism'.

John Paul Lederach has a compatible notion of peace to that understood by Galtung. However, he elevates some key elements that not covered in Galtung's essay, including the role of conflict transformation in relation to the concept of peace-building.

> Metaphorically, peace is seen not merely as a stage in time or a condition. It is a dynamic social construct . . . . [and] peacebuilding involves a wide range of activities and functions . . . . needed to transform conflict toward more sustainable, peaceful relationships
>
> (Lederach, 1997, p. 20)

Peace is a practical way of life. As part of this definition of peace, there are certain kinds of thought and action processes necessary to envision and then act in accordance with elements necessary for a long-term, positive peace. In *The Moral Imagination* (2005), Lederach stresses the need to continuously ask questions about the *status quo* in order to discover new ways of addressing what seem like the same old problems, such as how to encourage peace. He says that a commitment to living out or building peace requires a creative imagination as well as technical skill. At times, it even "requires a worldview shift" in order to facilitate "social change and break cycles of violence" while still living within them (Lederach, 2005, pp. ix–x). Used here, a 'worldview' is equivalent to a paradigm (Gladwin, Kennelly, & Krause, 1995).

Violence as the opposite of peace is discussed in Chapters 1 and 2. Lederach adds a characteristic whereby violence results from disregard of human inter-relatedness instead of "taking personal responsibility [for relationships] and acknowledging relational mutuality" (Lederach, 2005, p. 35). The argument here is to see relationships as central to conditions of peace; beyond that, there needs to be a willingness to suspend judgement and search for the least common social denominator. People need to think about peace from the following frame:

> live with a high degree of ambiguity . . . [while employing] paradoxical curiosity which approaches social realities with an abiding respect for complexity, a refusal to fall prey to the pressures of forced dualistic categories of truth, and an inquisitiveness about what may hold together in a seemingly contradictory social energies in a greater whole.
>
> (Lederach, 2005, pp. 36–37)

The relationships that result from these processes are characterised by "openness and accountability, self-reflection and vulnerability, mutual respect, dignity, and the proactive engagement of the other" (Lederach, 2005, p. 42).

5.3 Peace-Building with Conflict Transformation

Peace-building processes of conflict transformation address cultural, structural or direct violence and result in positive peace. Peace-building processes are rarely linear; thus, scholars have developed a number of diagrams that can be used to describe the nonlinearity of peace-building processes, the stakeholders involved and ways to conceptualise this distinct way of thinking about engaging people and groups experiencing conflict in their relationships (Curle, 2000; Francis, 2010; Lederach, 1995, 1997; Miall, 2011 [2004]; Nelson, 2000; Parlevliet, 2009; Schirch, 2004). Peace-building processes are dynamic, as described below.

> The crucial idea is to consider a peacebuilding strategy as an open, creative and dynamic process constituted by ongoing action and reflection. Instead of designing a peacebuilding strategy at the very beginning and then implementing it, a systemic strategy takes shape during the process itself . . . The idea is to leave enough space for defining the desired outcomes together with all relevant stakeholders during the process.
>
> (Korppen, 2011, pp. 86–87)

This contemporary description of what peace-building entails is more expansive than earlier iterations of the concept.

The term 'peace-building' originated with the UN's efforts to rebuild the international world order following World War Two. It originally described activities that helped States recover from armed conflict; establish a stable civil society and non-coercive governmental structures; and promote the model of a Western-style, liberal, democratic ideal. The UN's definition at inception was this: "peace-building refers to activities aimed at assisting nations to cultivate peace after conflict".[1] The current OECD definition of peace-building reflects the original UN use of the term.

> [Peace-building] includes activities designed to prevent conflict through addressing structural and proximate causes of violence,[2] promoting sustainable peace, delegitimizing violence as a dispute resolution strategy, building capacity within society to peacefully manage disputes, and reducing vulnerability to triggers that may spark violence.
>
> (Blum, 2011, p. 2)

Scholars within the discipline of International Relations have continued to expand the range and sweep of peace-building to encompass a wide variety of meanings and activities that include mitigation of both violent and non-violent conflict at local, State or inter-State levels (Bellamy, Williams, & Griffin, 2006).

Peace-building is different from peacekeeping or peacemaking. Aall (2011) from the US Institute of Peace identifies peacekeeping as a United Nations-sanctioned activity authorised by the UN Security Council under Chapter 6 or 7 of the UN Charter. Peacekeeping allows for the use of light military force to either institute or preserve order in support of peacemakers, comprised of diplomats and mediators who are engaged with disputants in negotiations to stop hostilities. *Peacekeeping* is generally not an activity associated with natural resources unless in a militarised zone, such as when an NRC calls on the state militia to intervene in a community-NRC conflict. In such instances, the state works with the NRCs on security issues, but the state is ultimately charged with the overall responsibility of co-ordinating that effort even if the NRCs hire their own security forces. *Peacemaking* typically refers to diplomatic activity with the goal of stopping open, armed conflict and achieving either a cease-fire or broad negotiated settlements (Aall, 2011). Furthermore, the 'order' peacemakers are aiming for is typically liberal, supporting the reformation or creation of a social-democratic state. It is based on achieving a limited or negative peace which is "based on the fragile equation of state interests, issues and resources, and often depends upon external guarantors" (Richmond, 2010, p. 18). The UN Department of Peacekeeping Operations unit (UNDPKO) represents the relationship between these terms and activities in Figure 5.1.

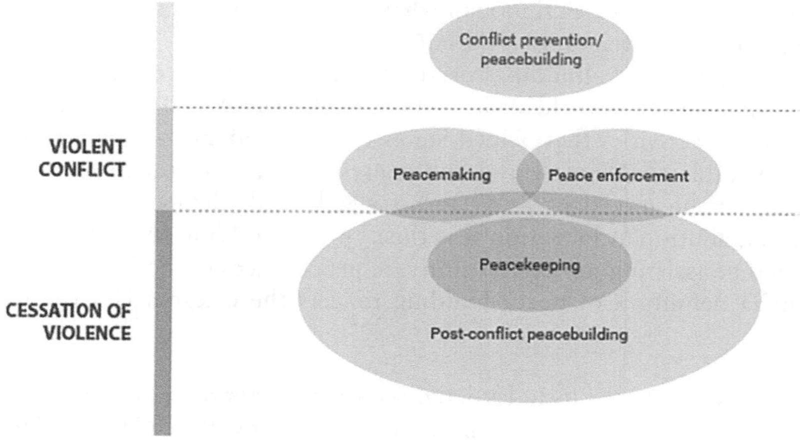

Figure 5.1 How Peace-Building is Related to Other Peace Concepts
Adapted Form: UNPKO

Peace-building includes a suite of activities involving actors from civil society, the business sector and advocacy groups (Jeong, 2000). These actors employ a wide range of strategies: helping disputants identify core and peripheral issues, assisting disputants in their own design of jointly held goals for both the short and long term and teaching disputants an ongoing mutual engagement process imbued with the qualities of integrity, non-violence and fairness. This book builds on the idea that *peace-building* strategies can be successfully expressed at the local level—even and perhaps especially when a conflict has not yet become physically violent. It is Galtung, Jacobsen and Brand-Jacobsen's (2002) and Lederach's (2003) perspective on the local applicability of peace-building activities which serves as further inspiration towards investigating their relevance in the NRC-community space.

Physical violence only breaks out in a minority of natural resource project sites around the world in any given year. However, most natural resource projects experience a range of less-violent yet still significant community-based conflicts at some point in their development or operation. Although positive peace and peace-building processes of conflict transformation are relevant in both sets of conflicts, this book is concerned with the larger group of non-physically violent NRC-community conflicts. Policy, NGO and research groups have covered physical violence, and natural resources are covered extensively elsewhere (*cf.* Amnesty International, IISD, UNDP).

This book proposes that NRCs are already employing versions of peace-building strategies to handle conflict with communities where both sustained and episodic, non-violent conflict is underway. However, the companies often do not label those activities as 'peace-building'. This book suggests that these activities might yield greater results understood within a paradigm of positive peace. Strategies and processes such as community consultation (Amat y León & Velarde, 2005), Free-Prior-Informed-Consent (Martin, 2007), Mine Development Agreements (Gibson & O'Faircheallaigh, 2010), participatory water monitoring (Atkins, 2008) and similar are consistent with peace-building strategies and an overall paradigm of positive peace.

Figure 5.2 represents a conceptual model for conflict transformation in this book, with the starting place as the *'Potential conflict trigger'*:

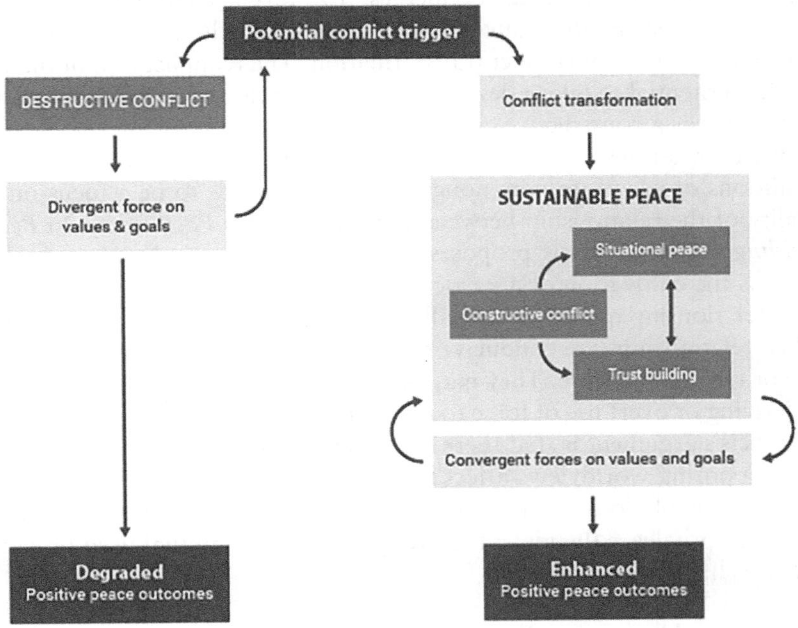

Figure 5.2 Positive Peace and Conflict Pathways

In other words, when there is a potential conflict trigger on an economic, risk or Human Rights aspect related to natural resources, the choice in peace-building terms becomes whether or not to respond to the conflict as a destructive force or a constructive opportunity for conflict transformation.

If two or more parties start with a potential conflict trigger and respond to it as a destructive conflict, the relationship between the parties to that conflict grows progressively confrontational. This potentially leads to increasingly polarised positions that separate the parties even further from agreeing on how to address the conflict. In those opposing positions, it is difficult to address conflicts successfully. This downward spiral leads to degraded positive peace outcomes.

Alternately, if parties respond to a potential conflict trigger as an opportunity for constructive change—for conflict transformation—the outcomes look much brighter. Conflict transformation emphasises the relationship between the parties as important to the overall conflict outcomes possible. In handling a conflict constructively, parties build trust and strengthen contextual/situational peace based on converging values and goals. The upward spiral results in enhanced or optimised positive peace outcomes.

Positive peace is not a static 'end goal' however. There are instances where parties handle a conflict is positively and positive peace outcomes are optimised, but then something happens or changes. Whether there is an incident, an argument between parties, a shift in previously agreed opinions—a potential conflict trigger again emerges. To prevent conditions of positive peace from degenerating into another destructive, the parties need to re-engage the process of conflict transformation. The reapplication of the process has potential to take a destructive conflict cycle and re-route the parties back towards a constructive cycle.

However, strategies and processes for practical steps towards creating conditions of peace are not enough. There also needs to be a focus on the quality of the relationship between parties. In *From Pacification to Peacebuilding* (2010), Francis proposes that the primary condition of positive peace is the cultivation of a particular quality of relationship between parties. Relationship quality is critically important to NRCs and communities. When relationships are conducive to peace, it means that they are not coercive or violent in nature. They may be intensively persuasive, but there is no underlying or overt use of force to maintain the integrity of the relationship.

Francis's argument is that there are two ways to view the world and that these opposing worldviews affect how people will enter into relationships. The way people look at relationships belongs in one of two categories: a view that privileges the idea of interdependence and mutual need or a view that sees life as a competition.

> Peacebuilding, as understood through conflict transformation, begins from the worldview in which interdependence is the point of departure, orientating [sic] people and institutions towards peacebuilding as cooperation, while the worldview that sees life as a matter of eating or being eaten leads to . . . 'pacification'.
>
> (2010, pp. 73–74)

The long-term benefit of the interdependence worldview is the focus on the quality, mutuality and continuity of a relationship needing adjustment in response to any number of conflicts during its life. The long-term benefit of the eat-or-be-eaten worldview can also result in the cessation of conflict, but control and violence are options to be exercised while people in the process are considered expendable instruments, useful only insofar as they help achieve goals. Applied in the context of natural resources, where natural resource leases may run anywhere from ten to 100 years, the 'long-term' view emphasises looking at the entire life-cycle of a relationship between an NRC and a community in addition to valuing the achievement

Table 5.1 Comparing Worldviews

Positive Peace	*Pacification or Negative Peace*
NOTION OF PEACE	
• Just relationships, mutual care. Shared economic and political power and responsibility. • Demilitarised world. Constructive conflict culture and systems. • Planet as home.	• Stability and hegemony. Top-down control, political and economic. • Strong military as guarantor of control. • Planet as resource to exploit
APPROACH TO INTERNATIONAL REGULATION	
• Principled and democratic (participatory)	• Conditional and instrumental
APPROACH TO CONFLICT AND CHANGE	
• Multi-level, bottom-up work; work of and in support of local actors • Nonviolent, constructive; achieving just outcome for all • Conflict Resolution to address human needs	• Top-down, hegemonic, interventionist • Military pacification 'if necessary' in own interest. • Win-lose orientation • Conflict Resolution to avoid destabilisation
APPROACH TO POWER, REALITY, PROCESS/OUTCOME, PEOPLE	
• Power as capacity to achieve things cooperatively • Process and outcome inseparable • All people are subjects and no one is expendable	• Power as ability to dominate • Process and outcome separate • Some people are instruments and may be expendable
VALUES	
• Common good • Respect and care for all	• Own success • Respect for power 'us' and 'them'
NOTION OF SECURITY	
• Interdependent	• Dominate or be dominated

(Table adapted from "From Pacification to Peacebuilding" Francis, 2010, p. 74)

of shorter-term goals. These two worldviews are represented Table 5.1 as 'positive peace' and 'negative peace', respectively.

This book privileges Francis's recommendation for genuine peace-building rather than for pacification as the perspective from which to evaluate the potential to achieve positive peace in the NRC-community space. History has repeatedly shown that when NRCs and their supporters, which sometimes include government bodies, prefer practices of 'pacification', such as the more metaphorically muscular, financially or legally persuasive methods of engaging conflict, then NRC-community conflict is not resolved in the long term and often results in recurring negative outcomes throughout the lifecycle of an NRC operation. Examples of these methods can be found in early community engagement activities at the Cerrejon mine in Colombia (Bond, 2009; Ringwood, 2011), where there was violent and forced resettlement, and in the history of mining at multiple sites in Indonesia, where environmental hazards were created that destroyed livelihoods, waterways and ecosystems (Ballard, 2001). Conversely, when mining companies and communities have chosen practices synchronous with long-term, non-violent peace-building methods, there has been greater success in realising acceptable outcomes from conflicts experienced during the lifecycle of a mine (Bichsel et al., 2007). Examples of these methods can be found in scholarship about the Tintaya *Mesas de Dialogo* in Peru (Barton, 2005; Echave, Keenan, Romero, & Tapia, 2004) and promising recent developments at the Three Gorges Dam in China (Wilmsen, 2016).

Finally, peace-building is an activity that can and does take place before, during and after a conflict of whatever size (Alger, 1999; Boulding, 2000; Graf, Kramer, & Nicolescou, 2007; Lederach, 2005; Vayrynen, 1999). Therefore, conflict transformation practices can intentionally create the conditions for positive peace by prevention as well as by helping disputants engage current conflicts or the aftermath of conflicts. This is because peace-building works at the cultural, structural and social levels of two or more groups who are experiencing conflict about opposed positions, interests and needs (Miall, 2011 [2004]). Since conflicts are always within distinct social environments, this chapter advances the idea that the social environmental context of NRC-community relationships is fertile ground for exploring how aspects of peace-building would improve the outcomes of those types of conflicts for all parties involved.

Admittedly, the history of natural resources projects in the 20th century alone reveals a legacy littered with outcomes that are not peaceful, such as involuntary resettlement, waterway pollution, significant health effects, poor labour conditions, grave environmental impacts, changing the contours of landscapes significant to Indigenous peoples and more. Communities in the Global South has borne the brunt of these effects. Consequently, it will become increasingly important for the 21st-century natural resources industries to develop the will and a holistic strategy towards both addressing these negative legacies and natural resources responsibly into the future. Peace-building practices of conflict transformation have potential to provide a vehicle by which to achieve these goals in co-operation with communities to deal constructively with the root causes of conflict and work on mending or improving relationships. Positive peace, then, is the endpoint towards which the transformation work is aiming and moving.

5.4 Positive Peace Paradigm

It is not enough to understand how the literature represents positive peace; it is also important to suggest a bridge towards practice. Paradigms could be that bridge between theory and practice, as well as being the potential foundation for CSR strategies. This section defines positive peace, describes a Positive Peace paradigm and evaluates what it offers as similar to and different from the three alternate CSR paradigms discussed in this chapter. The most distinctive difference is that a Positive Peace paradigm can incorporate other CSR paradigms, leading to improved conflict outcomes and less violence overall.

Following both Galtung and Lederach, a paradigm of positive peace is less about prescribing actions or listing a series of culturally or policy specific 'shoulds' and 'should nots' and more about cultivating an attitude both at the individual and at the group level. Positive peace focuses on outcomes beneficial to all because the process at arriving at those outcomes is inclusive, mutually co-created between stakeholders and retains mutual kindness at its core. The Positive Peace paradigm is different from the 'liberal peace' paradigm fashionable in international relations circles for the last 20 or more years (Chapter 3). "The liberal peace paradigm, views the development of democracy both as a goal of state-building and as a means to induce conflict transformation" (Galvanek & Mubashir, 2012, p. 81). In other words, liberalism equates democracy as a necessary pre-condition for peace. Zaum summarises the following characteristics:

> Across the literature, liberal peacebuilding has been used to describe external peacebuilding interventions that share several characteristics: first, they are conducted by liberal, Western states; second, they are motivated by liberal objectives such as responding to large-scale human rights violations or being conducted under an international responsibility to protect; and third, these interventions promote liberal-democratic political institutions, human rights, effective and good governance, and economic liberalization as a means to bring peace and prosperity to war-torn countries. Since the end of the Cold War, most peacebuilding operations have been characterized by a commitment to the promotion of these liberal values and institutions.
>
> (Zaum, 2012, pp. 121–122)

Zaum follows this description, citing major works by MacGinty and Richmond, to survey the relative lack of success of attaining peace or peaceful societies in periods following violent conflict and peacekeeping interventions, e.g., Cote d'Ivoire (ca. 2004) and Timor L'Este (ca. 1999). There are reasons for this failure: "the approach is laden with inherent contradictions, misses the specific socio-economic challenges of post-conflict countries, and exacerbates social and economic inequalities through marginalization and increased vulnerability to poverty" (Peace-building Initiative, 2009). Zaum concludes his comments on the liberal peace by saying that it does not sufficiently incorporate local culture or encourage local participation. Instead, he recommends looking at instances where peace-building has been successful. They have the structure of a hybrid peace, rather than a strictly liberal peace (Chapter 4).

As an alternative, scholars have begun exploring a hybrid peace as the preferred post-liberal concept of positive peace, as in *Hybrid Forms of Peace: from everyday agency to Post-Liberalism* (Richmond & Mitchell, 2012). In this volume, and in a related conference paper, hybrid forms of peace incorporate both international norms but also local customs (2012; Boege & Curth, 2011). Local customs are not unitary, nor are they static—they are constantly in flux. Additionally, they are inclusive of a wide variety of stakeholders, such as traditional authorities, women, group leaders or chiefs, affected community members as well as representatives from various levels of government. Finally, hybrid peace processes cannot be rushed according to political cycles or particularly Western standards of timeliness. The hybrid peace concept, and related peace-building practices, may have more potential than a liberal peace. Hybrid peace may indeed be useful to international actors, such as MNEs, who are in relationship with a wide variety of stakeholders in situations where natural resource company-community conflict is likely to emerge.

With an understanding of a Positive Peace paradigm, we now look at how to link the paradigm of positive peace to CSR. This book explores whether the paradigm of positive peace can function in one of two ways. The first way is to incorporate the other three CSR paradigms: Neoliberal Economic, Risk Management and Human Rights. Following the work of Masterman (1970) and Kuhn (1977), positive peace does not seek to supplant them but to provide a foundational paradigm that can prioritise and shape the use of the tools and frameworks that otherwise belong to the three influential paradigms described in the preceding chapter. They could ideally operate within an overall paradigm of positive peace (see Figure 5.3).

As an example of Masterson's reading of Kuhn, this construction conceptualises the relationship between the paradigms with positive peace in the following ways. In terms of the Economic paradigm, International Alert published that

> Peacebuilding . . . needs to be a comprehensive transformative process: . . . not as an adjunct to economic growth, but rather the function of economic growth in conflict contexts. It is also a process that intimately involves the private sector because of its core function in the economy.
> (2006, p. 78)

Regarding risk management, if violence and its outcomes can generally be seen as putting communities and businesses at risk in a variety of ways, then the use of peace-building processes—which, throughout the scholarship on peace, is resolutely focused on reducing and eliminating violence—can reduce those risks and improve the outcomes of using risk-based frameworks and toolkits. Finally, peace is inclusive of Human Rights: "elements in the culture

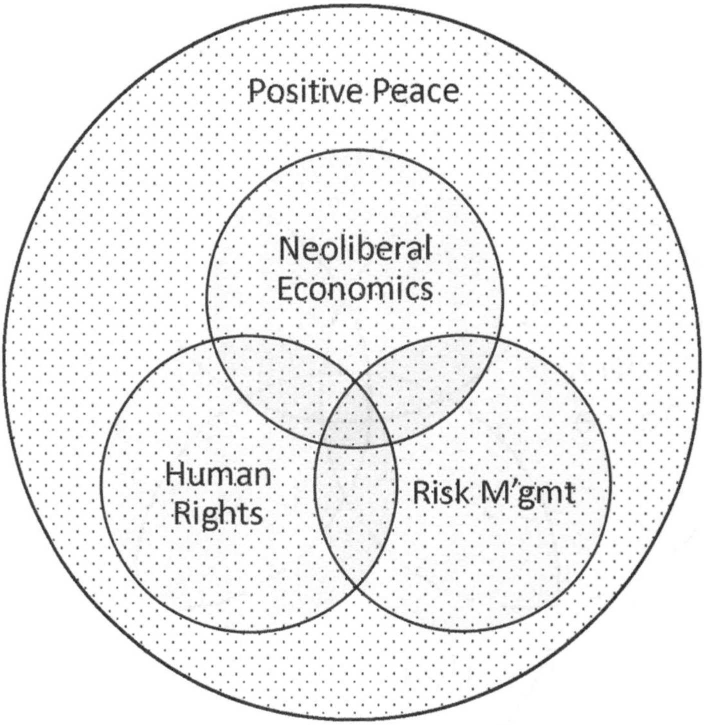

Figure 5.3 Positive Peace as a Foundational or Unifying CSR Paradigm

of peace paradigm . . . propose the replacement of hierarchical structures with equality values, understanding, tolerance, and human rights" (Fry, Bonta, & Baszarkiewicz, 2009, p. 24). Positive peace highlights a commitment to increased well-being, but not at the expense of the 'other', softening aspects of the Human Rights paradigm that can sometimes prioritise one person or groups rights over another's. The most unique aspect of the paradigm of positive peace is its ability to hold in creative tension the sometimes competing energies of the Neoliberal Economic, Risk Management and Human Rights paradigms in a way that prioritises finding non-violent or non-coercive solutions to those ambiguities and tensions.

A second, perhaps more convincing, way to conceptualise the relationship between the paradigm of positive peace and the other three paradigms is that they operate in an overlapping way. For practical purposes, different stakeholders within the NRC-community nexus will approach a conflict situation from within their own preferred paradigm. A CSR practitioner acting from within a Positive Peace paradigm would need to encourage processes and solutions that are acceptable to individuals operating from within these different paradigms (see Figure 5.4).

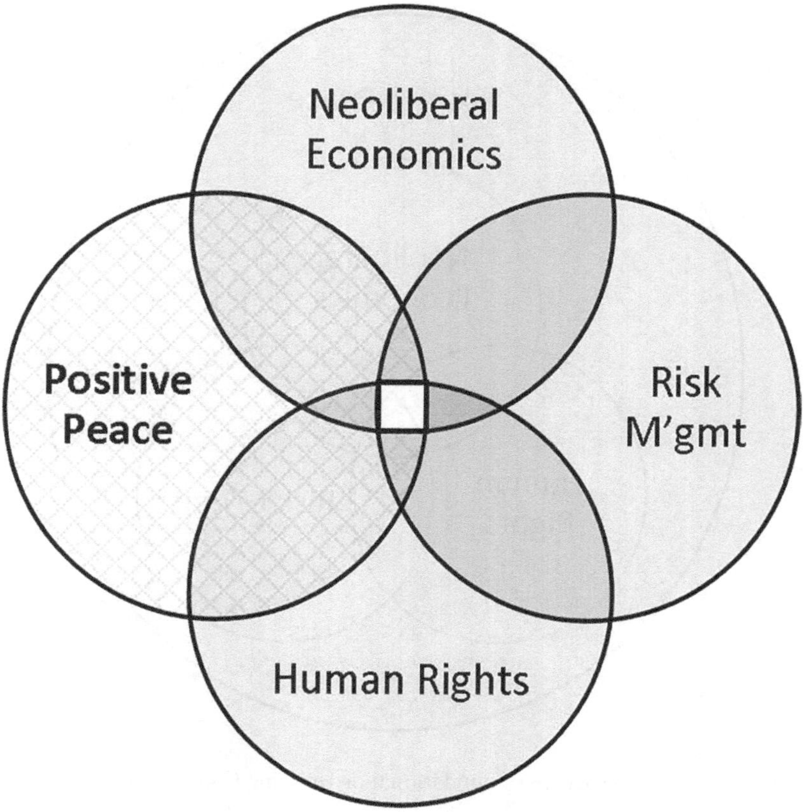

Figure 5.4 Positive Peace as a Complementary Paradigm

In this construction, the goal would be to find and enlarge the 'sweet spot' (*yellow circle, at the centre*) to support the relationship between the paradigms as described in the preceding paragraph. This 'sweet spot' would necessarily look different for each unique natural resources-company community conflict situation because they each have different characteristics. This construction, perhaps more so than the first one, would prioritise an emphasis on the quality of relationship between the parties as a central concern. An improved relationship would then increase opportunities to generate productive outcomes, including a combination of all four paradigms. Moreover, this model would allow more clearly for the consideration of other potential paradigms.

Comparing the two constructions suggests that they are both valid but at different times in a conflict cycle. The potential disadvantage of the first construction is that all parties to a conflict would have to agree—up front—that conditions of positive peace were jointly shared by all. In the heat of a conflict situation, this may not be possible, whereas it could be possible during an agreement-making period between an NRC and a community, as a statement of a goal held in common. A much larger program of research would need to be undertaken of NRC-community conflicts to test how these conceptualisations work in practice and with which CSR and/or peace-building methods. Within the scope of this book, however, it is enough to explore the degree to which a paradigm of positive peace has traction with CSR practitioners to determine whether it is feasible to pursue that larger program of research.

5.5 Why Make the Connection Between Positive Peace and CSR?

One purpose of exploring the paradigm of positive peace as a potential foundation for CSR strategies is to see if it can increase productive conflict outcomes. The word 'productive' refers to a range of beneficial conflict outcomes for most if not nearly all stakeholders in an NRC-community relationship. In business terms, Parker, Alstine, Gitsham and Dakin (2008) suggest that the word productive refers to value creation such as employee retention, increased NRC operational outputs and reduced human resource costs. Adding a social responsibility dimension to Parker et al.'s (2008) definition, the word 'productive' might also usefully refer to increased benefits for natural resources-affected communities. These benefits include but are not restricted to improved quality of life, infrastructure development, health care, education and training.

The word 'productive' has also had particular meaning in the peace and conflict literature since the mid-1950s. Three scholars highlight the term's positive aspects. Putnam (1994) summarises the inherent dynamism that characterises productive conflict between two or more stakeholders (*in the citation below:* 'groups') in the following way:

> Intergroup conflict is often characterized by an increased flow in communication between and within groups. Through engaging in controversy with another group, both groups can enhance their understanding of complex problems, broaden their perspectives on organizational life, and develop a foundation to manage differences.
>
> (Putnam, 1994, p. 285)

In other words, for a conflict to be productive means that it can harness the dynamic energy generated between stakeholders to achieve improved performance while co-creating innovative outcomes and solutions that would not be possible even in a static, harmonious, inflexible relationship. Bowman (2001) agrees and advances this position by suggesting that a conflict-free relationship leads to poor decision-making and sub-optimal outcomes for all parties. Respected peace scholar Schirch uses the analogous distinctions 'constructive' and 'destructive' to qualify the nature of conflicts in *Strategic Peacebuilding* (2004). She defines a constructive (productive) conflict as capable of addressing the needs of all involved and a destructive conflict as one in which communication has irretrievably broken down and violence is either immanent or active. Importantly, neither Putnam nor Bowman nor Schirch suggest that addressing conflict is either comfortable or easy to engage in a productive/constructive way. Nor do these authors advocate intentionally causing, manipulating or engineering circumstances of discontent to achieve an outcome. However, each cites a significant body of literature to indicate that productive/ constructive conflict, as opposed to unproductive/destructive conflict, has the potential to result in acceptable outcomes for the majority if not all parties who were engaged in the process.

In this book, then, the term 'productive' is preferred both for the scholarly reasons mentioned above but also because there is almost always an expectation of tangible material, financial and social outcomes from natural resources activities sought by both NRCs and communities. Examples include: generating positive cash flow, reducing organisational risk, maintaining or improving valuable aspects of a community's *status quo* in terms of socio-cultural heritage, employment opportunities and improved infrastructure. Table 5.2 illustrates this and compares productive conflict to its inverse.

The term 'unproductive' includes various forms of exclusion (*as above*) which have the consequence of diminishing how productive a conflict outcome can be considered, overall. If marginalised groups such as women, children, the elderly, Indigenous or disabled groups from a community are

Table 5.2 Illustrations of Productive v. Unproductive Conflict

Productive/Constructive Conflict	*Unproductive/Destructive Conflict*
Engagement of majority and minority groups throughout consultation and decision-making processes	Exclusion of women, elderly, children, Indigenous or marginalised groups from consultation or decision-making
Focus on long-term relationship building strategies that include short-term goals	Focus on short-term financial or production results with little to no long-term view
Intentional co-design of dispute resolution processes shared by company-community	*Ad hoc* or unilateral design of dispute resolution processes acted upon by one party at the expense of the other party
Mutually agreed outcomes (i.e. financial, material, social, cultural)	Predetermined outcomes set by one party without consulting the other party
High value placed on clear communication and the time necessary for it to occur	Communication channels have broken down; violence is immanent or active
Relationship between parties is dynamic, flexible, characterised by mutual regard and innovation	Relationship between parties is static, inflexible or even artificially harmonious

intentionally or unintentionally either partially or fully omitted from a conflict engagement process, then the capacity for that process to be considered productive is reduced by the measure that vulnerable people are under-represented in the process (Colchester & Ferrari, 2007; ICMM, 2010; Rio Tinto, 2010). Under-representation of marginal people increases the potential for negative outcomes for the parties who actually did engage in the process, no matter what side(s) of the conflict they were or are on (Martin, 2007). Increased negative outcomes (1) result from the process by which a conflict was handled and (2) affect the overall NRC-community relationship, diminishing the prospect for achieving positive peace. Examples of these negative outcomes can include: disease, unchecked in-migration, alcohol, drugs, sexual violence, environmental damage and cultural rupture. Each one of these symptoms of unproductive processes can become a conflict trigger.

Consistent with Richmond's (2010) fourth generation of Peace and Conflict Theory, a productive conflict successfully engages majority and minority group views from the design of the conflict engagement process through to the conclusion of the particular conflict situation between the parties. It also has the potential to improve the quality of the relationships between the local parties/groups and addresses the underlying issue(s) causing the conflict while contributing to the social, environmental and economic goals of the parties involved. Underlying a productive conflict engagement process from start to finish is the acknowledgement by all parties that any isolated instance of conflict is only one incident in a series of conflict encounters in the life of their relationship. The parties therefore recognise the iterative process regarding the way particular instances of conflict are handled can and will shape the ongoing relationship between the parties—setting up the initial conditions for how participants will view each other and the subsequent conflict. As in Figure 5.5, this iterative process can either result in a downward spiral that leads to greater frequency and more violent expressions of conflict, or it can result in an upward spiral that leads to the dynamic conditions of positive peace. The spiral can be represented alternately, as seen in the diagram.

Figure 5.5 Paradigm of Positive Peace

When a conflict engagement process is productive, transformative and by nature participatory, it is also peace-building (Richmond, 2010). Looking at conflict as a transformative opportunity rather than a threat is an intentional stance. Within the paradigm of positive peace, conflict is not seen only as a negative occurrence but, if handled properly, an occasion for positive change (Eurich, 2006). Lederach emphasises the following:

> Conflict is an opportunity, a gift . . . . Conflict can be understood as the motor of change, that which keeps relationships and social structures honest, alive and dynamically responsive to human needs, aspirations and growth.
>
> (Lederach, 2003, p. 18)

Lederach sees relationships and social structures as the locations where conflicts happen but also where peace is forged. His focus on relationships rather than on the content of any one conflict between parties allows the envisioning of a different future while finding a way to respond to a current conflict through constructive rather than destructive change (Lederach, 2003).

5.6 Conclusion

Although scholars and resource sector professionals have long recognised that natural resources activities often either precipitate or re-awaken conflict with and within proximate communities (Epps, 2003; Kemp, Owen, Gotzmann, & Bond, 2011; Zandvliet & Anderson, 2009), they have only begun to explore the potential for natural resources to contribute to ongoing conditions of peace at the community level as described in the second chapter on the literature linking business and peace. This book contributes to this newer body of knowledge by considering the NRC-community interface as a relatively new frontier for the application of peace practices and future peace research. In the next chapter, research data is presented and analysed to explore the level of traction a paradigm of positive peace could have in the CSR space in the natural resources context. Because a paradigm of positive peace is not directly linked to the use of legal means or threats and eschews physical, cultural or structural violence, it is uniquely suited to encouraging the development of peaceful relationships and outcomes from conflict between NRCs and communities.

Notes

1 www.un.org, [Accessed: 11 October 2010].
2 Proximate causes of violence are immediate precipitants or catalysts of violent episodes.

Bibliography

Aall, P. (2011). *Peace terms: Glossary of terms for conflict management and peacebuilding*. Washington, DC: USIP.

Alger, C. F. (1999). The expanding tool chest for peacebuilders. In H.-W. Jeong (Ed.), *The new agenda for peace research*. Ashgate: Sydney, Australia.

Amat y León, R. F., & Velarde, E. (2005). *Building stakeholder engagement through consultation*. Peru: Tintaya.

Atkins, D. (2008). *Participatory Water Monitoring: A guide for preventing and managing conflict*. Washington, D.C.: IFC.

Ballard, C. (2001). Human rights and the mining sector in Indonesia: A baseline study. England: MMSD.

Barton, B. (2005). A global/local approach to conflict resolution in the mining sector: The case of the Tintaya dialogue table (Master of Arts in Law and Diplomacy Thesis), Tufts University, Boston, MA.

Bellamy, A., Williams, P., & Griffin, S. (2006). *Understanding peacekeeping*. Cambridge, UK: Polity.

Bichsel, C., Dalby, S., Dama, A., Hagmann, T., Maurer, P., & Shiferaw, M. (2007). *Environmental peacebuildling: Managing natural resource conflicts in a changing world*. Bern, Switzerland: Swiss Peace.

Biskowski, L. J. (1998). Reason in politics: Arendt and Gadamer on the role of the eide. *Polity*, *31*(2), 217–244.

Blum, A. (2011). *Improving peacebuilding evaluation: A whole-of-field approach*. Washington, D.C.: USIP.

Boege, V., & Curth, J. (2011). *Grounding the responsibility to protect: Working with local strengths for peace and conflict prevention in the Solomon Islands*. Paper presented at the ISA Asia Pacific Conference, The University of Queensland, School of Political Science and International Studies.

Bond, C. J. (2009). Land, sacred sites and mining: Constructing dialogue to reduce conflict between transnational mining companies and indigenous/rural peoples. (Master of International Studies, Adv. (Peace Studies & Conflict Resolution)), University of Queensland, Brisbane, Australia.

Boulding, E. (2000). *Cultures of peace: the hidden side of history*. Syracuse, NY: Syracuse University Press.

Boulding, E. (1987). Learning peace. In R. Vayrynen, D. Senghaas, & C. Schmidt (Eds.), *The quest for peace*. London: Sage.

Bowman, R. F. (2001). Temptation #4: Harmony versus productive conflict. *The Educational Forum*, *65*(3), 221–226.

Brenes, A. (2009). Personal transformations needed for cultures of peace. In J. de Rivera (Ed.), *Handbook on building cultures of peace*. New York, NY: Springer.

Colchester, M., & Ferrari, M. F. (2007). *Making FPIC—free, prior and informed consent—work: Challenges and prospects for indigenous peoples*. Moreton-in-Marsh, UK: Forest People's Program.

Curle, A. (2000). Obstacles to peace. *Peace and Conflict: Journal of Peace Psychology*, *6*(3), 247–252.

Echave, J. D., Keenan, K., Romero, M. K., & Tapia, Á. (2004). *Dialogue and management of conflicts on community lands: The case of the Tintaya mine in Peru*. Peru: CooperAccion.

Epps, J. M. (2003). *Managing the social risk of mining*. Paper presented at the Mining Risk Management Conference, Sydney, Australia.

Eurich, H. (2006). *Factors of success in UN Mission communication strategies in post-conflict settings: A critical assessment of the UN Missions in East Timor and Nepal*. Berlin: Logos Verlag.

Francis, D. (2010). *From pacification to peacebuilding: A call to global transformation*. New York, NY: Palgrave Macmillan.

Fry, D. P., Bonta, B. D., & Baszarkiewicz, K. (2009). Learning from extant cultures of peace. In J. de Rivera (Ed.), *Handbook on building cultures of peace*. New York, NY: Springer.

Galtung, J. (1981). Social cosmology and the concept of peace. *Journal of Peace Research*, *18*(2), 183–199.

Galtung, J., Jacobsen, C., & Brand-Jacobsen, K. F. (2002). Peace: The goal and the way. In J. Galtung, C. Jacobsen, & K. F. Brand-Jacobsen (Eds.), *Searching for peace*. London: Pluto Press.

Galvanek, J. B., & Mubashir, M. (2012). Reflections on the CORE workshop: The potential of norms for conflict transformation. In J. B. Galvanek, H. J. Giessmann, & M. Mir (Eds.), *Norms and premises of peace governance* (Vol. 32, pp. 18–24). Tubingen: Berghof Peace Support and Institute for Peace Education.

Gibson, G., & O'Faircheallaigh, C. (2010). *IBA community toolkit: Negotiation and implementation of impact and benefit agreements*. Toronto: Walter & Duncan Gordan Foundation.

Gladwin, T. N., Kennelly, J. J., & Krause, T-S. (1995). Shifting paradigms for sustainable development: Implications for management theory and research. *The Academy of Management Review*, *20*(4), 874–907. doi:10.2307/258959

Graf, W., Kramer, G., & Nicolescou, A. (2007). Counselling and training for conflict transformation and peace-building. In C. Webel & J. Galtung (Eds.), *Handbook of peace and conflict studies*. London, UK: Routledge.

ICMM. (2010). *Good practice guide: Indigenous peoples and mining*. London.

International Alert. (2006). *Local business and the economic dimensions of peacebuilding*. -London: International Alert.

Jeong, H. -W. (2000). *Peace and conflict studies*. Burlington, VT: Ashgate.

Kemp, D., Owen, J. R., Gotzmann, N., & Bond, C. (2011). Just relations and company—community conflict in mining. *Journal of Business Ethics*, *101*(1), 93–109.

Korppen, D. (2011). Space beyond the liberal peacebuilding consensus—a systemic perspective. In D. Korppen, N. Ropers, & H. J. Giessmann (Eds.), *The non-linearity of peace processes*. Farmington Hills, MA: Barbara Budridge Verlag.

Kuhn, T. A. (1977). Second thoughts. *The essential tension*. Chicago, IL: University of Chicago Press.

Lederach, J. P. (1995). *Preparing for peace: Conflict transformation across cultures*. Syracuse, NY: Syracuse University Press.

Lederach, J. P. (1997). *Building peace: Sustainable reconciliation in divided societies*. Washington, DC: United States Institute for Peace.

Lederach, J. P. (2003). *The little book of conflict transformation*. Intercourse, PA: Good Books.

Lederach, J. P. (2005). *The moral imagination*. New York, NY: Oxford University Press.

Martin, S. (2007). *Free, prior and informed consent: The role of mining companies*. Victoria: Oxfam.

Masterman, M. (1970). The nature of a paradigm. In I. Lakatos & A. Musgrave (Eds.), *Criticism and the growth of knowledge*. Cambridge: Cambridge University Press.

Miall, H. (2011 [2004]). Conflict transformation: A multi-dimensional task. In B. Austin, M. Fischer, & H. J. Giessmann (Eds.), *Advancing conflict transformatoin: The Bergof handbook II*. Framington Hills, MA: Barbara Budrich.

Nelson, J. (2000). *The business of peace*. London: International Alert.

Parker, A. R., Alstine, J. V., Gitsham, M., & Dakin, R. (2008). *Managing risk and maintaining license to operate: Participatory planning and monitoring in the extractive industries*.

Parlevliet, M. (2009). *Rethinking conflict transformation from a human rights perspective*. Berlin.

Peacebuilding Initiative. (2009). *Economic recovery: Key debates and implementation challenges*. New York, NY. Retrieved from www.peacebuildinginitiative.org/index2ed1.html?pageId=1907

Putnam, L. L. (1994). Productive conflict: Negotiation as implicit coordination. *The International Journal of Conflict Management*, *5*(3), 284–298.

Richmond, O. (2010). A genealogy of peace and conflict theory. In O. Richmond (Ed.), *Palgrave advances in peacebuilding*. London: Palgrave.

Richmond, O., & Mitchell, A. (Eds.). (2012). *Hybrid forms of peace: From everyday agency to post-liberalism*. Hampshire: Palgrave Macmillan.

Ringwood, C. (2011). Afro-Colombian resistance in La Guajira. *Counter Punch*, 18 July 2011. Retrieved from http://www.counterpunch.org/2011/07/18/afro-colombian-resistance-in-la-guajira/

Rio Tinto. (2010). *Why gender matters: A resource guide for integrating gender considerations into communities work at Rio Tinto*. Melbourne.

Schirch, L. (2004). *The little book of strategic peacebuilding*. Intercourse, PA: Good Books.

UNPKO. (2008). *United Nations peacekeeping operations principles and guidelines*. New York, NY: United Nations.

Vayrynen, R. (1999). From Conflict Resolution to Conflict Transformation: A Critical Review. In H.W. Jeong (Ed.), *The New Agenda for Peace Research* (pp. 135–160). Sydney, Australia: Ashgate.

Webel, C. (2007). Introduction. In C. Webel & J. Galtung (Eds.), *Handbook of peace and conflict studies*. New York, NY: Routledge.

Wilmsen, B. (2016). After the Deluge: A longitudinal study of resettlement at the Three Gorges Dam, China. *World Development*, *84*, 41–54.

Zandvliet, L., & Anderson, M. B. (2009). *Getting it right: Making corporate-community relations work*. Sheffield: Greenleaf Publishing.

Zaum, D. (2012). Beyond the "Liberal Peace". *Global Governance*, *18*, 121–132.

6 CSR Practitioners and Peace?

This chapter presents examples of how CSR practitioners view the paradigm of peace in the natural resources environment. After establishing how peace could be conceived by CSR practitioners, the chapter presents examples of social and environmental outcomes within a peace-focused framework applied to natural resources industries at various stages of a project lifecycle. A practical framework is explained whereby the reader can analyse his or her own operations' activity similarly. Suggestions of how to encourage practice at all levels of an operation are woven throughout.

6.1 Overview

The primary question underpinning this book is: *how potentially useful is the application of a Positive Peace paradigm in the natural resources context?* The subsidiary question is: *how responsive are CSR practitioners to the paradigm of positive peace?* Using the conceptual, organisational framework on paradigms, described in Chapter 4, this chapter gives a better sense of whether or not a *paradigm* of positive peace is appealing to CSR practitioners as they choose or design strategies to support *conditions* of peace between NRCs and communities. Throughout the chapter are direct quotes from CSR practitioners who have each had between ten–30 years' experience in the natural resources sector. The country of their majority experience is indicated following each quotation.

This chapter presents examples from three natural resources industries: mining, timber harvesting and hydroelectric dams. The section on mining is the longest and based on a significant piece of original research. The reason to focus on one industry intensively here is to demonstrate how a peace-building paradigm operates at all stages of a resource project lifecycle. CSR practitioners and their managers, across other natural resources projects, can apply this peace-building paradigm to their projects analogously. Section 6.2 presents highlights from conversation with CSR practitioners in the natural resources industries to reflect how they approach their community-level work. Section 6.3, the centrepiece of this chapter, is a synthesis of how it is possible to frame CSR practice within a paradigm of positive peace. Section 6.4 presents several NRC-community conflicts CSR practitioners identified as exemplars of a Positive Peace paradigm. Following, section 6.5 provides a way to analyse conflict narratives from within a paradigm of positive peace. The chapter concludes that a paradigm of positive peace, framed carefully, indeed has traction with CSR professionals who handle conflict emerging within NRC-community relationships.

6.2 Heard on the Ground: CSR Practice in the Natural Resources Context

In principle, NRCs' CSR practitioners work with communities at all stages of resource development from exploration through to post closure. CSR practitioners come from all walks of life and all backgrounds. Some originally trained as engineers or environmental scientists; others have political or education sector experience, and another group comes from the development context. All, however, display an aptitude for working with people. This section describes how CSR practitioners themselves view their best work in natural resources-affected communities across the lifecycle of natural resource projects.

CSR practitioners understand their role to listen to community members' aspirations and concerns and serve as a conduit to communicate these views to their corporation. "*One thing you need to allow is the community to have a voice. I had the ability to listen and make the people who were telling their stories feel that I was taking them seriously*" *(Argentina)*. The CSR practitioners then relay to the community the content of whatever corporate action required in response. "*You have to tell people, from the very beginning, what you are going to do for them and what you expect them to do for you*" *(Ghana)*.

CSR professionals report being the first point of call for handling community-level complaints, negotiating access to land and water resources and working out the details of development and philanthropic assistance. CSR practitioners often work together with professionals from other business units:

- compensation teams that decide how much to pay for land/water resources;
- environmental teams that monitor the effect of natural resource related activities on flora, fauna and human health; and
- human resources teams that make decisions about whom to hire as employees, contractors, and supply chain providers.

Effective CSR practitioners either have or rapidly develop acute cultural sensitivities and spend more time 'in the community' than in their offices. "*You have to be accessible. Get out of the corporate environment; you can't be behind the fence*" *(Papua New Guinea)*, and "*It's about being very visible in the community, communicating as often and as transparently as possible*"

(Philippines). Ineffective CSR practice results from: lack of authority to implement solutions to particular issues, and insufficient corporate funding/support to accomplish the tasks to which they have been assigned and inadequate training and staff. When the technical and financial departments of a natural resources operation do not provide enough internal support for adequate, pro-active attention to the social impacts of natural resources, additional complications arise.

Three factors shape the activities of CSR practitioners in the natural resources sector. The first, and most influential, is their own personal experience and training. The second factor is corporate policies and procedures. Whether working directly for corporations or in some kind of consultancy or advisory capacity, CSR practitioners couch their community-level advice within the parameters of the corporations with or for whom they work. The third factor is the range of international best practice, toolkits, guidance notes and regulations regarding the natural resources industry. However, most practitioners find the broad array of sometimes competing claims of these instruments to be a usage barrier.

To address community-level concerns most efficiently, CSR practitioners describe developing their own systems to balance (1) their responsibility to the corporation and (2) their commitment to doing as much as possible for the communities affected by natural resources operations. Sometimes their systems work well, with practitioners able to handle conflict situations effectively and institute a range of development programs that positively changed the lives of people affected by natural resources. However, there are others times when, despite 'all best efforts', practitioners report that CSR strategies collapse. At this point, community level conflict may escalate with operation-halting and community-distressing consequences, or worse.

Certainly, room remains to improve CSR outcomes from NRC-community interactions. However, most CSR practitioners are familiar with tools such as corporate policies, international guidance and best practice frameworks and use them in their work. If anything, there may be too many policies, procedures, guides and frameworks. Nevertheless, CSR practitioners acknowledge that the implementation of this suite of CSR tools did not always ensure successful CSR outcomes. Given the volume of material on CSR practice and the uncertain results, perhaps the natural resources sector would benefit from another approach to conceptualising CSR practice rather than the application of more tools and rules.

6.3 Starting Places: Using the Tools and Rules Available

Before making suggestions to change how CSR practitioners operate, it is worth understanding how they frame their work. Many CSR practitioners tend to contextualise their roles within the three influential paradigms discussed in Chapter 4: Risk Management, Human Rights or Neoliberal Economics. The Risk paradigm is the most prevalent of these three. When asked how they view risk, one practitioner said, "*We take a very conservative, risk-averse approach. We don't want to inflame a situation" (Indonesia).* Another said, *"I am looking for the implicit assumptions that guide [natural resources company CSR practitioners]. Do they see the community as a risk or an asset?" (Peru).* A second practitioner explained, *"We had a process called non-technical risk assessment" (China).* Another echoed, *"Risk management is a language that works very effectively in the resources sector" (South Africa).* A government regulator of social risk reflected on the Impact Benefit Agreements (IBAs) in Canada as an effective way to lower the risk profile for both communities and NRCs. *"All parties are seeing that it is to their advantage to go to the negotiating table rather than go to the courts" (Canada).* One CSR practitioner was critical of not having an explicit paradigm out of which to work, *"Just because you have all the standards and guidelines, it doesn't all necessarily hang together" (Australia).* In other words, this practitioner identified that it is not sufficient to have CSR frameworks, standards and guidelines in order to achieve conflict-minimising outcomes. There needs to be some way of linking these tools of practice into an effective and coherent whole.

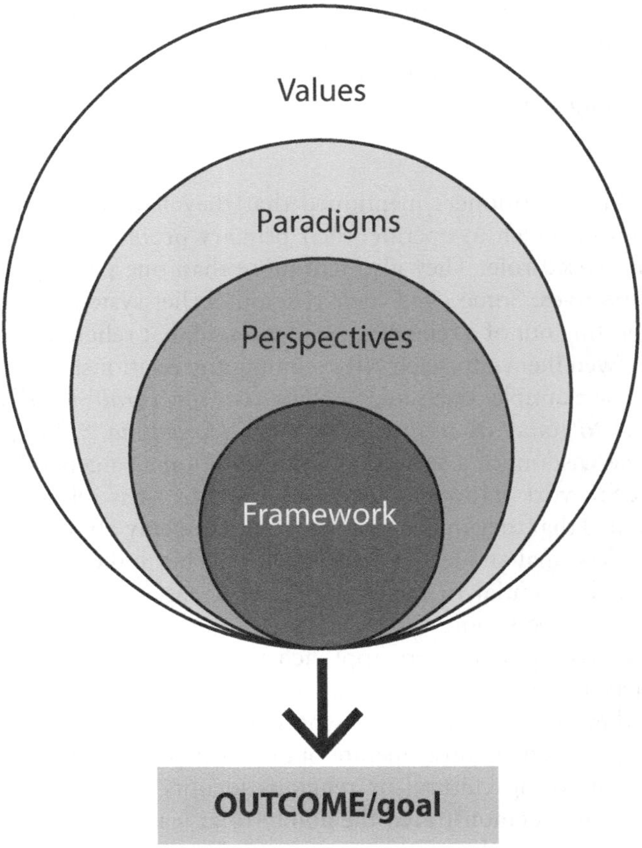

Figure 6.1 Relationship of Classifying Concepts to Outcomes

Most CSR practitioners do not approach their roles paradigmatically, but rather from the perspective of their current role and position. A perspective is nested within an over-arching paradigm. CSR practitioners working for NRCs define their perspective by the role they play in achieving certain objectives within the corporate structure. CSR practitioners contracted, but not employed, by NRCs are able to view and critically evaluate CSR opportunities from different perspectives as necessary (e.g., NGO, legal, civil society, government, corporate). Whereas CSR practitioners working for NGOs and academic research centres balance various perspectives in their work. On the one hand, these professionals work for organisations with perspectives privileging sustainable development. On the other hand, they work with NRCs as a *"critical friend" (Australia)* to create *"transformational" (Peru)* change. These perspectives can be complementary but may also compete, or appear to lack integrity. One practitioner summarised the conundrum as follows:

> *NGOs often look at natural resources companies as bad, [our organisation] doesn't take that perspective . . . Working with industry has risks. We work with companies—develop a position. So the community perception of [our NGO] is coloured because the company is paying for the work . . . it's very difficult to engage communities if you are seen as being bought by a company.*
>
> *(Australia)*

Some CSR practitioners mentioned that they had more than one perspective out of which to operate: their primary professional role and their community-based role. They also had more than one paradigm informing these perspectives. Some cited their religious belief system as a paradigm. Those operating out of a religious paradigm said that religion was meaningful and allowed them approach NRC-community relationships in more than one way. For example, one said, *"I think that the Torah*[1] *is full of wisdom that speaks to today as well as yesterday" (Argentina)*. This practitioner drew on the wisdom of a sacred text and tradition as a general foundation for their CSR work. However, those informed by their religious paradigm also cautioned that they might hesitate to speak openly about that paradigm in their professional and leadership capacities. They indicated that religious language had potential to make communications with colleagues and/or community members more complex.

To summarise, practitioners approach their work in several ways. CSR practitioners referred to 'risk management' as the primary paradigm out of which they operate. For those who conceptualise their work from an individual perspective, most operate out of their primary professional role. Those with a strong cultural or religious identity (e.g., operating out of those paradigms) demonstrated the ability to at least evaluate or approach CSR work from more than one perspective and/or paradigm simultaneously.

6.4 Approaching Peace

This section investigates whether either the word or the concept of 'peace' has traction with CSR practitioners in the natural resources context. If it does, the book argues it would then be possible to expand the potential for using a paradigm of positive peace to inform CSR practice. A Positive Peace paradigm, used alone or in combination with the other influential CSR paradigms, would represent a true paradigm shift. A paradigm of positive peace emphasises balance in addressing the concerns of NRCs and community stakeholders in the distribution of natural resources benefits. As described in Chapter 4, the Neoliberal Economic and Risk Management paradigms prioritise the concerns of the company; the Human Rights paradigm prioritises the concerns of the community and individuals, while the Positive Peace paradigm prioritises the *relationship* between companies and communities. The paradigm of positive peace is a true shift in the highest values with potential to accommodate, more fairly, all stakeholders to natural resources operations, thereby (1) reducing provocations for violent or structural conflict between them and (2) increasing potential for long-term, sustainable and productive conflict outcomes overall.

Before assuming that 'peace' is simply an under-acknowledged concept with transformational potential, it is important to establish whether or where the concept of *peace* occurs in the natural resources context, specifically, in environments where there are not episodes of active or recent physical violence. Of the CSR professionals interviewed in the research project underpinning this book, 34% had encountered the word or concepts relating to peace in the natural resources context, whereas 21% had heard '*peace*' used by colleagues as specifically relevant to developing country contexts. Only one respondent was specific in saying that *"[peace] comes up in post-conflict contexts" (Lao PDR)*. For the 55% who had either encountered or had colleagues who used the word or concept of 'peace', this question did not seem entirely out of context for CSR practice. However, the topic seemed surprising to the majority of these practitioners, despite their ability to give an immediate example of the kind of contexts and situations where they or their colleagues in developing countries had encountered the word or concept of peace.

Of the 45% of practitioners who had *not* encountered the word 'peace' in their work, most laughed when I initially mentioned the word. When I probed why the word 'peace' was humorous, it was because the practitioners had never even thought of using that word in the natural resources context. The word's mention provoked surprise and often the reiteration of the word as a query, "*Peace?*" Then there would be a pause, followed by a reflection. During that reflection period, often respondents would locate either what peace means for them or what contexts they thought were appropriate in which to mention peace.

Within the group who found the word 'peace' comical, 40% thought that the word 'peace' was not helpful in the natural resources context at all. These respondents all took the question seriously and couched their objections contextually within a Realist framework (*see:* Chapter Three) as something that the state should address.

> The word 'peace' for me is about civil unrest within the citizenry not necessarily between governments.
>
> (Australia)

> Peace is often associated with macro-economic political processes. If you talk to mine managers they'll tell you they don't care about peace, peace is for the country.
>
> (Ghana)

> I don't think that there would be a knee jerk reaction against it necessarily but I think that the connotations about the word that we all derive from our reading of the newspapers and headlines is that it is a word bandied about in terms of 'Peace in the Middle East' or fairly far out examples like that.
>
> (Tanzania)

Of these respondents, only one said that the word 'peace' was on the "*blacklist*" *(Canada)* in the natural resources context; the others could see that the word might have traction in particular in-country contexts where civil unrest was a real and present risk (e.g., South Africa, Peru or Papua New Guinea).

6.4.1 Responses to Peace

The initial mention of the word 'peace' with CSR practitioners tended to provoke polar responses. This was a curious finding, because 'peace' typically evokes feelings of equanimity and calm. Significantly, some CSR practitioners indicated that the word 'peace' evoked discomfort or conflict between parties. "*[If you say] we are striving towards peace or peaceful engagement, you are implying that there isn't peace and that we are in a situation of conflict" (South Africa).*

Those who view 'peace' as a helpful word or concept offered the following. Peace evoked 'trust' for 14 respondents and 'justice' for six respondents. Two quotations are illustrative. *"Peace for me is intertwined with justice" (Chile)*, and "*Trust is the key word and the other one . . . is justice [. . .] the beauty about trust is that you cannot achieve it by an IFC performance standard. You can only achieve it by your own behaviour" (PNG)*. The word 'peace' suggested *"achieving a balance" (Tanzania)* and dealing with differences through *"mutual respect" (South Africa)*. It also suggests that *"effective self-interest" (Australia)* is at work between the parties, that everybody can see that they will 'get' something out of a consensus-building process. Peace is conceptually a welcome *"alternative" (Canada)* to talking about conflict and an indication of the *"absence of violence" (New Zealand)*. The paradigm of positive peace is implicit in community work, and it underlies some frameworks and good practice guidance. One respondent said,

> It means finding solutions and dealing with difference [in ways that] are not going to be inherently undermining basic human rights: rights to a livelihood, to not be killed, to have somewhere to live, for the children to have a future.
>
> (Australia)

Nevertheless, 'peace' remains a problematic word or concept to some. The reason practitioners gave is that the word 'peace' surfaced discomfort and statements, perhaps assumptions, that engineers, technical people and executives would not even think about peace as relevant to the work they do. "*I can't see Marius Kloppers*[2] *signing up for peace [laughs]. Not in our lifetime" (South Africa)*. Furthermore, it was a word or concept some respondents associated with the resolution of particular conflicts, such as with *"artisanal miners" (Canada)* or *"people clearing old growth forests to grow crops" (Indonesia)* or in non-Western contexts where there is either more civil unrest or, in the opinion of eight respondents, outright war. One South African respondent said,

> [Peace] is such a strong word and it relates to an extreme scenario, if we have to talk about peace then we have to talk about war. I don't think that natural resources companies ever see themselves as at war with communities or that communities see themselves as at war with the natural resources companies.
>
> (South Africa)

Finally, a few respondents thought that peace implied *"tension" (Australia)* or negatively charged *"compromise" (Australia)* in terms of losing ground or bargaining power.

The line of questioning shifted from asking about how respondents thought generally about peace in the natural resources context to whether or not using language or concepts related to peace would encourage cooperative conversations between NRCs and communities experiencing conflict in their relationship. One point of view indicated that peace was "*incompatible with raw capitalism*" *(Australia)*. In other words, executives might not be able to uncouple peace from the global scenarios such as war and large-scale conflict in order to see it as *"relevant to their bottom line" (Chile)*. Another point of view is that it is difficult to relate the concept of peace to the military regimes located around the world that control state-owned natural resources projects. "*[W]hen you are dealing with a natural resources company that is heavily supported by a by-and-large military government, or secured by people that the government has either sponsored or authorised, some of the nice words don't get you anywhere" (Canada)*. Finally, some practitioners saw the word '*peace*' as difficult to use in technical, financial or scientific circles. However, there are analogous words; these are grouped according to theme in Table 6.1:

Table 6.1 Analogous Expressions for 'Peace'

Theme	*Examples*
Peace	"Peaceful co-existence", "Peacefulness", "Peaceful", Peaceful communities"
Harmony	"Harmonious/ness", "Harmony", "Living and working in harmony"
Benefits	"Win-win", "Reciprocity", "Mutual benefits", "Partnerships", "Beneficial gain"
Sustainable Development	"Social Responsibility", "Sustainable Development", "Social License to Operate"
Positive	"Progress", "Unity", "Positiveness", "Well-being", "Proactive"
Mutuality	"Common ground", "Collaboration"
Legacy	"Enduring value", "Legacy"

Follow-up research could test whether or not a discussion of other CSR concepts, such as Social License to Operate (SLTO) or Free Prior and Informed Consent (FPIC), would elicit a similar group of words as in Table 6.1 or whether these analogous words are specific to the conceptualisation of peace.

Among CSR practitioners who were reluctant to use the word 'peace' and who preferred analogous language, there was consensus that the word 'peace' as a starting place was more evocative or helpful than a focus on 'conflict' or 'violence'. This is despite 'peace' having *"baggage due to its association with over-zealous activists" (Australia)*. This group of practitioners stated, *"the word 'conflict' also has baggage" (Canada)*, which was much more inhibiting, overall, towards achieving a positive outcome from NRC-community conflicts. At a minimum, one practitioner conceded that NRCs would understand that *"you don't want to cause conflict; you don't want a war to break out because of you" (Indonesia)*.

The third set of comments—from those who saw peace as either a potentially or actually helpful word or concept—was creative in nature and evoked positive, pragmatic responses about the possibility of using peace in the natural resources context. One respondent *(Australia)* supposed that 'peace' is something you could embed in a memorandum of understanding (MOU) at the beginning of a project's life and that 'peace' would grow in meaning between the project and the community as the project matured. Some were particular about using the word or concept of 'peace' after the initial stages of establishing a natural resources project were over, during the longer operations phase. This group viewed 'peace' broadly as a way to engage conflict mitigation strategies and arrive at a collaborative end-state of a functioning community or society. 'Peace' is the kind of word or concept you use *"when you are learning how to live and work together when you have differences" (Brazil)*. In other words, practitioners saw 'peace' as a helpful word or concept for NRCs to use when fostering and building community-level relationships.

The final set of responses reflected larger cultural reasons of why 'peace' might not come up in natural resources contexts. Some Australian and Canadian practitioners said, *"peace doesn't come up in civilised societies"*. Without labouring the choice of the word 'civilised', a number of practitioners thought it unusual to invoke the concept of peace within what are generally considered peaceful societies. In other words, *"[peace is] too heavy handed . . . [it] brings up images of much more violent conflict than we have in Australia"*. However, practitioners agreed that in all cultural contexts, *"there will be no peace with communities who don't want their natural resources developed" (Tanzania)*.

6.4.2 Be Careful About Your Definitions of Peace and Conflict

Respondents emphasised the necessity of being clear on use of terminology. The three words that repeatedly emerged as needing contextual definition were these: 'peace', 'conflict' and 'violence'. Having discussed 'peace' above, practitioners' understanding of 'conflict' and 'violence' is briefly addressed here. One practitioner joined their understanding of the two words. They wryly commented that they would reserve the use of the word 'conflict' only for expressions of physical violence, as robust disagreement was normal in the CSR space in the natural resources context.

> I have just come from [a site] last week where we had 39 shooting incidents and 14 fatalities. I think there is conflict there. We use our careful social science training to make these hairline judgments.
>
> (UK)

However, most other respondents separated the two words when juxtaposing them to 'peace'.

Some practitioners saw conflict, not violence, as the opposite of peace, which is the inverse of how peace scholars understand conflict. One practitioner put it this way: *"peace being the opposite of conflict, companies can put a dollar figure on conflict because it disrupts their operations" (Papua New Guinea)*. Others has a view in line with peace-building scholarship, with violence as being the antithesis of peace. *"[Peace] would not be the absence of conflict, like people would still discuss things and have disagreements, but the absence of violence" (Australia)*. Another practitioner said, *"[peace] comes up for me in terms of the alternative to violence" (New Zealand)*. One practitioner expressed a general understanding of the word 'conflict'. *"Conflict is a symptom—not a disease . . . All long-term relationships have conflict" (Canada)*. Some practitioners see conflict as a tool to generate action from stakeholders to an NRC-community disagreement.

> Greenpeace Argentina recommends that communities never ever talk with a natural resources company, to stone the vehicles, etc. Greenpeace knows it's possible for communities to be persuaded so they try to stop the conversation from ever taking place.
>
> (Argentina)

> If I was a community, sometimes what you are trying to do is create conflict. You are trying to create a situation where an organisation needs to respond and act.
>
> (Peru)

> Earthworks is responsible for the 'No Dirty Gold' campaign—their tactic was to increase conflict and contention in order to solve the problems, they found in this instance that increasing conflict had the result of motivating people to do something and clarifying the situation.
>
> (Canada)

One NGO respondent summarised that no matter how the words 'peace', 'conflict' and 'violence' are defined, the question NRCs needed to ask themselves about their community engagement strategies was this: *"How do you insure that conflict is not happening? That you are not contributing to conflict?" (Madagascar)*

6.4.3 Upon Further Reflection

Having established that practitioners from around the world have a basic understanding of what peace is, the next step is to understand whether or not practitioners could use the concept of 'peace' in their work. Most CSR practitioners were able to come up with at least one scenario in which peace could be used as a word or a concept—whether explicitly or with the analogous set of words in Table 6.1. The range of scenarios include the following:

- where there are security concerns; in open conflict environments (e.g., war);
- to characterise a situation or relationship (e.g., as being peaceful); during industrial relations negotiations;
- where there is conflict between NRCs and communities over water; when developing local procurement strategies with SMEs;

- to discuss global natural resources contexts; within a collaborative community planning framework;
- as a way to use language that emphasises a commitment to resolving and issue or problem; and
- as a way to identify processes in situations where reconciliation is needed.

There are enablers and barriers to using the concept of or word 'peace'. Enablers include the reality that peace is not a completely foreign word or concept, either to NRC employees and contractors or to communities, *"although they might look at it differently" (Papua New Guinea)*. Another practitioner suggested that when you *"foreground trust" (Papua New Guinea)* in an NRC-community relationship, peace is the end result. Still another said that *"peace, as a concept, is less judgmental and more facilitative" (UK)* especially if you *"provide pragmatic examples and not just talk about peace in the abstract" (Australia)*. Barriers and challenges include the language of peace itself and the *"perceptions" (Chile)* it elicits. Context is important. In situations that are highly militarised or where there is rampant government corruption, peace was seen as less likely to be of immediate relevance—although definitely needed in the long term. There also needs to be *"credibility" (UK)* as well as an *"openness and a willingness" (Papua New Guinea)* by both NRCs and communities to use the word or concept of peace. Finally, the success or failure of using 'peace' can depend on the possibility of breaking down a conflictual situation into manageable *"action steps" (Indonesia)*. However, most respondents surmised that if CSR practitioners can adjust their use of the word or concept of 'peace' to fit their context, it had the potential to enhance outcomes from the CSR strategies that are used to handle NRC-community conflict.

6.5 Summary

Just over half of the practitioners reported encountering 'peace' in the work that they do. They were definitionally and contextually careful about how the word and concept of 'peace' is constructed in the natural resources context. Once constructed carefully, however, the majority of practitioners were then able to take the next step to allow that positive peace had potential as a foundational paradigm for determining how to choose the most appropriate perspectives and frameworks for effective CSR practice, especially in handling conflict situations between NRCs and affected communities. The general consensus was that peace invokes a number of valuable and related concepts, such as justice, trust, reconciliation and harmony. *"Peace represents an opportunity [especially] in . . . situations where nothing much else has worked" (Australia)*. Despite a range of opinions on how a peace paradigm could be introduced, the majority of practitioners thought it has real potential to augment productive outcomes from NRC-community conflict.

Although the sample size is limited, the practitioners were encouraging about peers using 'peace' in their work.

Nevertheless, it is important to acknowledge the minority CSR practitioners felt that NRC workers, especially at the executive, financial and technical levels, might respond negatively to the use of peace in the natural resources context. Practitioners were cautious about 'peace' as an imprecise word or concept without pragmatic outcomes or actionable business steps. Practitioners sceptical about the use of the word and concept of peace did agree that NRC-community conflict continues to happen despite the proliferation of guidelines, tools, and standards during the last 20 years. Consequently, there was consensus amongst all practitioners that there is still room for improvement in the CSR space. Further, to the extent that there is a Kuhnian paradigm shift, practitioners said defining certain concepts more clearly (e.g., structural violence and positive peace) would address the potential for scepticism about the paradigm of positive peace in the natural resources context. Perhaps because peace has an ability to encourage people to think *"laterally" (Papua New Guinea)*, a paradigm of positive peace might emerge as a new way to underpin existing frameworks, standards, guidance notes and toolkit to address conflicts.

Throughout the interviews, practitioners offered 65 scenarios as illustrations (Table 6.2), with varying degrees of detail, indicative of a paradigm of positive peace. The scenarios were offered in response to questions asking practitioners to imagine or reflect on what peace between NRCs and communities might look like—even if it was not labelled as such. The range of scenarios across the Americas, Africa, the Asia-Pacific and Eastern Europe was geographically diverse. They include examples from across the full range of project lifecycles and represent both developed and developing

Table 6.2 CSR Practitioners' Suggestions of Places Where Positive Peace Has Been or Could Be Encouraged

Country	*Country*
Australia	Mongolia
Azerbaijan	New Zealand
Bolivia	Nicaragua
Canada	Papua New Guinea
Chile	Peru
Colombia	Philippines
Ecuador	Solomon Islands
Fiji	South Africa
Ghana	Tanzania
Guatemala	Timor L'Este
Indonesia	Turkey
Madagascar	USA
Melanesia	Venezuela
Mexico	West Papua

country contexts. The significance of the breadth of these scenarios cited by practitioners is that, when they were able to define peace in their own way, conceptualising peace in the natural resources context was not limited to war zones, where scholars and policy makers have tended to focus. Nor was peace in the natural resources context limited to far-flung corners of the world with limited prior contact to natural resources and/or the West. In other words, the practitioners were able to able to see the paradigm of positive peace as applicable in a variety of situations and did not appear to reflect the limits on its potential to increase productive conflict outcomes (Chapter 2). The following chapter looks at a series of cases where CSR practitioners demonstrated an ability to view conflict situations through the paradigm of positive peace

Notes

1 The Torah is Judaism's most important text. It is composed of the Five Books of Moses and also contains the 613 commandments (mitzvot) and the *Ten Commandments*. The word "Torah" means "to teach".

2 Marius Kloppers was the CEO of BHP Billiton at the time of the interviews for this book.

Bibliography

Amat y León, R. F., & Velarde, E. (2005). *Building stakeholder engagement through consultation*. Peru: Tintaya.

Anglo American. (2012). *SEAT toolbox, version 3*. Anglo American: London.

7 Learning to 'See' Within a Peace-Focused Paradigm

This chapter presents examples of social and environmental outcomes within a peace-focused paradigm applied to natural resources industries at various stages of a project lifecycle. A practical conceptual model provides an analytical method to re-envision cases as described by CSR practitioners. Using the conceptual model and applying to their own situation, the reader can learn to analyse their own operations' activity similarly.

7.1 What Might 'Positive Peace' Look Like in the Natural Resources Context?

This chapter presents cases from four natural resources industries: mining; oil and gas; timber harvesting; and hydroelectric dams. CSR practitioners and their managers across natural resources projects can apply this peace-building paradigm to their projects analogously. The presentation of cases on mining is the longest and based on a significant piece of original research. The reason to focus on one industry intensively is to demonstrate how a peace-building paradigm operates at all stages of a resource project lifecycle.

All nine cases are consistent with a paradigm of positive peace. The stories represent both geographic diversity as well as how they epitomise creative examples of conflict transformation within a peace-focused paradigm. They also represent developed and developing country contexts. Each case was described in response to the following question: "Whether the word 'peace' was used or not, can you recall a CSR conflict in a non-war context which had the outcome of more peaceful relations between your company and affected communities?" The way the practitioners presented each case demonstrates that it is possible to view the potential for a Positive Peace paradigm to encourage productive conflict outcomes.

It is important to 'hear' directly from CSR practitioners what a paradigm of positive peace looked like to them. The cases are presented *verbatim* and then analysed using a conceptual framework. The cases demonstrate that practitioners were able to describe a conflictual situation in a way that did not emphasise the negative or 'worst case' aspects of these NRC-community relationships. Analogously, practitioners were able to describe the conflict situation as a glass half-full rather than half-empty opportunity. This subtle shift in emphasis proves that it is indeed possible to look at community-level conflict, in non-war-affected regions, without relying on the negative outlook embedded in the three dominant CSR paradigms: Risk, Economics and Human Rights (Chapter 5). Instead, the practitioners responded to the question about peace by emphasising structures, situations and relationships that are non-coercive and harmonious in nature to achieve productive outcomes consistent with a paradigm of positive peace.

There are a few caveats in the presentation of these stories. First, in protecting practitioners' identities, personal and site-specific details have been altered. Second, practitioners mentioned Tintaya (Peru) as an outstanding example of the concept of peace being enacted in the natural resources context. The case has already been well documented and linked in a tangential way to positive peace (Amat y León & Velarde, 2005; Barton, 2005; Echave, Keenan, Romero, & Tapia, 2004; Oxfam, 2003; Rangan, Barton, & Reficco, 2006); therefore it will not be recapitulated here. The third caveat is not to be seduced into thinking that once the parties have achieved peace, the relationship no longer needs attention. The cases presented recount success stories supporting the conclusion that a *paradigm* of positive peace emphasises CSR strategies supportive of *conditions* of peace between NRCs and communities. However, it does not mean that these situations have remained stable. In other words, even though these cases represent various examples of the kind of CSR responses that fall within a paradigm of positive peace, peace is a journey—not a destination. Because human relationships are continuously in flux, it is important to actively maintain the relationships between the NRCs and the communities in order for conditions of peace to endure.

Finally, those familiar with NRC-community conflict may recognise other scholars have written about some of these cases to highlight themes including, but not limited to, environmental concerns, economic consequences, Human Rights, security issues and social license to operate. It is ancillary to the scope of this book to compare how practitioners viewed these cases to how other scholars have described them. The purpose here is to take the cases at face value as described by practitioners and look at these otherwise different cases through the lens or paradigm of positive peace. In so doing, there is increased potential to make connections and look for overall characteristics linking these cases within a larger set of data that might be missed by focusing on a more fine-grained, or thematically limited, analysis.

As you read the cases, keep in mind Banfield's conflict typology (Table 2.4) as well as Lederach's (see Figure 2.1) and Nelson's (see Figure 2.2) identifications of which actors have responsibility for particular peace-building activities. The goal is to determine how these cases serve as examples of the paradigm of positive peace. To recapitulate (Chapter 4), the term 'paradigm' is:

> a generally accepted or widely shared set of concepts, assumptions, values and practices that constitute a way of understanding [. . .], a practical model for how to think through or handle a particular class of problems, rather than as a set of explicit rules we might follow
>
> (de Neufville, 2010, p. 1014)

with the capacity to

> 'frame language, meanings and relationships' (Wilkinson-Maposa & Fowler, 2009, p. 33) by 'guid[ing] acts and behaviour'.
>
> (Jonker & Pennink, 2010, p. 26)

From the *insider's* perspective, practitioners identified these cases as exemplifying a paradigm of positive peace. If these cases can be classified together within one paradigm (rather than separated by risk, Human Rights or economic paradigms), it would then be possible to identify more cases as examples of a paradigm of peace. Companies can construct their own practical model for how to think through or handle a particular class of problems using the paradigm of peace as a lens. When CSR practitioners use a peace paradigm to frame language, meanings and relationships using the toolkits, guidance notes and voluntary initiatives already in use by CSR practitioners in the natural resources sector, it is possible to increase productive outcomes from conflicts with a root cause in one or more types of violence.

Within the paradigm of positive peace, it is vitally important to identify and address conflicts at all levels, including the level of any root cause for the conflict. The typology below represents three levels at which conflicts are typically analysed are:

1) ***Root causes***—(*foundational issues*) pervasive factors built into structures, situations and relationships that contribute to violence. These are commonly categorised as structural, cultural or physical according to Banfield's typology (*see: Section 1.3.2*).
2) ***Proximate causes***—(*symptoms*) factors that are the immediate precipitants of violent incidents and are symptomatic of the root causes but are not actually the root causes.
3) ***Triggers***—(*flash points*) single acts, events or the anticipation thereof that set off or escalate violent conflict.

This categorisation allows practitioners to work at a structural level towards isolating and then supporting conditions of positive peace rather than simply addressing individual symptomatic conflicts with potential to re-emerge periodically. The typology helps practitioners avoid the mistake of thinking that if they handle a conflict at either the trigger or proximate level that it has been conclusively resolved.

Once identifying the source of community-company conflict, the next stage of analysis is to determine how conflict outcomes are illustrative of 'peace' from an *outsider's* perspective. This analysis stems from the paradigm of positive peace in line as described in Francis's (2010) typology (Table 5.1).

- A focus on the quality of the relationship between the parties
- Non-violent methods are used to affect conflict outcomes
- No threat of legal force is evident
- Processes of handling the conflict and the outcome are inseparable
- Co-operative conflict handling occurred
- Multi-level, bottom-up work happened

In terms of this narrative analysis, I would expect that many people operating from within the Positive Peace paradigm would provide a broadly similar analysis. However, other people might describe these conflict outcomes differently, perhaps even significantly so.

7.2 Cases From the Full Project Cycle in the Natural Resources Context

Case 1: Malaysia—Operation Phase (Timber)

There was a poor community that lived in a forest near Sarawak. The people have a subsistence living on close to or below $2/day. Education is not a priority and most residents in this community were illiterate and had only basic numeracy skills. The community depended on the forest to meet their subsistence needs but also to supply a livelihood. There are not many other sources of income in the region except agricultural and small handicrafts. Families in desperate situations are forced to turn to illegal activities harmful to themselves and the viability of the next generation. These activities attract police raids, heavy judicial penalties and fines the families are not able to withstand.

One way people manage to earn a living is to engage in the practice of illegal logging and selling the timber on the black market to companies and countries without strong environmental or Human Rights records. The perversity of this situation is that the deeper the community members go into the forest to engage in illegal logging, the more they are reducing the footprint of the forest on which they depend for firewood, edible plants, timber for houses and furniture, and habitats for animals that supply their protein.

A non-profit environmental organisation became aware of this community and wanted to intervene on their behalf to teach them sustainable timber harvesting practices according to REDD+ principles. They served in a CSR capacity by establishing a trusting presence within the community. The NGO served as an intermediary between the Malaysian government, firms that wished to purchase the timber and the community. The de facto CSR practitioners began teaching the community how to appropriately log timber, mark it as 'theirs' using alpha-numeric codes, and trained several members of the community how to keep a register of which families had farmed which pieces of timber, and sold for an appropriate price on the open market to reputable companies and countries. They also taught the community how to replant trees and nurture saplings to provide ongoing income for themselves and the next generation. The community did so well, they were able to use their increased income and livelihood stability to improve community dwelling spaces and establish a primary school for their children.

Root causes and types of violence indicated:

Structural Violence: unaddressed poverty and lack of education contributed to poor choices available to the community

Proximate causes (conflict characteristics):

Sporadic police raids designed to stop the illegal logging

Triggers:

Potential trigger: the illegal logging threatened the very livelihoods and well-being of the community that the activity was trying to address

Corporate Actor:

Non-profit CSR practitioners (local NGO)

Outcomes indicative of conflict transformation and a paradigm of positive peace:

The CSR practitioners were able to work with the community to identify a lack of training in appropriate timber harvesting practice. They were able to teach the community appropriate forest management practices in line with REDD+ principles. The community was able to lift itself out of abject poverty and provide a brighter future for themselves and their children.

Case 2: Canada—Expansion Phase (Hydroelectric Dam)

Canada is a land covered with abundant water resources including a myriad of riverine systems. In order to harness the power of these rivers for power production, Canada has built around 600 dams to provide a reliable source of electricity. However, there not all the communities affected by dam construction experience only benefits.

Two communities of First Nations people has lived for thousands of years near Lake Winnipeg, the 7th-largest lake in the world, and the largest watershed in North America. The eco-system is in disarray due to drainage, farming, fertilisers and poor water management practices. The complexity and scientific uncertainty of these systems is overlaid with the diverse and divergent government, businesses, and communities with competing needs makes for a very difficult situation.

The First Nations peoples, Cree and Ojibwe, have rights over the use of water and environmental resources all of which have cultural significance. The First Nations people and the European descendants have framed the history of the region very differently. Differential memory is the foundation of conflict over who has the right to use the natural water resources. The Canadian government and private industry see Lake Winnipeg as part of the Nelson Drainage Basin that extends from Canada into Minnesota and the Dakotas (USA). Whereas, the First Nations people remember a history of trying to share the resources, including a brisk trade in beaver pelts, only to find that the Europeans abused their generosity. Based on this history, the First Nations people doubted it was possible to achieve their preferred goal of social reciprocity rather than social responsibility as the hydro-electric project expands.

Hydro engineers wanted to expand the use the aquatic resources of the Nelson River, part of the Nelson Drainage Basin (NDB), to generate electricity. The problem for the communities is the way in which the Nelson River Hydroelectric Project is developing, would change the nature NDB. A CSR practitioner was engaged to assist the NDB engineers come to an agreement with the Cree and Ojibwe Nations about a possible way forward for the project. His approach was to reach backwards to reach forwards. His approach is to respect and work with history. For the NDB engineers, there is no holistic sense of history for the region, whereas the full sweep of history imbues the communities around the project. Differential memory became a huge dilemma. The parties needed to arrive at a mutually written story or the differential memory would continue to grow and create problems.

The CSR practitioner made a decision not to force the processes around problem solving in the space between people, groups and organisations. His insight was that people do not act according to their self-interests but where they perceive their self-interests lie. Therefore designing a conversation between stakeholders in conflict, means that the structure of a conversation or a dialogue matters—if the structure is wrong, the outcome will be wrong. You might win your points, with an inappropriate structure, but you will also get important people off side that will fuel conflict down the track. In these circumstances, social license sounds and feels more like a permit than genuine reciprocity.

The stakeholders agreed to engage in a back-ended conversation about how to negotiate the way in which they would make explicit their implicit values. In other words, the practitioner assisted them in talking about how to engineer a conversation that allows the problem to be addressed by all parties. The underlying principle, consistent with a peace paradigm, is that relationships are assets. When relationships go wrong, they do not go to zero they become a liability. Climbing out of the negative space becomes really tough.

In working with the community-based stakeholders, the CSR practitioner encouraged them not to argue with the approach of the 'evil' corporation, but then say, 'what are you really trying to accomplish here? Where are the exit ramps? How does this approach achieve successes without creating more problems along the way? How does each party understand closing a deal? How long is it going to take? How many other people will it involve?' The practitioner encouraged the community to make their process tactile and use role-plays.

A critical factor of moving two parties closer to an agreement is to think about time ahead of time—before starting the conversation. It limits the stunt-pulling. The CSR practitioner made sure to have milestones along the way. There needed to be opportunities to re-commit or exit. The more they were able to keep the clock going, with alarm bells at regular intervals, the more likely they would get to the end of the conversation together. The second critical factor the CSR practitioner used was to know the community involved—he made sure everyone had ownership of the process from the beginning to the end—as equal partners. In this way, the CSR practitioner exercised tremendous leadership.

The practitioner explained that the most important insight is that it is not necessary to get two or more parties to an agreement to agree to the WHY of sharing an end goal in common, just to get them to agree on the goal (for whatever reasons are interior to their group). The idea is to fill the negative space with positive islands of possibility. You will never bring two banks of a river closer together, but you may fill the river with stepping-stones. In this instance, the First Nations communities and the NBD project were able to negotiate a way forward for the expansion of the hydro power project.

Root causes and types of violence indicated:

Structural and Cultural Violence: pre-existing tensions between First Nations communities and descendants of European settlement in the region resulting from differential memory

Proximate causes (conflict characteristics):

Simmering conflict between the First Nations communities and the NBD project which was changing the eco-system of the Winnipeg Lake area

Triggers:

Proposed expansion of the hydro-electric dam system

Corporate Actor:

External CSR consultant

Outcomes indicative of conflict transformation and a paradigm of positive peace:

The CSR practitioner led the First Nations communities, in particular, in understanding new ways to negotiate the terms of the expansion so that the outcome of the project would be culturally and environmentally appropriate. It was not important how they came to terms with the natural resources project, but that each set of stakeholders was able to articulate and satisfy their needs for a shared resource.

Case 3: West Papua—Exploration/Pre-Construction Phase (Oil and Gas)

In the early days, before anything was built, there were pre-existing tensions between villages proximate to the site. One village group, in particular, was very aggressive. Compounding the existing tensions was how local people perceived the distribution of benefits from the extraction project. The operation was to be built on one side of the bay and the villages on the other side felt that they were not being adequately compensated. Their perception was that more was being done for the villages living closer to the plant. Furthermore, one village was being relocated; which they supported because the company provided them very high standard accommodation, a school, a mosque and a church. Villages on the other side of the bay felt that they weren't receiving comparable benefits. Consequently, a great deal of work went into trying to resolve that situation as well as to manage potential in-migration before it happened; which was successful.

Couple that situation with the fact that from early exploration it was very important to keep the Indonesian army and Special Forces out of the area. They wanted in because they make money out of providing

'protection' for the operation from disgruntled villagers. The Special Forces, called the green mob, are feared and hated by villagers because they are ruthless and cruel. The company understood this and put in place ways of keeping them away, which involved agreements and setting up local processes to persuade them or demonstrate to them that they weren't needed.

The CSR team devised one particular innovation to establish a secure facility without resorting to the 'green mob'. This innovation had the result of creating conditions of peace both inside and outside the fence. The company put into place a community-based security policy. In other words, security team members were recruited from all the local villages to be security guards. The company trained them, gave them uniforms, and hired them as the fence security. The basis for the idea is that a villager is not going to attack his brother doing security detail on the gate. The army and professional security companies hated it. They kept saying the West Papuans cannot provide adequate security, the usual kind of stories about the lack of capacity and trainability of Indigenous people; but it worked. There have been no conflicts with the villages and there is an up-and-running operation.

This is a significant success story about a process that resulted in peace between villages as well as between the company and the villages. The situation had the potential for an entirely different outcome, where the situation could have easily degenerated into a bloodbath, as was seen at Aceh in the 1990's. In that instance, and as a counterpoint to the story above, to secure their facility, ExxonMobil hired and turned a blind eye on the practices of Indonesian Special Forces (the 'green mob')[1].

Root causes and types of violence indicated:

Structural and Cultural Violence: pre-existing tensions between villages proximate to the site

Proximate causes (conflict characteristics):

Compounding the existing tensions was how local people perceived the distribution of benefits from the project

Triggers:

Potential trigger: the Indonesian army and 'special forces' threatening to have a presence in the area

Corporate Actor:

CSR team

Outcomes indicative of conflict transformation and a paradigm of positive peace:

The CSR team devised one particular innovation to establish a secure facility without resorting to the 'green mob'. This innovation had the result of creating conditions of peace both inside and outside the fence. The company put into place a community-based security policy. In other words, the company recruited security team members from all the local villages to be security guards. The company trained them, gave them uniforms and hired them as the fence security thereby increasing community level peace for all.

Case 4: Chile—Construction Phase (Mining)

There was a situation in Chile where a mine needed to construct a water storage facility, due to its topographic situation, and was facing the potential of running out of water during drought periods. Complicating the water security issue was the local farming community, of half a million people, that lived below the mine site. They also faced climatic water variability. The question was: how can this mine site increase its water security without exacerbating a simmering conflict between the mine and the farmers over water availability, especially during dry periods?

The answer ended up creating a situation of peace although, initially, it did not look likely. The solution was for the mine to enter into an arrangement with the local community. The mine would build a water supply dam for storage which, most of the time, would be used for agricultural irrigation. However, they made an agreement the water, under particular conditions, would be made available to the mine site during the worst of the drought. The community benefit was that, most of the time, the agricultural community had greater access to water than it would have without the water storage facility. The company's view was that the water storage facility represented a kind of insurance policy. In other words, the business case for it was not around investment in infrastructure to increase production, it was an effort to address to potentially problematic vulnerabilities: water security and the social license to operate.

Root causes and types of violence indicated:

Structural Violence: inadequate government involvement to adjudicate claims for water between business and local communities

Proximate causes (conflict characteristics):

Simmering conflict between the mine and the farmers over water availability

Triggers:

Potential trigger: the mine needed to construct a water storage facility

Corporate Actor:

CSR team, Environmental team and General Manager

Outcomes indicative of conflict transformation and a paradigm of positive peace:

The answer ended up creating a situation of peace when the mine entered into an arrangement with the local community. The mine agreed to build a water supply dam for storage, which would be used for agricultural irrigation. However, the company and the town agreed that the water, under particular conditions, would be made available to the mine site during drought periods. The community benefit was that, most of the time, the agricultural community had greater access to water than it would have without the water storage facility.

Case 5: South Africa—Expansion Phase (Mining)

A community in South Africa lives near a platinum operation. There were issues around the community opposing further drilling for a license project, an extension of an existing mine. In trying to understand why the community was publicly opposing the license, and stopping the drilling from happening, the company engaged the various stakeholders through two Section 21A companies. These companies speak on behalf of the community and manage the community's interests in relation to the mine. However, the situation was escalating and people were going out to the site to march, in a very provocative way. The CSR team realised that the first thing needed was a mechanism to manage the public protests by understanding why the situation had escalated. This was particularly concerning because, in this instance, the existing stakeholder platforms were obviously not succeeding in preventing expressions of community discontent.

What the three-person CSR team did was to talk to the various stakeholders, directly, to find out why the existing platforms were either not working or were insufficient. The answer clearly indicated that the community was not happy because the Section 21A companies were not communicating well with the communities nor where they giving them sufficient feedback about the needs and concerns that were supposed to have been brought to the attention of the mining company. Therefore, the communities did not know what was going on nor were their needs being addressed. This was compounded by the fact that the Section 21A companies were not comfortable saying, on the community's behalf, that the mine was not doing enough for them. Adding to the communication problems, the traditional leader was being difficult and was not representing the community's interests either. He was unwilling to be present at the any meeting that local government officials would also attend, a situation the Section 21A companies were supposed to help mitigate.

The answer resulting in peace between the stakeholders, as well as between the stakeholders and the company, was to create various structures and platforms with which people would be happy. In addition to that, the company increased the capacity of the Section 21A companies by teaching them how to do community engagement better. This skill training also addressed an issue with the executives of the Section 21A companies who had insufficient financial management knowledge to understand, for example, the financial statements that they were supposed to report back to the community.

Root causes and types of violence indicated:

Structural Violence: Section 21A company was not serving the structural role as an effective mediator

Cultural Violence: The traditional leader was being difficult and not representing the community's interests

Proximate causes (conflict characteristics):

Community members were going out to the site to march in a very provocative way

Triggers:

Potential trigger: expansion of the mine without community consent

Corporate Actor:

Three-person CSR team

Outcomes indicative of conflict transformation and a paradigm of positive peace:

The resulting peace between the stakeholders, as well as between the stakeholders and the company, resulted from the creation of various structures and platforms with which people would be happy. In addition to that, the company increased the capacity of the Section 21A companies by teaching them how to do community engagement better.

This skill training also addressed an issue with the executives of the Section 21A companies who had insufficient financial management knowledge to understand, for example, the financial statements that they were supposed to report to the community. These interventions resulted in community level peace.

Case 6: Venezuela—Operations and ASM (Mining)

The case of the mine was about the presence of Artisinal and Small Scale Miners (ASM) who were constantly on a mining lease without permission from either the company or the government. The company wanted an assessment of the situation so they called the CSR practitioners in to assist with the situation. The CSR practitioners put their cards on the table, they went in with a certain perspective and position. The CSR practitioners expressed their commitment as advocates for poor people and their livelihood sustainability. Their condition for doing the assessment was to come up with an idea for a solution that is not going to cause further distress.

The assessment revealed that people were angry at the government of Venezuela because, in their view, the gringo company was stealing their national birth right. The other thing was when they were displaced by the government to make room for the mine the people, who lived on the property and had the means to do so, were able to relocate somewhere else. Those left behind were the poorer people. They were less able and less literate and more vulnerable to manipulation by opportunists. Recognising those facts was very important. It was these people who turned to ASM as a last resort in terms of a livelihood. They also turned to violent protest to engage the company, since nothing else had worked. For example, the ASM miners had kidnapped the camp manager and were throwing rocks at the loaders and the machinery, especially during periods when geologists were digging trenches to prevent the ASM miners from entering the property. In a last ditch effort to keep the ASM miners out, the company had resorted to hiring armed guards who eventually used their weapons on individuals who were illegally trying to access the property. There was also just a high level of tension in the community which resulted in emotional as well as physical violence.

The CSR practitioners had a preliminary meeting with the communities dependent on ASM. They went into the community at the invitation of one of the groups. The community sat them in chairs in the middle of the room, and rounded up all the women and old men who were left in the village, since the younger guys were out mining—illegally—on the property. This began a year and a half process of listening to the community, which had an ameliorative affect. This process resulted in greater overall communication because the CSR practitioners wrote up versions of the reports they were giving to the mining company and shared the edited versions, in Spanish, with the community members. The CSR practitioners therefore became conduits of information and to some extent mediators. Part of the solution, therefore, was being prepared to take the time to understand what the situation was, and be as responsive as possible even though the CSR practitioners didn't have any power or authority. They were able to build confidence and trust and then take advantage of those opportunities to change things or encourage the company to do things a little bit differently. However, more work needed to be done in order for the situation not to deteriorate again.

To help devise a long-term solution and achieve peace the CSR practitioners recalled the wisdom in two stories from the Hebrew Bible. In the book of Leviticus there is a passage of scripture about putting part of the field aside, and leaving the gleanings so that the poor could come and gather enough grain to feed their families. 'When you reap the harvest of your land, do not reap to the very edges of your field or gather the gleanings of your harvest. Leave them for the poor and for the foreigner residing among you (Lev 23:22)'. The second biblical reference comes from the book of Genesis (41:41–56; 47:13–24). In this story, Joseph—a Jewish man—was elevated to the position of manager for Pharaoh. Part of his mandate was to consolidate Pharaoh's assets. Ahead of a seven-year famine which Joseph prophesied, Joseph was tasked with filling granaries with seven years' worth of food. During the last year of the drought, people were coming to Joseph and willing to give up title to their land for food. Joseph accepted transfer of title to the land to Pharaoh. According to one of the commentaries, Joseph told the farmers his rationale. He wanted to keep the Jewish people together as a community and would resettle them into the urban centres so they could be fed more easily. After the famine, he wanted them to go back to their lands and continue to farm them as they had always done but they would now pay some sort of tax to Pharaoh for the use of the land. The important part of this story is this concept of maintaining the integrity of the community and recognising that in removing them from their place, it was necessary to be able to restore their livelihoods in a holistic way.

Without actually mentioning the source of the idea, the CSR managers suggested were able to make the following suggestion which led to the restoration of conditions of peace for the community and peace between the community and the mine. It was revealed in the community consultation that the fundamental source of the problem at this stage was in regard to accessing prospective ground. The mining company had taken over the piece of property that the miners used to work on. The government had provided alternative areas, but they were far away. It was clear that they were not very good. Taking inspiration from scripture passages cited above, the CSR practitioners suggested setting aside a portion of the mining lease, near where the ASM community lived. They allowed them to mine, keep their community whole, and—with the increased communication facilitated between the mining company and community—eliminate the violence both within the community and between the mining company and the community.

Root causes and types of violence indicated:

Structural & Physical Violence: the National government had sold the natural resources rights to a large multinational without community consultation and only poor people, who couldn't afford to move, were left

Proximate causes (conflict characteristics):

ASMs were constantly on a natural resources lease, without permission from either the company or the government

Triggers:

ASM miners kidnapped the camp manager and threw rocks at the loaders and the machinery. Initial company response was to hire armed guards who shot at the ASMs

Corporate Actor:

CSR team

Outcomes indicative of conflict transformation and a paradigm of positive peace:

Part of the solution meant taking the time to understand what the situation was and be as responsive as possible, even though the CSR practitioners did not have any power or authority. They were able to build confidence and trust and then take advantage of those opportunities to change things or encourage the company to do things a little bit differently. However, more work was needed in order for the situation not to deteriorate again. The CSR practitioners suggested setting aside a portion of the natural resources lease, near where the ASM community lived, to allow them to mine, keep their community whole and—with the increased communication between the natural resources company and community—eliminate the violence both within the community and between the natural resources company and the community.

Case 7: South Africa—Operation Phase (Mining)

A major mining company had a lease which was located close to two communities. The situation was such that every time the mine needed to detonate a blast, the mining company had to relocate, repeatedly, communities of 1000 people. It was very much a contractual process. The mining company sent buses and food, and said for example at 2 pm you will all leave your houses, we will blast, and when it is safe you will come back. There was no kind of peaceful process or open dialogue, it was just 'we'll pay you to move.'

"That degenerated pretty quickly into a bad relationship. It just promoted a culture of resentment where the communities would ask for more money whenever the company wanted to move them, because that was the basis on which the company was talking to them. Then people would be like, 'oh, they are extorting us.' But the company created that problem.

"To change the situation, a social responsibility department of 10–15 people was created to manage this situation. They were in constant communication with the community and the tribal leaders. It was their dialogue that diffused the situation and eventually successfully relocated the entire village, permanently. This created conditions of peace between the community and the mining company.

Root causes and types of violence indicated:

Structural Violence: natural resources company set up a structure of paying community members to move, temporarily, every time they needed to blast in exchange for compensation

Proximate causes (conflict characteristics):

A culture of resentment developed between natural resources company and community

Triggers:

Potential trigger: communities might refuse relocation next time a blast needed to be detonated

Corporate Actor:

Social responsibility team

Outcomes indicative of conflict transformation and a paradigm of positive peace:

A social responsibility department of ten–15 people was created to manage this situation. They were in constant communication with the community and the tribal leaders. Practitioners engaged in dialogue that diffused the situation and eventually successfully relocated the entire village permanently. This outcome created conditions of peace between the community and the natural resources company.

Case 8: Indonesia—Operation Phase (Mining)

There was a mine that in very early years had strained relationships with the local communities. The owner is an American company that would bring people in from Nevada who had never even had a passport before they were sent in to manage a mine in Indonesia, which was not a terribly sensitive cultural process. Additionally, the mining company did a poor initial job of involving local people; they did not understand that they needed to hire local people to help negotiate difficult permitting processes as well as to develop really good and robust CSR processes at the local village level. This resulted in high community tensions that could have become as tense, obstructive and violent as the situation at Minahasa which ended up being prematurely closed.

However, in this instance, the company took a more strategic view and they listened to the communities. They became respectful of local customs and powers. Over time, the company developed an effective investment program around shared futures, schooling, sharing of benefits, and respecting local structures to do that. I think it's fair to say now that at our site, the senior people say that the most effective defence they have against terrorism is that all of the local villages look after them. Anybody wandering in would be identified and known. It seems to me that this is a really good example of peace in the mining context. It's not to say that they don't have disputes occasionally, and that they haven't had issues, but I think that there is this underlying feeling of being safe in one another's company.

Root causes and types of violence indicated:

Structural and Cultural Violence: the Indonesian government sold a natural resources lease to a foreign national company without community consultation by either party

Proximate causes (conflict characteristics):

The company failed to hire local people to help negotiate difficult permitting processes as well as to develop really good and robust CSR processes at the local village level

Triggers:

Potential trigger: high community tensions that had potential to become obstructive and violent

Corporate Actor:

CSR team

Outcomes indicative of conflict transformation and a paradigm of positive peace:

The company took a strategic view and they listened to the communities. They became respectful of local customs and powers. Over time, the company developed an effective investment program around shared futures, schooling, sharing of benefits, and respecting local structures to do that. These interventions contributed to an underlying feeling of peace, being safe in one another's company.

Case 9: Queensland, Australia—Closure (Mining)

In Queensland, Australia's Bowen Basin there are dozens of coal mines. Blair Athol is one of the oldest mines in Queensland. It's about 20 minutes outside of the town of Clermont which was originally established as a farming/agriculture community but developed a coal industry beginning in the 1960s. A few years ago it was announced that Blair Athol was going to close and the community became very depressed about that prospect since it had built a lot of the town infrastructure which was subsequently transferred to shire council. The community was becoming very concerned, made worse by the fact that the mining engineers could never give a date for definite closure nor could they adequately communicate with Clermont their plans for a new mine to take its place. Consequently, there was a fair bit of mistrust in the community around what they were doing and what their intention was, which led to a situation that was definitely unpeaceful between the community and the mine at the point at which a new mine was proposed.

When the Clermont mine was announced as the successor to Blair Athol, the community came up with a rather heavy list that they gave to Rio Tinto, the owner of the mining leases for both properties. For example, the community asked for an indoor, heated swimming pool and various things of that nature. Basically, they were making their statement of claim. What Rio Tinto did was to say, 'What we'd rather do is deal with the fact that the Clermont mine will also shut in about 16 years or so, therefore we would like to work with you on what we call 'Preferred Futures' to design what Clermont, the town, would look like in 16 years' time. Rio Tinto then embarked on a process that included an external facilitator to work with the community and the councils. In the process, Rio Tinto gave the funds to the councils to manage the community development process and as well as to offer some gentle guidance. That basically calmed everything down and restored a condition of peace between the mines and the community through methods of sharing information through open processes.

Root causes and types of violence indicated:

Structural Violence: the mine had built a lot of the town infrastructure, which was subsequently transferred to shire council—which was unable to support it financially

Proximate causes (conflict characteristics):

The community mistrusted the mine consultation process.

Triggers:

Potential trigger: closure of a mine and potential to open a new mine without a clear plan of intent

Corporate Actor:

CSR team

Outcomes indicative of conflict transformation and a paradigm of positive peace:

The company initiated a 'Preferred Futures' planning process to design what the town would look like in 16 years' time. The company hired an external facilitator to work with the community and the councils. In the process, the company gave the funds to the councils to manage the community development process and as well as to offer some gentle guidance. That basically calmed everything down and restored a condition of peace between the mines and the community through methods of sharing information through open consultation processes.

7.3 Implications

An initial common theme of these cases is that the solutions occurred at the grassroots level, consistent with Richmond's (2010) fourth-generation emphasis on peace-building as a bottom-up as well as a top-down process. He argues that,

> there is space for a hybridised form of peacebuilding that can develop international approaches and consensus for peace while also developing and assisting the localised dynamics for peace . . . These would be designed to capitalise on the core of the original conflict resolution and peacebuilding agendas, addressing needs and root causes, connecting the new liberal state or polity with older, locally recognizable and

> contextual, customary, political, social, and economic traditions, and engaging with grass roots and the most marginalised.
>
> (Richmond, 2010, p. 32)

NRCs as non-state actors can participate in peace-building process at the grassroots level, whether or not they use the word 'peace'. Importantly, if companies choose to engage at the grassroots level in peace-focused CSR work, NRCs are able to maintain their position as not taking on the roles of a state towards natural resources affected communities.

The following illustration (see Figure 7.1) demonstrates this point. This figure builds on the initial presentation of corporate 'levels of influence' presented in Chapter 2 (see Figure 2.2). Both figures are useful in locating the level of a conflict as: (1) international (*top*), (2) national (*middle*) or (3) local (*bottom*). If the conflict presents at the local level, it is possible to identify the most appropriate actors from both the company and the community. Non-state actors operating at the local level (e.g., business actors, local NGOs and community actors) have an opportunity to co-construct peace at the local level in culturally appropriate ways. The bottom-up, grassroots approach to positive peace as a response to or prevention of violence can and should be connected with middle- and top-range efforts for peace at national and international levels but do not need to be dictated from the top down in order to achieve productive conflict outcomes. Consistent with the fourth generation of Peace Theory, the cases related in this chapter indicate that NRCs could and in some instances already do operate in a peace-building capacity at the grassroots leadership level without needing to try

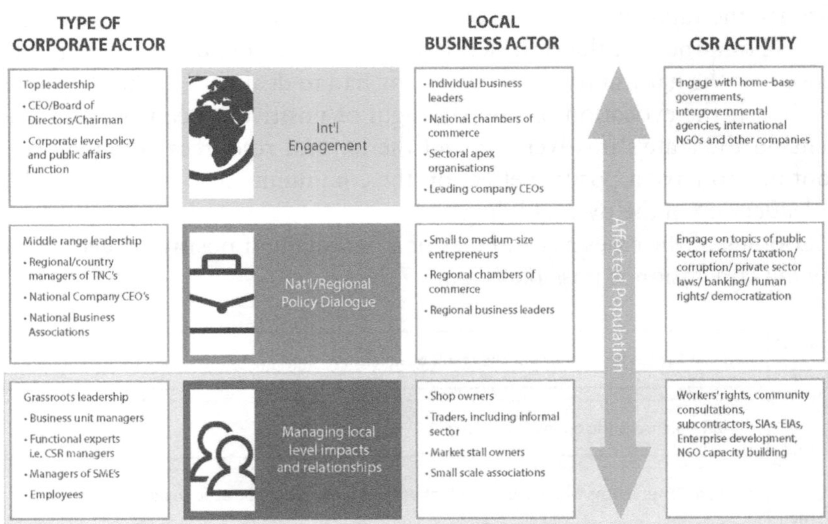

Figure 7.1 Location of the Narratives on the Pyramid of Business and Peace: Local-Level Impacts and Relationships

to change the system at the middle-range or top leadership levels. Furthermore, in these examples, the peace achieved really did not exemplify or 'push' a liberal peace-building agenda from the national or international spheres. Instead, the companies worked with communities at a clan, tribal or within other regionally traditional structures. In no case in this chapter was war, of any kind, a factor. Nevertheless, peace-focused action resulted in an improvement in the conditions of peace between the natural resources company and the affected communities.

A second aspect to these cases was a quick analysis of the background information to identify the cause of the conflict according to a root cause of one or more of types of violence: structural, cultural or physical. The root cause of violence underlying each case was disaggregated from the proximate causes, the symptoms. It is also possible to identify at least one trigger factor in each case with the potential to escalate the conflict further and lead toward unproductive and even destructive conflict outcomes for the natural resources company and/or the community.

Thirdly, the cases focus on relationships within a Positive Peace paradigm characterised by an absence of either physical violence or legal force. As each of these conflicts developed, there was a CSR team, either alone, in partnership with another department or in coordination with a General Manager of an operation. In each case, the CSR team chose to respond to the emerging conflict in a constructive, relationship-affirming way at the local level. With local, external stakeholders, the CSR practitioners were able to co-create the conditions supportive of peace both *for* the natural resources affected communities as well as *between* the communities and the operations. This is true even in situations where the violence was not directly the fault or result of actions taken by the NRCs. For example, in Cases Four and Six, the state actor was a significant contributor to the violence that the natural resources company had to deal with at the community level. Yet, the evocation of the paradigm of positive peace was not dependent on the state's involvement and the natural resources company could continue to have a positive effect on the community at the grassroots level of leadership in the pyramid diagram.

Looking at the cases as examples of a paradigm of positive peace, the following conclusion is possible (Figure 7.2):

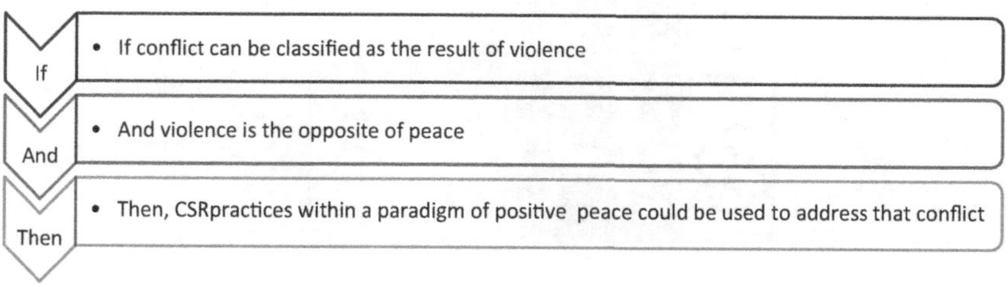

Figure 7.2 Peace and Violence Syllogism

Thinking this way makes it possible to identify the following themes from the cases as consistent with a paradigm of positive peace. First, the relationship between the natural resources company and the community improved as a result of how the conflict was handled. Second, practitioners did not indicate that specialists or use of specialist language was required in order for a solution to be co-created with the natural resources affected community. Third, the key to handling these conflicts was a willingness to take the time to develop trust between the parties and devise creative solutions. Fourth, no threat of physical violence or force was exercised by any of the parties to the conflict. Thematically, then, each of these cases can be considered from an *etic* or external perspective as the kind of conflict outcomes possible between NRCs and communities when elements of a paradigm of positive peace are present.

Overall, the lack of awareness of positive peace by CSR practitioners, when contrasted with the ability of more than half of the practitioners to describe outcomes characteristic of a paradigm of positive peace, suggests that the paradigm of positive peace is relevant but largely unexplored within the natural resources sector. There is potential, then, to collect even more cases characteristic of a paradigm of positive peace from CSR practitioners to begin creating a new way to both view and approach natural resources-company community conflict. It is possible to conceptualise the phenomenon of natural resources company-community relationships from several different paradigms. However, it is no longer necessary to look at these cases solely from the established, influential CSR paradigms (e.g., Neoliberal Economics, Risk Management, Human Rights). Certainly, one or more of these have been used by others to classify what happened at these sites. However, thinking about cases within a peace paradigm, a new pattern emerges and generates the potential to identify opportunities for synergy, sharing best-practice success stories and the achievement of productive conflict outcomes. If paradigms govern how groups of people understand phenomena (Kuhn, 1996 [1962]), and paradigms inform perspectives and guide which practical frameworks are chosen to achieve particular outcomes or goals, then *shared examples of successful practice* could provide the coherence necessary for a CSR practitioners to solve puzzles, problems or conflicts (Kuhn, 1977) within the Positive Peace paradigm.

7.4 Conclusion

In this chapter, I have walked through an analytical process to examine conflict cases in the natural resources-company-community nexus (the CSR space) within a paradigm of peace. Using a series of tables demonstrating key concepts characteristic of the paradigm of positive peace, it is possible to ground what positive peace in the natural resources context looks like. This chapter has shown that it is possible to analyse conflicts having a basis in structural, cultural or physical violence, at all stages of an NRC operation's life and in both developed and developing countries, from within the paradigm of positive peace. Once the orientation is made to view conflicts from the Positive Peace paradigm, peace-focused thinking can be harnessed by CSR practitioners in the field to provide a foundation for the use of the various toolkits, guides, voluntary initiatives and company protocols already at their disposal (e.g., Anglo American SEAT toolkit, Rio Tinto Guiding Principles, Conflict Analysis Handbooks). The chapter has shown that most of the CSR practitioners in this sample are indeed receptive to the paradigm of positive peace; especially once they recast conflicts themselves using the Positive Peace paradigm according to their own, context-specific definitions. Furthermore, and more importantly, the cases indicate that it is possible within a very short period of time and without additional specialist training or elaborate explanation for CSR practitioners to shift an *emic* or internal understanding of productive conflict outcomes within to a paradigm of positive peace at the local, grassroots level. Of course, it is critical not to overstate this point from an *etic* or external point of view. It remains to be seen what degree of traction this paradigm shift has in practice, either as an

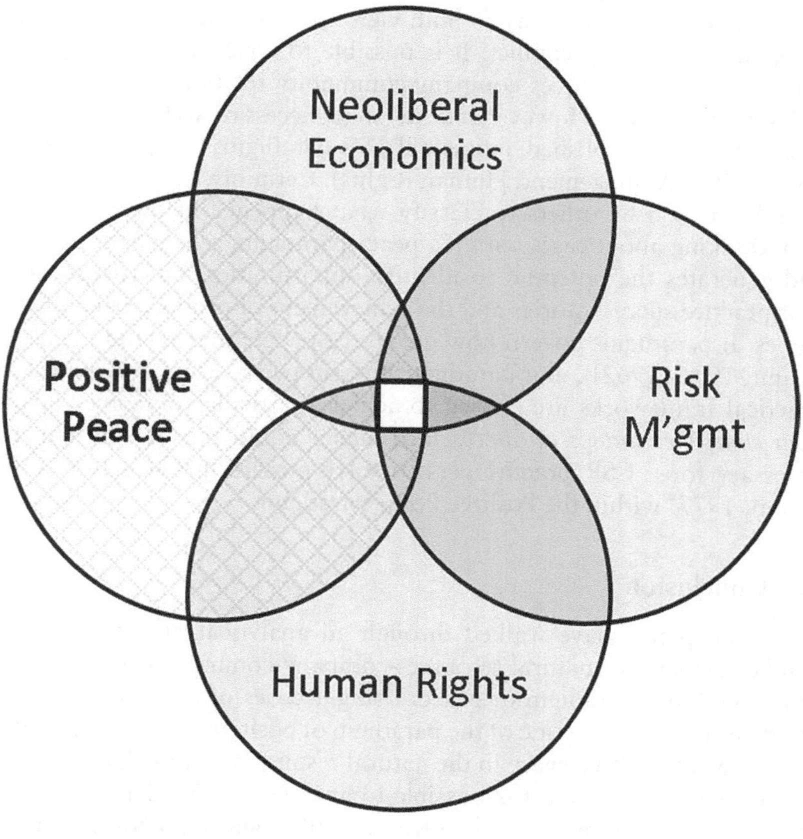

Figure 7.3 Positive Peace as a Complementary Paradigm

overall paradigm for or in combination with the three influential paradigms affecting CSR practice and, consequently, conflict outcomes.

Note

1 The 'green mob' is alleged to have committed systematic and horrific human rights abuses on the Acehnese, including: torture, rape and genocide (Frost, 2001)

Bibliography

Amat y León, R. F., & Velarde, E. (2005). *Building stakeholder engagement through consultation*. Peru: Tintaya.

Anglo American. (2012). *SEAT toolbox, version 3*. London: Anglo American.

Barton, B. (2005). *A global/local approach to conflict resolution in the mining sector: The case of the Tintaya dialogue table* (Master of Arts in Law and Diplomacy Thesis), Tufts University, Boston, MA.

de Neufville, R. (2010). Paradigm. In M. Bevir (Ed.), *Encyclopedia of political theory* (pp. 1014–1015). Thousand Oaks, CA: Sage.

Echave, J. D., Keenan, K., Romero, M. K., & Tapia, Á. (2004). *Dialogue and management of conflicts on community lands: The case of the Tintaya mine in Peru*. Peru: CooperAccion.

Francis, D. (2010). *From pacification to peacebuilding: A call to global transformation*. New York, NY: Palgrave Macmillan.

Frost, S. (2001). Aceh: ExxonMobil accused of 'ethnic genocide'. *Green Left Weekly*.

Jonker, J., & Pennink, B. W. (2010). The essence of methodology. In *The essence of research methodology: A concise guide for master and PhD students in management science*. London: Springer.

Kuhn, T. A. (1977). Second thoughts. In *The essential tension*. Chicago, IL: University of Chicago Press.

Kuhn, T. A. (1996 [1962]). *The structure of scientific revolutions*. Chicago, IL: University of Chicago Press.

Oxfam. (2003). *Mining Ombudsman annual report*. Australia: Oxfam.

Rangan, V. K., Barton, B., & Reficco, E. (2006). Corporate responsibility & community engagement at the Tintaya Copper Mine (A). Cambridge MA: Harvard Business School, Harvard Publishing. 9–506–023.

Richmond, O. (2010). A genealogy of peace and conflict theory. In O. Richmond (Ed.), *Palgrave advances in peacebuilding*. London: Palgrave.

Wilkinson-Maposa, S., & Fowler, A. (2009). *The poor philanthropist II: New approaches to sustainable development*. Cape Town.

8 Conclusion

8.1 Review

The primary question that drove the research underpinning this book is: *how useful it is to apply the concept of positive peace, as a paradigm, in the natural resources context?* The answer to this question reframes natural resources company-community conflict. Instead of NRCs focusing on a wide range of risks and avoiding negative outcomes, this book suggests there is merit to also considering natural resources-linked conflict in terms of (1) the emerging literature on business and peace and (2) peace and conflict theory. First, the literature on business and peace has not sufficiently engaged NRCs as having potential to contribute towards societal conditions of positive peace other than in war-affected contexts. Second, peace and conflict theories within the international relations literature have not yet expanded to include natural resources activities as either a contributing source of conflict or a potential context for enhancing peace. Therefore, the book features natural resources company conflict in non-war-affected contexts, as this context accounts for the majority of conflicts associated with natural resources activities around the world. If it is possible to marry the literature on business and peace with Peace and Conflict Theory in this space, there is the potential to enhance conflict outcomes in the natural resources company-community nexus, with consequent implications for CSR practice.

Within Peace and Conflict Theory, NRCs represented a particular kind of 'non-state actors', with the capacity to enhance or diminish conditions of positive peace at the grass roots level in the regions where they operate. It was theorised that CSR practitioners might be able to participate with local-level people in developing their own vision of what positive peace looks like on the ground, day in and day out, in relationship to NRCs. Richmond (2010) provided the basis for the argument that building positive peace allows for benefits from natural resources-related development to actually result in overall conditions of positive peace, rather than sowing the seeds of violent conflict. The theory chapter concluded that it is important to articulate the manner in which NRCs are classified as 'non-state actors'.

The coherent expression of that role sets appropriate limits for shaping CSR practice in responding to community-level conflict linked to expectations about deriving benefits from natural resources. It also helps contextualise how NRCs can contribute to conditions of positive peace at the local level as articulated in the business and peace literature.

Informed by Peace and Conflict Theory, business and peace literature and terminology from CSR practice, a conceptual model was developed using Kuhn's work on paradigms. The paradigm of positive peace was compared to the influential neoliberal economics, risk management and Human Rights paradigms to show what it offers in comparison. The conceptual model made it possible to explore how different CSR concepts could be classified and compared at particular levels of analysis. Positive peace, as a paradigm, was shown to have potential that is not prioritised by the three influential paradigms. A Positive Peace paradigm emphasises the quality of relationships between NRCs and communities, rather than privileging particular conflict outcomes. Following the peace literature, relationships characterised by trust, good will and a commitment to use non-violent conflict handling strategies have the necessary resilience to handle conflict, such that the achievement of productive conflict outcomes is increased.

The theoretical basis and conceptual framework provided scaffolding to engage the subsidiary research question: *how responsive are CSR professionals in the natural resources context to using positive peace in shaping their work?* Their receptivity to the concept of 'positive peace' was tested via a series of individual interviews, transcribed and analysed for content and themes to determine whether or not the paradigm of positive peace had potential for uptake by them. All of the respondents were able to identify structures, situations and relationships that are non-coercive and harmonious in nature to achieve the kind of productive outcomes that are consistent with a paradigm of positive peace. Even those who were disinclined to use the actual term 'peace' found that the term had analogous words which they would use in practice.

In addition, thematic analysis was used to compare elicitive cases offered by practitioners on whether or not they had observed positive peace as a conflict outcome in the natural resources company-community nexus. From the point of view of the respondents, they had an *emic* or internal/insider way of constructing a 'peace' narrative out of the cases whereas I, as the researcher, had an *etic* or external/outsider way of looking at these cases as 'peace' narratives. The book showed that it was possible to link CSR practitioners *emic* understanding of their narratives to an *etic* reading that recast those narratives as representative of a larger group of narratives illustrative of the paradigm of positive peace. Thus accomplished, the possibility for a paradigm shift in the way natural resources company-community conflicts could be viewed, responded to and handled by CSR professionals, was confirmed. The book concludes that the paradigm of positive peace has potential to influence other paradigms as well as how individual practitioners use CSR strategies in the natural resources sector. By extension, there is potential for CSR practitioners to engage in positive peace-building strategies with communities at all stages of NRC operation life.

8.2 Opportunities for Further Research

Because the application of peace and conflict theory to the natural resources context is relatively novel, there are a number of different directions for future research that will emerge as I and other scholars engage this material further. Six indicative projects are sketched here. The inspiration for these potential research projects has grown out of responses to my work on positive peace and natural resources at conferences, from the suggestions of my students and in conversation with other researchers.

The first is to explore in more depth the relationship between influential paradigms. This would require further theoretical and conceptual work. As well, the paradigmatic conceptual framework could be tested for applicability in other disciplines (e.g. legal, environmental, spiritual). Further theoretical and conceptual work could point to opportunities where the paradigm of positive peace could be used effectively as an overall foundational paradigm and when it can be used in conjunction with other CSR paradigms.

The second is to work with the toolkits and guidance notes identified in this book in earlier chapters. It would be useful to conduct a detailed analysis of how they might actually configure with the achievement and maintenance of positive peace in the interface between companies and communities. It would also be instructive to compare these strategies to known, effective peace-building processes developed by Lederach and Francis. A detailed analysis would articulate the emergent possibilities from strengthening operational principles of CSR practice.

A third opportunity for research was inspired by conversations with government officials in Ghana and Liberia. In these countries, the language of peace is already accepted and used within the natural resources context. It would therefore be fruitful to do fieldwork in natural resources communities in such locations to explore exactly how this Positive Peace paradigm affects the natural resources company-community relationships.

Fourth, one of the greatest areas of concern for NRCs is the health and safety of their own workers. When accidents and fatalities routinely occur as a result of natural resources extraction, peacelessness can result. For example, while the causes of the Marikana massacre in South Africa ca. 2012 were complex, the conflict occurred against a backdrop of a long history of dangerous working conditions in which little regard was paid to the well-being and safety of employees. Consequently, synergies between a paradigm of positive peace and a health and safety risk management paradigm is worth exploring. Again, it would be worthwhile to see if certain peace-building processes could be adapted for use in the human interface of a risk management paradigm.

A fifth opportunity for research is to test Richmond's fourth generation of Peace and Conflict Theory for applicability in regard to Indigenous peoples. For example, according to one interview respondent for this book who hails from Canada, First Nations people have a holistic understanding of peace as the foundation for all activity and relationship between peoples. It could be rewarding to explore a First Nations concept of peace and see if it is possible to articulate that vision more clearly for use in the natural resources context.

Sixth, it would be worth extending the interviews to include a larger and more diverse sample size to see if the openness to the paradigm of positive peace was idiosyncratic to this group of respondents or more indicative of a wider receptivity to using this paradigm as a foundation for CSR practice. A larger sample could also include community voices, directly, to see if the paradigm of positive peace would have traction with natural resources affected communities especially in situations where a legacy of mistrust and violence of one form or another has affected natural resources company-community relationships.

8.3 Implications for Practice and Further Theoretical Analysis

My aim in this book is not to rebadge CSR practitioners as peacebuilders. However, I have argued that there may be some advantages for international organisations, governments, IFIs, NGOs and civil society actors to engage these practitioners functioning as peacebuilders within NRCs. Currently, CSR practitioners and people in the peace-building space are operating on parallel tracks, even though they are often committed to activities designed to provide certain outcomes for the communities in question. If it is possible to create a conceptual and dialogical bridge between these two groups of practitioners operating at the local level, both NRCs, communities and local-level actors stand to benefit by working together within a broadly shared paradigm.

The potential advantages gained by doing so depend upon being able to use the concept and paradigm of positive peace within the CSR space and to include CSR practitioners in the peace-building space. Embedding the paradigm of positive peace in the CSR space could provide language for the natural resources/business sector to connect with those who are more formally engaged with peace-building. It also gives businesses the opportunity to speak on their own behalf in the peace-building dialogue, should they choose to exercise that option. Presently, the formally recognised peace-building actors talk **about** natural resources/businesses, but not **with** natural resources/business actors. If CSR practitioners and people engaged in peace-building can use similar language and concepts related to peace, they can engage one another as partners in peace-building processes rather than as adversaries or competitors. Working together, the possibilities expand for sharing the benefits of natural resources in a peaceful way.

The Positive Peace paradigm can encourage a pause in the automatic, well-trodden response processes to focus on prioritising relationships and making choices that don't resort to the violence. Such a focus may result in more productive outcomes within the natural resources sector. This book opens up the explicit, rather than implicit, opportunity to engage the relational aspects of conflict that peace-building specifically addresses.

> For peace to be built, it is necessary for conflicting groups to negotiate the means of coexistence . . . For there to be positive peace, in the sense of general well-being and peaceful relationships, there is a need for transformation: personal, cultural and structural.
>
> (Francis, 2010, pp. 82–83)

If NRCs can be categorised as non-state actors, and conflict in the natural resources context can be classified as one or another kind of violence, then peace-building practices can be adapted to reduce or eliminate effects of natural resources-related conflict. Positive peace is not a panacea, and it is not going to provide an instant solution to situations of entrenched and deeply experienced conflict. At a minimum, there needs to be political will, trust and robust relationships for positive peace to emerge. However, focusing on a paradigm rather than any one particular definition of peace is inclusive and provides greater opportunity for dialogue and relationships to build towards creating conditions of positive peace between NRCs and communities at the local level.

This book represents a first step towards understanding that improved CSR practice in the natural resources context lies not merely in developing a new guidance note, toolkit, or voluntary initiative. Instead, I have sought to show in the book that when conflicts with a root cause in violence are viewed at the paradigmatic level, it is possible to use the paradigm of positive peace to improve analysis, view new connections and identify novel ways to use existing CSR strategies more effectively.

Consequently, NRCs, like other large-scale industries, have an opportunity to create positive social value and increase conditions of peace in their operating environments. This is due to their long presence in the regions where they operate as well as the extent of the effects they will have on local populations and environments. In order to deal with the challenges related to natural resources-related change, there are several aspects NRCs can consider towards building peace, as a coherent and accessible goal, with the communities affected by their operations. The first is that they do not take on the role of the state in their local contexts but that they work with the state in a capacity-building way. The second is that they have the personnel (CSR and otherwise) at the appropriate level of skill, knowledge and empathy to interact constructively with different sectors of society. The third is that they engage and empower other stakeholders in their operating environment, including NGOs, International Organisations (IOs) (e.g., the UN) and civil society groups to design and deliver development programs. The fourth is that they pay special attention to culturally and socially appropriate ways to include local people as employees, contractors and suppliers. The fifth is that they uphold and model to the best of their ability the highest standards in regard to revenue transparency, Human Rights and security. The sixth is to use the guides and strategies that have already been accepted and used by the natural resources industry in a way that fosters an increase in the conditions of peace at the local level. In these ways, as part of a multi-stakeholder, multi-level web of relationships, NRCs can indeed make a contribution to peace while pursuing their core business activities.

Bibliography

Francis, D. (2010). *From pacification to peacebuilding: A call to global transformation*. New York, NY: Palgrave Macmillan.

Richmond, O. (2010). A genealogy of peace and conflict theory. In O. Richmond (Ed.), *Palgrave advances in peacebuilding*. New York, NY: Palgrave Macmillan.

Glossary

ASM	Artisanal and Small-Scale Mining
CEDAW	Convention on the Elimination of All Forms of Discrimination Against Women
CR	Community Relations
CSR	Corporate Social Responsibility
ECOSOC	United Nations Economic and Social Council
EIA	Environmental Impact Assessment
EIS	Environmental Impact Statement
FPIC	Free Prior and Informed Consent
GP	Guiding Principles (*also* UNGP)
IFC	International Finance Corporation
IFI	International Finance Institutions
IISD	International Institute for Sustainable Development
ILO	International Labor Organisation
IO	International Organisation
IR	International Relations
MMSD	Mining, Minerals and Sustainable Development
MNE	Multinational Enterprise
MOU	Memorandum of Understanding
NGO	Non-Governmental Organisation
NRC	Natural Resources Company
REDD+	UN collaborative programme on Reducing Emissions from Deforestation and Forest Degradation in Developing Countries
SD	Sustainable Development
SIA	Social Impact Assessment
SLTO	Social License to Operate
SME	Small and Medium-Scale Enterprises
SRSG	Special Representative of the Secretary General of the UN
UDHR	Universal Declaration of Human Rights
UN	United Nations
UNDPKO	United Nations Department of Peacekeeping Operations
UNGA	United Nations General Assembly
UNGP	United Nations Guiding Principles on Business and Human Rights (*aka* Ruggie Principles)

Index

Note: Page numbers in **bold** indicate tables.

For Product Safety Concerns and Information please contact our EU representative GPSR@taylorandfrancis.com Taylor & Francis Verlag GmbH, Kaufingerstraße 24, 80331 München, Germany